I0169543

Lean Startup Branding
WORKBOOK 2: BRANDING

Step 2 of the 3-Step RAF Marketing Method of Branding and Marketing an Offering of Value, for Profit

Real-World Marketing, Step-by-Step, Idea to Launch and Beyond

Entropy Publications, LLC, San Francisco, CA
query@entropypublishing.com

Entropy Press® is a registered trademark of Entropy Publications, LLC.

Library of Congress Cataloging-in-Publication Data is available.

ISBN-13: 978-1-7325431-1-9 (Entropy Press)
ISBN-10: 1-7325431-1-9

1. Entrepreneurship. 2. Small Business Marketing. 3. Branding.
4. MVP, Minimum Viable Product. 4. Digital Marketing. 6. Social Media Marketing.

Printed in the U.S.A

Cover design by TargetMediaDesign

◆◆◆◆◆◆

Lean Startup BRANDING (LSB)
<u>Workbook 2</u> CONTENTS

<u>LSB WORKBOOK 2</u>: BRANDING PREFACE

MODULE 13
Identity Development: Name your startup *and* offerings. Purchase URLs for your web addresses. Write taglines for your new venture *and* your offerings.

MODULE 14
Design Fundamentals: Utilizing the psychology of Design. Applying color theory to graphic design. Effective color reproduction, online *and* in print.

MODULE 15
Identity Design: Design your offering *and* startup logos. Working with type (typography). Rebranding your identities. Create Brand Standards for your products *and* company.

MODULE 16
Visual Content: Design effective layouts. Responsive design development. Identifying and creating imagery with impact.

MODULE 17
Image Capture: Obtain low to no-cost images and video clips. Create and maintain a visual content library.

MODULE 18
Online Marketing: User interface (UI) and user experience (UX) design. Search Engine Optimized (SEO) content marketing.

MODULE 19
Online Technology: Understanding computing basics. Webhosting. Cloud computing. Utilizing free and low-cost content management systems (CMS). Setting up secure e-commerce. Working with VARs.

MODULE 20
Website Development: Develop, produce, and maintain your digital storefront.

MODULE 21
Digital Campaigns: Create cost-per-click (CPC) and low-cost click-advertising campaigns. Develop video branding and advertising campaigns. Utilize Landing Pages for sales and email capture.

◆◆◆◆◆

Lean Startup BRANDING
Workbook 2: Take Aim—BRAND
Step 2 of the 3-Step RAF Marketing Method of
Branding and Marketing Your Offerings of Value, for Profit

-

-

-BRANDING Preface-

Do you have an *iPhone*? When you purchase tablets, laptops, and other electronics, do you only consider buying from *Apple*? Why? Perhaps you got used to their user interface—the layout and icons on their device screens. Or maybe, *Apple* convinced you that you'll be 'more creative' using *their* products over their competitors. Whatever your reason for buying only *Apple* devices, it's likely you have become one of their many 'brand advocates,' a true believer that *Apple* will continually deliver you offerings of value.

In just 30 years, *Apple* has become one of the most recognizable brands of all time. How did they do this? What convinced you to become a brand advocate of *Apple*? And if you are *not* an *Apple* devote, why not?

Branding is a powerful tool to market products, services, and messages. The Branding *process*—garnering awareness of your offering/s and business—is essential for startup success, but also to build a sustainable company.

LSB Workbook 2: Take Aim, in the **RAF** (Ready; Aim; Fire;) **Marketing Method** examines the process of **Branding**. This workbook takes you step-by-step in creating, producing *and* publishing branding and advertising campaigns with impact, that grab attention, and motivate the *action* your marketing efforts direct. **LSB Workbook 2** also provides startups struggling to get traction with their marketing campaigns a clear and direct process to achieving much greater response on their marketing efforts, at launch and beyond.

Engaging in marketing your offering and company with branding and advertising campaigns should begin *before* your product is completely developed. You, or someone you hire, should be creating and producing your startup's marketing efforts for pre-launch and launch *simultaneously* with the development of your offering. But before we take the first step in the Branding process, we must review LSM Workbook 1—PRODUCTIZATION, to be sure your offering is READY to brand and sell.

LSE Series and the RAF Marketing Method
The **Lean Startup Entrepreneurial (LSE)** series is a three-step process that

gives innovators practical, doable steps to build a marketable, *sustainable* business. Originally taught live at Stanford, UC Berkeley, and other accredited universities in L.A. and the Bay area, for the past six years the LSE series has helped hundreds of students launch and *market* a startup with the **RAF** (Ready; Aim; Fire;) **Marketing Method**.

> 1. **Get Ready**, and **Productize** your offering.
> 2. **Take Aim**, and **Brand** your offering.
> 3. **Fire**, and **Launch** your marketing efforts.

The **RAF Marketing Method** in the **Lean Startup series** has been developed to *actualize* marketing theory—put it into a step-by-step *process*. Each of the three workbooks, filled with slides, challenges and projects, are **step-by-step guides** you'll refer to again and again, to assure you are on the proper path to building a thriving business. Each workbook in the **LSE series** provides specific, low-budget, *actionable steps* for marketing your offerings, to sell directly, or launch your first offering, of many others to come, as a *profitable* company. Every step presented in each workbook guides learners through the process of creating and producing marketing tools and material that gets greater response to your campaigns, generates conversion (try; sign-up; subscribe), and ultimately sales for your new venture.

LSM Workbook 1: Step 1, examined the process of Productization, step-by-step, to actualize an idea, or effectively *market* an existing offering, for profit. Remember, implementing the **RAF Marketing Method** *in order,* will vastly increase your odds of startup success:

LSM Workbook 1. Step 1—Get <u>R</u>eady, and PRODUCTIZE.

LSB Workbook 2. Step 2—Take <u>A</u>im, and BRAND.

LSL Workbook 3. Step 3—<u>F</u>ire, and <u>L</u>AUNCH marketing campaigns.

Simply follow the steps of the **RAF** (<u>R</u>eady; <u>A</u>im; <u>F</u>ire;) **Marketing Method,** *in order*, and you'll be able to actualize most any idea you have now, or any that may come in the future, into a *marketable* offering of value, for profit (kind of like working a math equation... ;-).

Getting <u>R</u>eady to BRAND your offering and startup *begins* with **Productization.** Productizing our ideas, or even fully developed offerings, helps us define 'product/market fit,' i.e. where our offering *fits* in the marketplace of sellable items. It also helps us pinpoint target markets and potential users who will find benefit, or value in the features of our products, services, and company. We perform competitive analysis during Productization, to make us aware of our competitors, and define what makes our offering unique, and *better* than theirs. We project horizontal and vertical markets so we'll have continuous groups of people to sell to. And we identify profit models, to be sure we'll make money with our offering, out of the gate and beyond.

After Productization is established, and well underway, we **Take <u>A</u>im** in this workbook, **LSB Workbook 2,** and develop marketing efforts directed at the likely target audiences we've identified in LSM Workbook 1. We'll take the step-by-step process of creating and producing branding and marketing tools and collateral, from **product** and **corporate names**, **identities** and **taglines**, through establishing **brand standards**, to **websites**, as well as **digital and video advertising** to **social media marketing** (**SMM**) campaigns.

The LSE series assumes you have the knowledge and means to *produce the offering* you envision. **LSM Workbook 1**—PRODUCTIZATION does *not* require that your offering already be actualized. Producing branding and advertising campaigns during **LSB Workbook 2—BRANDING**, the development of your offering should at least be in the works before releasing your pre-launch, and roll-out marketing efforts. **LSL Workbook 3—LAUNCH**, however, you must have a complete and *quality-tested* offering to sell.

-

-

STOP! Do CHALLENGE #1 before moving on.

◆◆◆

CHALLENGE #1: PRODUCTIZATION

A thorough understanding of Productization is required to effectively apply the principles and practices of BRANDING. Do NOT move on to Workbook 2: Take Aim —BRAND, until you've completed all the modules *and* projects in Workbook 1.

1. Eight (8) Productization lists for *your* **productized** offering:
- Features
- Benefits/solutions
- Target Markets
- Target Users
- Competitive Analysis
- Differentiators/UVPs
- Horizontal Markets
- Vertical Markets

2. A **working draft of an ELEVATOR PITCH** for your offering *and* company.

3. A **PROFIT MODEL timeline** of **expected revenue** in the first year through the fifth year after the launch of your new venture, including how your company will generate this income. What sources—target markets and users—will purchase your offering/s, and for how much?

If you are reading the LSE series hoping to launch a specific idea you are in the process of producing, or you want to get more traction with your marketing efforts on a fully developed offering, be sure to DO ALL THE PROJECTS in

Workbook 1: PRODUCTIZAITON. **Get Ready**, and productize your offering *before* moving on to the steps in this workbook. The lists and documentation you produce in productizing your product, service, or nonprofit message are essential to effectively begin the Branding process.

◆◆◆

Step 2: Take Aim and BRAND Your Offering

Branding is the marriage of marketing and design, applied to build awareness of your product and company, and ultimately sell your offerings. **Startup branding** is the process of 'giving birth' to the marketing of your productized offering. Creating an identity for your product and business, you are effectively giving your offering a form, a body of marketing material, so it becomes something real, virtually physical, instead of just an idea or concept in development.

Have you actualized *and* productized a software application? An online bakery delivery service? A new widget that adds value or offers a solution to an existing problem? Whether a product or service, and/or new company, branding your offering/s begins with a name—like naming a newborn.

Your new venture must have a pleasing face, a look and feel that is attractive, and even better if the identity is striking, stunning, captivating. A **corporate I.D.**, also known as a **logo**, must be as powerful on a Twitter feed, as the side of a building. You must create a logo for your startup, but also for each product or service your company releases.

We give children language to communicate. We must give our offering and startup a voice with **Taglines**—an essential component of the corporate identity, to communicate who we are and what we have to offer. Taglines are the voice that define the names and faces we create for our offerings and company, in affect, making the company whole. Taglines also provide the fabric, or *skin* that describe the primary mission or function of your products and business.

Beyond the corporate identity, you must produce branded marketing tools and campaigns to launch and grow any business. Creating advertising that builds brand awareness and gets response requires an understanding of graphic design, to produce effective campaigns that motivate action. Design and color theory, reproduction for print and digital marketing, layout, eye-tracking, photography, photo editing, video capture, are all covered, here, in LSB Workbook 2.

You'll begin a professional **visual library** of free and low-cost pictures and video clips to use in your marketing material. You'll add to this library with free music to enhance the messaging in your video campaigns. You'll include free typefaces in your library that reflect the tone of your words to garner your target audience's interest. You'll learn tips and tricks of **SEO content** for creating attention-grabbing click-advertising, email campaigns, and micro-posts that improve your **search ranking**, and get response.

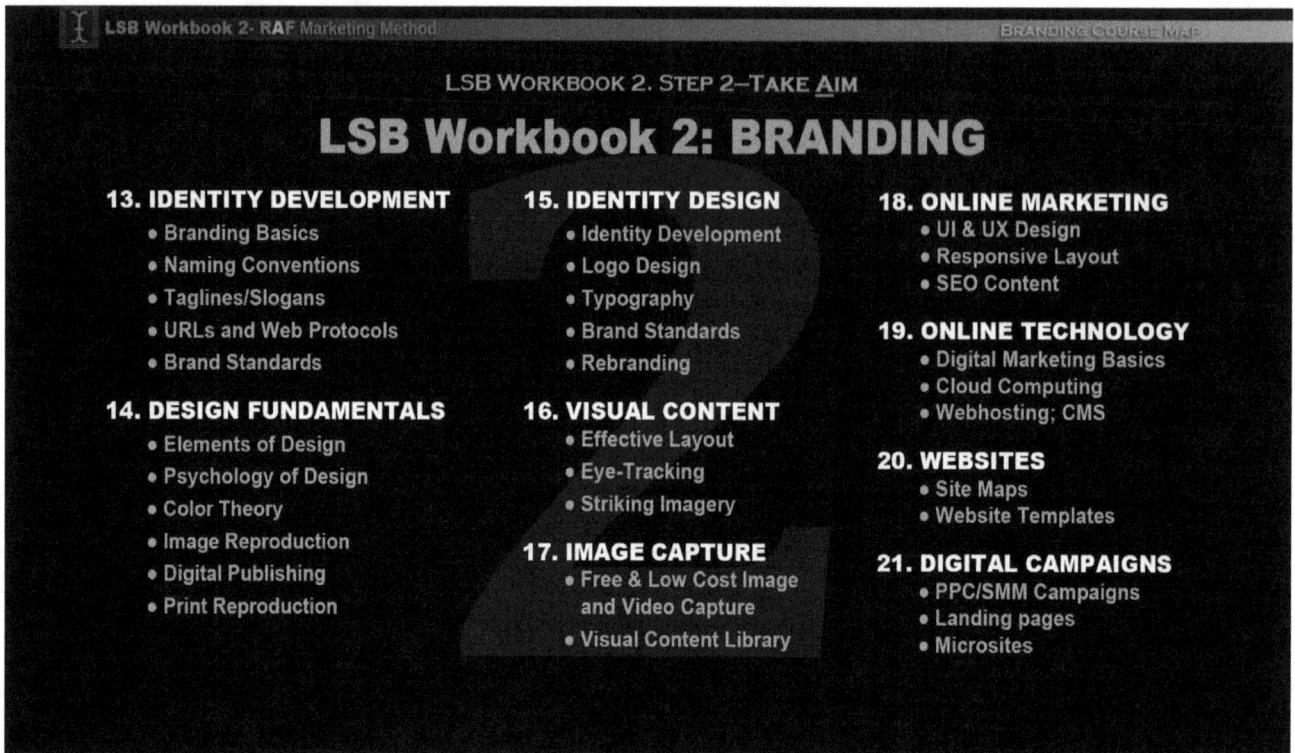

Branding is an ongoing process. Marketing must be continually developed, produced and published for pre-launch, as well as launch campaigns, and beyond. **LSB Workbook 2: Take Aim** covers understanding online technology basics, from how to *write* and purchase URLs for your company that improve your search (SEO) ranking, to responsive **user interface** (**UI**) design that looks great on any computer monitor, as well as mobile devices. We'll explore effective **User Experience** (**UX**) design, to help you keep your audience engaged with your marketing efforts. Then we parlay this knowledge into building stunning websites and **social media marketing** (**SMM**) campaigns at little to no cost.

Step 2, of the RAF Marketing Method presented in LSB Workbook 2, gives you the tools, techniques, and step-by-step *process* to creating identities, and advertising and marketing campaigns that build awareness of your offering and company, and convert viewers to try, subscribe, or buy.

Projects for LSB Workbook 2: BRANDING

There are **five multifaceted projects throughout this workbook**. Completing each of the BRANDING projects will give both your potential offering *and* startup **names**, including one to several **online addresses** (**URLs**), a face—**logo**

identities, and a voice with **taglines** for your offering *and* company. You'll implement **brand standards** that will keep you, and those you hire, producing marketing efforts that will build brand awareness of each offering you create, as well as give your new venture a memorable brand.

You'll learn how to produce **websites, landing pages**, video advertising, and social media marketing (SMM) campaigns for the pre-launch of your new offering, to sell directly, or to actualize a startup with your first product of many to come. (In LSL Workbook 3: Step 3— Fire, you'll learn how to LAUNCH the marketing efforts you create in both LSB Workbook 2, and LSL Workbook 3. You'll create multichannel branding and advertising campaigns and publish them online, as well as in print, for maximum impact, and the greatest possible response to your marketing efforts.)

LSB Workbook 2- RAF Marketing Method   BRANDING PROJECTS

LSB WORKBOOK 2. STEP 2–TAKE AIM

LSB Workbook 2: PROJECTS

Step 2: Take Aim—Brand Offering & Startup

1. BRAND IDENTITIES
Company & Product **NAMES**
Company & Product **TAGLINES**
Company & Product **LOGOS**

2. VISUAL LIBRARIES
Image, Video, Music, Font Libraries

3. WEBSITE
5+ web pages (minimum)

4. PPC/SMM AD SERIES
Pre-launch Campaign

5. LANDING PAGE
Pre-launch Campaign

Of course, it's your choice to engage in producing your own branding and advertising campaigns, or hire an ad agency or graphic designer to create the marketing required to launch your new venture. However, *working the process* of branding will help you intimately understand the branding process. So, even if you want to hire an agency or designer to create your marketing, I highly recommend walking the process of naming your offering and company, designing logos, coming up with product and corporate taglines, and starting a visual, audio and type library of usable images, video clips, music, and fonts, for your marketing efforts.

The knowledge you'll gain in producing your own marketing, even if you don't use it, will aide you in directing those you hire to economically produce advertising and marketing material for your offering, since you'll learn what it costs, in time, and real dollars, to produce a campaign by producing some yourself. You'll also be better equipped to direct the designer or agency you contract to produce tightly targeted branding advertising that gets the greatest response. A thorough understanding of the Productization and Branding process allows you to be the conduit that keeps marketing and design married, and producing better campaigns together.

You can read each of these workbooks twenty times, memorize them in fact, and not learn as much as you will from doing the projects. To *really* understand how something works—you must *work the process*.

Welcome to LSB Workbook 2: Branding. I hope you'll engage in this learning opportunity to BRAND your newly productized offering (LSM Workbook 1). It's time to meet your creative potential, give birth to the marketing of your new venture, and manifest a job you'll love.

Challenges

There are a few challenges scattered throughout this workbook, usually at the end of important content to remember. Completed challenges will *not* be used to market your offering or startup, but are provided as an adjutant to your understanding of the Branding process.

If you already have a complete offering, but want to get more traction with your marketing efforts, working the challenges will help broaden your knowledge of the intricacies of branding, as well as the marketing process.

As with the projects, I strongly suggest you do all the challenges! Beyond working each project to create and then produce your marketing campaigns, both the projects and challenges in the LSE series have been designed to accelerate your learning of the Lean Startup Marketing process.

The Private Language of Any Industry

Most every industry, from baked goods to software, has its own private language. Learning the language of business marketing is essential for startup success. Throughout LSB Workbook 2, as well as the entire LSE series, you will see words in **bold**. You'll also find acronyms—abbreviated initials of broader concepts—used every day in the entrepreneurial industry. It is imperative these terms and acronyms get inside your head. Pay extra attention to the words and phrases in bold, and the acronyms that follow them. Even if you don't always remember their meaning, over the course of the entire LSE series, you'll see them in context often enough to learn the language of Startup Marketing.

Access to LSB Workbook 2 Slides

You will find all the **slides in LSB Workbook 2** at this URL address:
https://idea2product4profit/lsb-workbook2-slides
Password: LSBWorkbook2-Branding

◆◆◆◆◆◆

MODULE 13: IDENTITY DEVELOPMENT

-Personal Branding-

So, what *is* **branding**? Let's take it down to the personal level. YOU are being branded. We *all* are! From how you look, to the clothing you choose, to what you buy, and even *say*—the words you use both in-person and online—IS your **brand**.

You have a persona you wear in public. You'll likely dress different, and use different language at work than you will in your home environment. Your personal brand is your *public* persona.

Do you have a personal *Facebook* page? Is it separate from your business profile page? It should be! Apply for a job, a college, or going on a first date, and it's likely the business, university, or your upcoming date is looking you up to learn about you through your social media accounts. Your social media profile pages are part of your public persona—your brand.

Your public persona—your personal brand—begins with a name. It is wise to make up a fake name to separate your personal social media accounts with your public-facing accounts. If you choose to use your real name, be sure to keep all your posts 'clean.' Don't cuss online. Don't identify your religion, or get political, or take any position that will brand you as a 'liberal,' or 'conservative,' or an atheist. Don't get angry at a business for their poor products or customer service. Don't take an argument with your boss, or even your partner or friend online. Take your issues to your therapist and keep your personal problems offline. Trust me, it will not help your professional life, and often hurt you personally as well to brand your public persona as a whiner, or too outspoken, or angry.

It takes time to build a positive brand image, and only minutes to destroy it, like posting a rant, or engaging in a flame war (a hostile interaction) online. Protect and nurture your public persona—your personal brand. Represent yourself as you wish others to see you. Make no mistake about it, more than just a potential employer or date is looking at you, and watching your every move.

Marketing to Our Personal Brands

Your personal brand is valuable to advertisers. Marketing uses our personal brand —our public persona—to sell to us. LSM Workbook 1, Module 6: Target Marketing and Targeting Users, illuminated how marketing categorizes each one of us to fit into a segment, or group of people with similar characteristics to ours. All of us are likely segmented by advertisers with **topic classifiers**, essentially *labels*, from four primary data sources:

- **Demographic**—age, sex, education level, income level, marital status.
- **Geographic**— location, ethnicity, climate, environmental conditions.
- **Psychographic**—personality traits, values, attitudes, interests, beliefs, religion, lifestyles.
- **Behavioral**—purchase data, customer loyalty, web-surfing habits, social media posts.

As we age, our personal brand changes. What categorized each of us at 10 years old is going to be different at 15, or 21, or 35, or 50. Some of our **demographic data** changes, from our age, to our marital status, to even our gender, if we chose to change our sex. Our **geographic data** usually changes. We move from our parents house to living on our own, sometimes close by, sometimes far from home. Our **psychographic data** changes. What we think, do, and react to changes with the passing of time, and life circumstances. Our **behavioral data** changes over time as well, from our food choices, to our fashion statements, to our health requirements, to our web-surfing and purchase habits.

People have become a valuable *product* in most business transactions today. Our information is bought and sold for billions, daily. Marketers, and affiliate networks like *Google, Microsoft, Apple*, or *Facebook*, even the 'loyalty' cards issues by our grocery, or box-chain stores track our behavior. These companies gather information on each of us in *real-time*, on what we search for and look at online, to what we click on, try, and buy on the internet, as well as in-person with our credit cards. The only way to avoid tracking of what you purchase is to pay with cash, or cryptocurrency, like *Bitcoin*, as long as you don't allow your receipt to be sent via email.

With all this information businesses and affiliate networks are gathering about us today, you'd think it'd be easy to motivate people to buy our products and services with our marketing efforts, or at least *remember* our company name— our corporate brand. So why aren't response and conversion rates greater than ever before? Because people lie. We lie to ourselves—tell ourselves we need things we don't, or make promises we never keep, like dieting, exercise, control spending, less time on our electronic devices, *YouTube*...etc. We lie to each other, because we believe it ourselves, or we want to appear smarter, kinder, wiser. We ALL fib, exaggerate, fabricate, remember wrong because memory has been proven to be faulty. Humans are fickle, which is what makes figuring out what motivates us particularly difficult when we often don't know ourselves. Our public persona simply reflects what we want to show, to ourselves, and whoever else is looking at us. It doesn't necessarily reveal what we really think, or actually do in private (offline, and with no one watching), or *will* do.

Algorithms that collect and analysis all our data position each of us into segments —broad target markets that classify our personal brand with people similar to us, who are potentially interested in the same things we are. However, assessing and categorizing our behavior only tells marketers what we *do*—where we go online, and offline (your cellphone has an accelerometer and GPS tracking in it showing your route and location), how long we stay at any given place, or on a website, if we take an action, like purchasing a product, or filling out a form. It does *not* automatically give the reason *why* someone chooses to take an action.

In the past, the value of our personal brand was not defined our actions, but by our last name. In days of old, your family linage (and gender) defined the job, wealth, and position in society you could attain. While this is still true in some countries, most modern cultures today offer the opportunity to rise above, or disassociate ourselves from our parentage. While our personal brand is still under the umbrella of our name, whether from our linage, or a moniker we invent for ourselves, our public persona—our brand—is now defined by what we choose to do with our time, the actions we take over the course of our lifetime.

Just like with our personal brand, a company brand takes time to establish. Companies change, hopefully grow over time, just as people do. For a company to thrive requires a healthy mix of new features to their existing products and services, as well as new offerings that are well-received, to garner 'brand advocates.' If the startup is branded effectively, the company's name recognition usually grows as the business mature.

We begin the branding process by creating a name for your offering, *and* your new venture. Even if you plan to sell only one type of offering, directly—a book on *Amazon*, an algorithm to *Oracle*, or your pottery on *Etsy*—this offering will likely be your first offering of many to come. You must put your very first offering under a 'corporate umbrella,' effectively creating a *house* to put your current and upcoming products and services (a place to grow each new creation).

-Corporate Branding-

Apple did not become a brand name without any products. The *Apple II*, and then the *Macintosh*, running software from spreadsheets to *Pagemaker* (one the first desktop publishing packages) branded *Apple* into the mega-corporation it is today. You must have an *offering*—a product, service, or [nonprofit] message such as a religion, or a cause—to create a company brand.

We begin the branding process by establishing names for your offering and startup. There are only a few subtle variations between branding a startup and branding a new product, service, or message (which we'll review in a minute). They both require at least five (5) components to create and produce effective identity packages.

1. Corporate I.D., also known as a LOGO.

2. **Corporate Tagline**, also known as a 'slogan,' that captures the essences of the offerings the company plans to sell.
3. **Product Logos** and **Taglines** must be developed for *every new offering released.*
4. **Brand Standards**, strict guidelines for use and display of logos and taglines that build brand awareness with every campaign, across all media channels.
5. **Productization lists**, which were produced in LSM Workbook 1.

Naming Your New Venture

You already have (or *should have* by now) your Productization lists of features, benefits/solutions, target markets, and **unique value propositions** (**UVPs**). You even know (or *should know* by now) some of your competitors, as well as a few additional horizontal and vertical markets—potential new audiences to sell your offering. These lists are going to help you build your brand components, so it's important at this point that you have these lists fully populated, or, at least, implemented.

Corporate branding is **"umbrella" branding**—directed at *very broad* target markets. You want to focus your corporate brand name and image (logo icon) on what your company will produce overall. *Ford Motor Company* produces automobiles. Sure, they produce other things, like tractors, buses, even financial services for financing their vehicles, but most everything they produce is related to vehicles of some type or another.

Your startup may be producing different offerings five years down the line than the product or service you've launched with, but it is likely your company will still produce offerings in the same general category as you began. *Apple* began with computers, then segued into music players, and cellphone, but most all *Apple* products are electronic devices, or services for their devices. Every offering you release at launch and beyond, will be housed under the *umbrella* of your corporate brand.

Your company's name should be ambiguous enough that it doesn't pinpoint your business to any specific product or service. Remember, your startup's offerings will change over time, likely even before launch. You'll discontinue obsolete products, and add new, and (hopefully) improved offerings. During its time, each product or service has its own name. The candy maker, *Nestlé*, has *Crunch Bars,* and *Butterfingers,* but their corporate name remains the same. When choosing a corporate name for your startup, make sure that it captures the essence of what you plan to sell. Your startup name should *not* change over time, but build brand awareness and instill trust in your company, throughout the life of your business.

Begin the process of choosing a name for your new company using one of the three typical naming paradigms:
- **Founder's Name, or Factitious Name**
- **Product Feature or Benefit**
- **Location**

Founder's or Factitious Name
Wells Fargo Bank began with Henry Wells and William Fargo in the 1850s, who started an east coast banking services for the west coast gold rush.

Prada is a fashion label by the Italian designer, Miuccia Prada. It began in Milan, Italy, in 1913.

HP is *Hewlett Packard*, named after Bill Hewlett and Dave Packard. In 1939 they formalized their partnership, and the two men, working from a garage in Palo Alto, CA, tossed a coin to see who's name would go first.

Nestlé, known for their candy and chocolates, began in Switzerland, in 1867, by Henri Nestlé, who created one of the first infant foods for women who couldn't breastfeed. (*Nestlé* now owns *Gerber* baby foods.)

Are you creating your own fashion line, or food label, or even a commercial blog or vlog (video blog), like *Martha Stewart*—the home-lifestyle celebrity? A typical naming convention for these types of *personal* products and services is using part or all of the founder's name for their corporate identity. It can be a pseudonym, a 'stage name,' but branding a personal name to a uniquely custom product unconsciously represents an *artist*, or an important, trusted individual, and adds the *perception* of value to your offering.

Founder's often use bizarre, seemingly random names, like the gaming company *Zinga,* named after the founder's dog. The electric car company, *Tesla*, uses the name of the famous physicist, Nikola Tesla.

A founder's name, or the name of their dog as the company name, doesn't make the brand. Remember, a blogger's *content*, or company's *offerings* initially make their brand [name] memorable (*"A rose by any other name would smell as sweet."* —Shakespeare).

Product's Feature or Benefit

Corporate names are often derived from the product or service itself—the features or benefits of the offering. These may be real or *perceived* benefits, and can be taken directly from your Productization lists that you began in LSM Workbook 1. You've already identified your offering's features and benefits (List 1A and 1B), and the unique value, or UVPs of your offering (List 3B). Create a name that reflects these features and benefits.

Jack Dorsey, co-founder of *Twitter*, came up with using an SMS (short message service) to communicate online. The original project name for the service was *twttr*, after the five-character length of American SMS short codes. During an all day brainstorming session, Dorsey claims they came across the word 'twitter,' as a perfect definition for 'a short burst of inconsequential information,' as 'chirps from birds'. Since the *Twitter* domain name was already taken, six months after the launch of *twttr,* they purchased the domain and changed the name of the service to *Twitter*.

Originally an online directory, "*the facebook*" offered profile pages to Harvard students that included a photo of their face. Their first logo, reflecting their 'face' feature, was a header across the top of each page. It had a sketch of the actor, Al Pacino's face, in the upper left corner, and the words *[thefacebook]* in the upper right corner, in a similar blue that is used in their logo today. Designed by Andrew McCollum, who was a co-founder of *Facebook's* original team, as [thefacebook] extended beyond Harvard students, they dropped Pacino's face, and the brackets around the text, but kept the logo text identity. Their current logo is similar to the san-serif typeface of the original [thefacebook].

Google founders Larry Page and Sergey Brin originally considered the name *Backrub*, for their program's analysis of "back links" that categorized a website's contents. Sean Anderson, a fellow graduate student, came up with "googolplex," the number 1 followed by 100 zeros, to amplify the indexing engine's benefit of returning virtually limitless amounts of information. Sean searched the web to see if the name was available, but misspelling "googol" as Google. And so the name was registered as *Google.com*.

Nike's co-founder Phil Knight wanted to name the brand, "Dimension Six." Geoff Hollister, an early employee, wanted to stay in the zone of Puma, after the cougar, and suggested the name "Peregrine," a type of falcon. Another employee suggested "Bengal." None of these options were popular with other employees.

Popular brand names, such as Kleenex and Xerox, had no more than two syllables and at least one exotic letter or sound, as with Z, X or K. Johnson, who ran their east coast factory, came up with Nike—the Greek winged goddess of victory. All but Phil Knight's name suggestions gave the perception of fast, nimble, agile, reflecting the benefit that *Nike* sports shoes offer.

Location
Like founder's names, naming a company after a specific location probably goes back pretty far, but we still use this naming convention today.

Adobe Corporation carries products like *Photoshop* and *Illustrator*. The company began in co-founder John Warnock's garage. Their name comes from the Adobe Creek in Los Altos, California, which, at one time, ran behind his house.

Southwest Airlines launched with very smart marketing all around, but especially in their corporate naming convention. When they first rolled out as an independent airline, they only flew to the southwestern United States. *Southwest* originally **niche marketed** to fliers interested in going only to the southwest U.S. No major airline took you directly to the southwestern states at that time, often routing passengers with several stopovers just to get from L.A. to Phoenix or Tuscon, only a few hundred miles away. *Southwest Airlines* offered many direct flights to get you to the southwest and back quickly. Their company name is not only the location they first serviced, but it was also their greatest benefit!

The name *Amazon.com* came from its CEO, Jeff Bezos. He started looking for a company name in the dictionary to find a word that broadly represented his upcoming online bookstore. Knowing much of the internet was, and *is* alphabetically ordered, Bezos started his dictionary search in the 'A's,' so his company name would be on the top of most lists, and, in effect, be the first returns in a search as well.

The Amazon river is the largest river in the world by volume. Bezos planned to make his bookstore the largest in the world, so he chose the name Amazon, as it begins with an 'A,' and represented the massive volume he planned for his online store. Starting his company name with the letter 'A' was smart branding, and something that you should consider when naming your company.

Corporate Divisions

If your company buys another, or breaks up the original company into multiple divisions, a corporate division name and identity are required. Corporate divisions typically have the original company name, and even corporate logo, with the addition of the primary feature or benefit of that division. *Nike Golf*, *Amazon Web Services*, *Xbox Live* (MMOG gaming). Each of these corporate divisions not only begins with the original corporate name *and* logo, but also identifies the key feature each of the divisions provides. When naming corporate divisions, be sure to begin with the corporate name (and logo I.D.), then add the primary feature or benefit the new division offers.

What's in a [Company] Name

Whether naming your company after the founder's name, a factious name; the offering's features, or real or perceived benefits; or you name your company after a real or imagined location, the name of your company isn't all that important.

Yahoo!, originally a web directory, renamed from *Jerry and David's Guide to the World Wide Web* (Jerry Yang and David Filo founders), did not become famous because of their name. As cool as it was for a technology service, at the time, in 1995, its **user interface** (**UI**) was simple, and user-friendly for everyone, as were their marketing campaigns. They were funny, and non-technical, verging on absurd, the opposite of most other web services of their kind.

Facebook did not become the most popular social network online because their name is so profoundly brilliant. Nor was the name *Nike*, or even *Amazon*. These companies got famous because the features of their offerings gave (and still give) real *value.* Their products and services provided real or perceived benefits to *a lot* of people, and still do, which is why they are still in business. In 2017, *Yahoo!* was sold to *Verizon Communications* after its user-base, and stock price, had been stagnate for years.

Remember, your company name is the *beginning* of your brand. Your corporate branding only becomes recognized and remembered by **continually delivering products or services of value**. So, don't dwell on what to name your company! Pick a company name using any one of the three naming conventions, buy the URL (we'll review how to purchase domains, next), and move on to the mountain of work ahead of you. Building your brand name will happen organically if the products and services your organization continually delivers has benefit to users.

-Product Branding-

Naming Your Offering

Naming products and services differs from 'umbrella' branding of corporations. You'll give your offering a name, logo, and tagline, but all three should be focused on a feature or benefit of the offering itself.

Branding the products and services within your corporation, your offering's identity should be much more focused on a real or perceived benefit that the features of your offering provides.

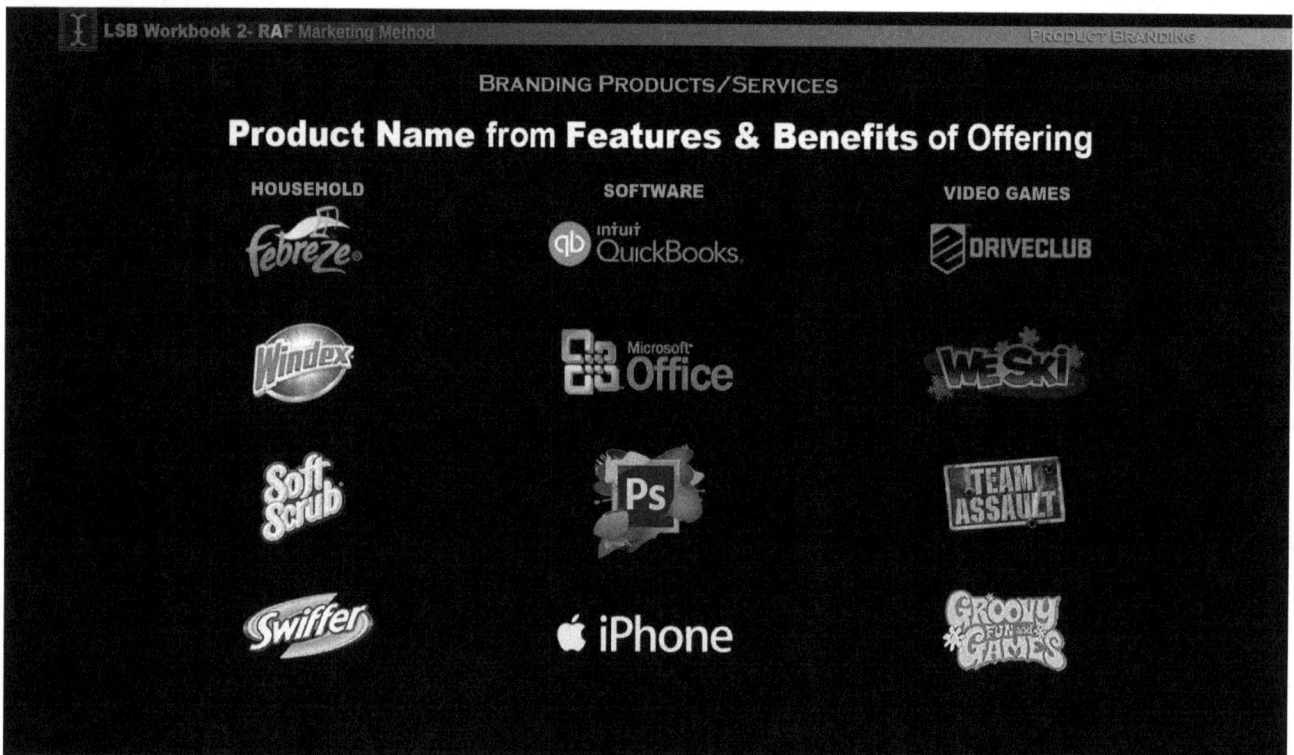

Household products, like cleansers, or dish soap, generally have a combination of **visual words** representing their best feature and benefit.

Soft Scrub, is a *mild* cleaning fluid. The offering's name is describing its key feature *and* benefit, and what sets it apart from competitors like *Comet*, which is a grainy powder cleanser.

Windex, is a window cleaner—the EX evokes high tech, or 'extra powerful, extraordinary, exceptional,' imagery.

Fabreze, a spray to mask odor—FABulous bREZE, evokes fresh air imagery. These names represent a benefit of the product that they're branding. (We'll examine visual words in the Copywriting Module of LSL Workbook 3.)

Naming software programs or applications is the same as naming any other offering. The name should be derived from *the* feature or benefit of what the offering does. You [should] already know what your offering does, in detail, from your Productization lists. List 1A—FEATURES and 1B—BENEFITS explicitly explain what your product or service IS and DOES.

Quickbooks, by *Intuit*, is accounting software. "Keeping the books" is a common colloquialism for business accounting. Doing the 'books' quickly and simple is a direct benefit of their software.

Microsoft Office is software that performs office administration functions. They are touting the key feature of their software in their offering's name.

Photoshop is a photo-editing program. Adding "shop" to "photo" implies *working* on photography, which is what their software enables users to do.

Even *iPhone* speaks to the perceived benefit of owning an *Apple* product, as most of their consumer-friendly products begin with an 'i.' *iPhone. iPod. iPad*.

Video games have the same naming convention as any other offerings, describing a feature and/or benefit of the game itself.

DriveClub, a *PS4* (*Sony PlayStation*) game is clearly an **MMOG** (**massive multiplayer online game**) car racing game. *DriveClub VR* also describes the addition of **virtual reality** (**VR**) to this gaming experience.

Team Assault, speaks for itself. It is clearly a **FPS** (**first person shooter**) game, and its logo screams this with the bullet holes in the panel the name is visually stenciled on.

We Ski, speaks for itself, a **FPP** (**first person perspective**) virtual skiing and downhill racing experience.

Naming products, services, or even messages, such as *Global Climate Action*, a United Nation initiative to stop global warming, choose or invent names that describe what the offering *does*, the key feature and/or benefit of the product itself. When naming your offerings, be sure to review your Productization lists: 1A, 1B, *and* 3B—your UVPs—to accurately describe *and* position, or 'fit' your offerings in the marketplace of sellable items.

-The Mechanics of URLs-

Give Your Company a Web Address
So, you've chosen great names for your offering *and* company. Congratulations!

You're on the way to turning your productized offering into a real, marketable product, service, and startup. LSB Workbook 2 takes you step-by-step through the process of creating an effective logo for your new offering and company in few modules forward, but for now, you need a web address to give your new venture a place to live.

Remember, if you have no wish to create a startup, and are only looking to sell your offerings through a **VAR** (**value added reseller**), such as *Amazon, Etsy,* or even license your software to *SAP* or *Oracle,* you still should create a corporate name. It's likely your first book, or clothing line, or software solution, won't be your last, especially if you realize success creating what you love. You'll need a web address for your corporate name, of course, even if it's *your* name as an author, or clothing designer, or software developer.

It is wise to buy many web addresses—domain names—URLs. You may purchase several for your company, all of which 'point,' known as 'mapping,' to your website. It's often smart marketing to have a separate web address for each of your offerings as well, though it is common to use subdomains—an addition to the end (or beginning) of your URL. We'll examine why in a minute, but for now, let's drill down on what a web address actually *is*.

URL means **Uniform Resource Locator**. Your URLs are your online addresses, aka your company and product **Domain Names**.

You need a URL for everything you put online that does *not* reside on another's platform, such as *LinkedIn, Twitter,* or *Instagram*. These platforms have their own URL addresses. Your company profile page becomes a **subdomain** to *LinkedIn's* platform URL: www.linkedin.com/**in/jericafesin**. Your posts and adverts are embedded into these platform's feeds, which is why you don't need a URL when you post an update, or run an ad campaign on these sites. *Your* websites, *your* landing pages, *your* commercial blogs or vlogs, all must have a URL—a web address—to publish your digital campaigns online.

There are three (3) levels, or distinct parts, to a domain name (URL):
- **3LD**: 3rd level domain.
- **2LD**: 2nd level domain.
- **TLD**: Top level domain.

My author website URL: www.jcafesin.com, breaks down into three (3) domain levels. **3LD:** www; **2LD:** jcafesin; **TLD:** com.

3rd Level Domains
3LDs indicate who the **host server** is—where what you see on your screen is coming from. A **webhost** stores the code and components—text, images, video—

of the [web]pages of your website, landing pages, microsites…etc., on **servers**, then *serves up* your marketing efforts to the internet. We'll drill down on webhosting, along with exploring the range of online technology you'll need to know to launch a startup, in Module 19 of this workbook.

The 3LDs (often referred to as sub-domains) is the location of the server that we are sent to when we click on a site link, or put a URL into our browser widow. WWW means World Wide Web, and at this point you don't even need to put 'www.' in your URL searches because all 3LDs default to the world wide web now.

An exception to this rule is web addresses that use a different protocol, like **FTP**, (**file transfer protocol**), that allows you to upload and download files, documents, code, music, and imagery directly to (upload) or from (download) a specific server. A web address for FTP transactions would look something like this: ftp.somecompany.com.

Another exception to leaving off the 3LD www in a web address is when you are searching for, or sending something *within* an organization. Known as the **intranet**, it is a private network **within a business**. Within intranets, your 3LDs must be *where you want to send people within the company*, to download or upload content from your company's private network. For example, help.yourcompany.com, will send people to a live person, or instructional videos or presentations, or documentation for 'help,' depending on what the company makes available on their help.yourcompany.com web page. Email 3LD might look like this: mail.yourcompany.com, and this address would be an email server. These URLs are NOT public-facing, like your website, but in a safe space on secure (from hacking) servers. These servers can be located at your company, or at a third party vendor such as *Amazon Web Services (AWS)*, or *Wix* webhosting.

2ⁿᵈ Level Domains

2LDs are your *unique* identifier: your **company name**, and can also be your offering's names as well. Shorter, easy-to-spell names and common words are best to use as your company identifiers, but it is hard to find these available with a .com extension (TLD), as most have been taken already. And a .com extension is a must to immediately identify and market your company as a substantive commercial business today.

Your 2LD is the name of your company or offering. I'm *Jeri Cafesin*, and I'm using my name to brand myself as an author, just like *Stephen King*, the horror writer does (stephenking.com). I got lucky because my name isn't common, so I was able to get my URL with *my* name: **jcafesin**.com.

What happens if you aren't as lucky as I was, and can't get the URL you pick for your company name with a .com TLD?

Let's say you sell electronics, like *Best Buy*, and choose the company name *Tech Giant*, after the benefit of the wide range of devices your company offers. We can pretty much guarantee the name *Tech Giant* is already taken by some other tech company. If you still want to use the company name *Tech Giant*, you can find out who has it, and offer to buy it from them, but that can get very expensive, and it's not necessary.

If you can not get the name you want as your 2LD, *and* a .com extension, you should change the name of your company, or *adapt* the 2LD of your company's URL.

Instead of just your company name, consider using a phrase for your URL, to be sure that you retain the .com extension. *TechGiant<u>Outlet</u>.com* ("outlet" = inexpensive); *TechGiant<u>MegaStore</u>.com*; *TechGiant<u>Bargins</u>.com*. In this way, you get to have your company's name in your 2LD, but you also have a **UVP** (**unique value proposition**) of what your company *does,* which makes it even more powerful, especially in terms of **search engine optimization** (**SEO**)! Your URL will rank higher in search results, be closer to the top of returns, *if* your URL text matches what your company *does,* literally. If my URL says, *TechGiantOutlet.com,* and *Tech Giant* really does sell cheap, but well-rated electronic devices, and this messaging is concertized by all of *Tech Giant's* websites, landing pages, public relations and related online marketing efforts, this URL will likely increase my startup's SEO ranking. (Think <u>Southwest</u> Airlines. Their 2LD concertized the messaging that *Southwest* only flew to the southwestern states when they launched their airline. Throughout their initial marketing efforts, when they only flew to the southwest U.S., this URL also helped rank their business higher whenever their website link appeared in their campaigns, or articles, testimonials, and other PR about their company.)

Top Level Domains
Top Level Domains (TLD) are your **type of business** identifiers. You want a URL for your company with a **.com TLD**. At *least* one. The .com extension, or Top Level Domain, is globally recognized as a real, commercial business (regardless if this is true, or merely a shell company). Just because a TLD extension, such as .net, or .io (originally stood for *Indian Ocean Territory*—India) has more 'space' available to pull the 2LD name you want, it does NOT mean it is more valuable. The .com TLD is more common, and is more popular than any other option. It is memorable. At this point, we are wired to think "dot com," for a business.

Don't forget that it's important to change your 2LD to insure you get a .com URL for your business, if necessary. TLDs can be a very powerful marketing tools, telling all viewers of your URL, as well as all internet search crawlers like *Google*, what type of business you are.

- **.com**—for global, commercial and wholesale businesses.

- **.org**—non-profits, charities, online schools, religions, social causes.

- **.net**—commercial internet businesses, but less recognized than .com.

- **.edu**—for accredited schools, universities, and education companies.

- **.gov**—for most sectors of local and national government.

As mentioned, an excellent SEO technique is to buy multiple URLs for the same company. Multiple URLs will increase your digital footprint, and assure your company ranks higher in your industry sector. Once you've purchased your corporate .com URL, you may get URLs with .net, or similar trending TLDs, as second and third (or more) domains for your company, then *point*, or *map* them to whatever URL you want, from your website, to your landing page campaigns. If a viewer clicks on a search result for *TechGiantSavings.net,* you can *map* that link to land them on the *TechGiantOutlet.com* main website.

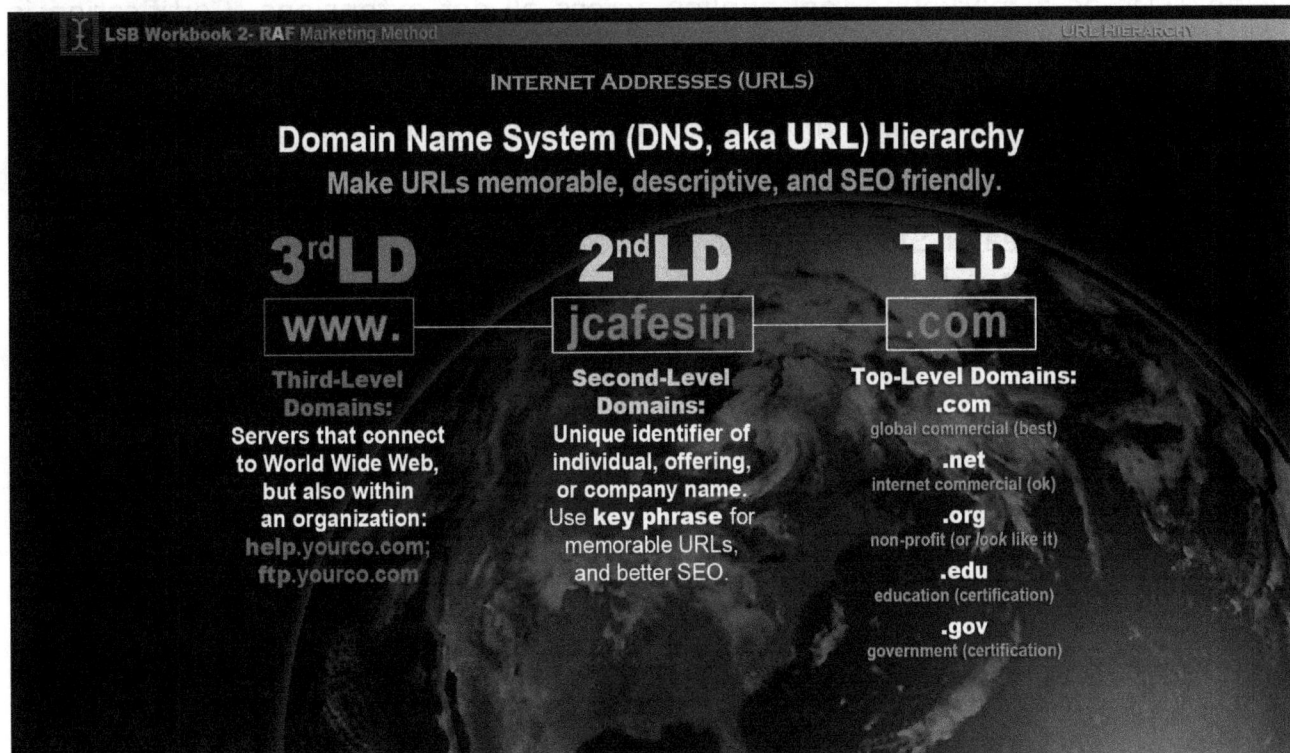

All the URLs you purchase *must* pay off what your venture DOES, to keep your URLs on top of search returns (SEO) in your business category. The URLs *TechGiantMegaStore*.com, *TechGiantSavings.net, and TechGiantBargins*.com, may link to your main website, *or*, they may be utilized as landing page addresses (URL), but the content on that landing page must concertize the messaging that *Tech Giant sells tech devices at a discount* to increase the company's SEO ranking. (We'll closely examine using subdomains for your online marketing efforts in Module 21—Digital Campaigns, of this workbook.)

In addition to .com, and trending, more 'available' TLDs, like .net, or .io, you may consider purchasing a .org TLD as well. Most of us think of .org as a nonprofit business, or even a charity. Your company does not need to be an online school, or a charity, or a nonprofit organization, but sometimes it sure helps in marketing your business to *look* like one.

An example of using the .org TLD in the URL to give an *impression*, or perception of philanthropy, is the company *Change.org*. They are a social advocacy platform, where people can create petitions to protest everything from global warming to losing their local fire house to budget cuts. *Change* is *not* a nonprofit company. It is a for-profit, commercial business that collects money when you sign, or give money to their promoted petitions. We all want to feel like we are doing the right thing when we sign our name to back a cause. Knowing *Change.org* is making money on our engagements, would make it less likely for us to engage, as social morality says, *doing the right thing,* should not be equated with making a profit.

Using TLDs as a marketing tool applies across all dot-extensions. Certification is required for .edu, and .gov. EduCause is the managing registrar to get a .edu TLD, and it requires that your business be an accredited institution. To get a .gov domain name your business must be a federal, state, local or tribal government organization within the U.S.

Remember, for greater SEO, first buy your .com TLDs, then several other domains with .com and other TLD extensions. More important than search ranking, URLs are an effective *first impression*, especially when they include the best bit about what our startup has to offer, as most of us are now wired to notice the web address when we're visiting a website, landing page, or receiving an email.
-
-

STOP! Complete LSB PROJECT #1a before moving on.

◆◆◆

LSB Workbook 2: PROJECT #1a
Corporate and Product NAMES

Make the *process* of coming up with your **corporate name** easier by choosing from one of the **three (3) naming conventions**. Don't get too hung up on creating the *perfect* name. After all, the value of a rose is that it smells fragrant and looks beautiful. The *value your offering/s provides* to your target audiences will **brand your company name** (not the other way around).

1. **Give your new COMPANY a name.** Use **'umbrella' branding**, and give your new venture a **corporate name** that encapsulates a *broad idea* of the offering/s your company plans to produce, or the industry to which your business belongs. Use the **founder's name/s**, or *your* name if you are creating a company with a unique, personal signature, like a commercial blog or vlog, a clothing line, or artistic venture. (Examples: MarthaStewart.com for the homemaker's blog and products. StephenKing.com, the horror author's website.) Use a **key feature or benefit** of your potential offerings for products and services, even software, to identify what your new venture *does*. Use a place, a **real or imagined location** if it has any significance to the offerings you are planning to sell.

2. **Name your initial OFFERING.** Create a **name** for your **launch offering** that is **related to what the offering does**. Use a **key feature or benefit** of your product, service or message, which you will find on your Productization lists: 1A—FEATURES, 1B—BENEFITS, and 3B—UVPs. Add visual words or letters to your key feature. (Example: EX for 'extra' or 'extraordinary.' TEC, for 'technology.') Try to keep your **offering's name** aligned with your corporate name. (Example: the *Apple* computer line, *Macintosh*, is a type of apple we eat. The *iphone, ipad,* and *ipod*, are part of *Apple's iOS*—operating system).

The Naming Process

1. **Come up with a list of** [at least] **five (5) CORPORATE names**, *and* **five (5) names** for your initial **launch OFFERING**. If you selling a product directly, through a VAR like *Amazon* or *Etsy*, you do not necessarily need a corporate name, though it is highly recommended, even if just *your* name, i.e. *MaryJane Pottery*. As the artist/creator of what you are selling, you'll likely want to create and sell more items if you find success doing what you love, though a VAR, or creating your own company down the line.

2. **Go to a domain registrar**, such as *Name.com* or *NetworkSolutions.com*.

3. **Input each name on your list in their search bar**, adding a **.com TLD** to each. Check if the URL is already taken. Likely, most of the names on your list will have existing (even if inactive) URLs owned by other companies, or individuals.

   If you can *not* get a **.com URL TLD** with any of the names on your list, pick the company name you prefer, off your list of 5 names, and come up with a **phrase for your 2nd Level Domain (2LD)** that includes the company name you prefer. Be sure the phrase concertizes a key feature or benefit that your new venture will offer, and the URL is not already taken. For better SEO, so the search crawlers will delineate your company name from your keyword addition, you can use a hyphen between them. The only issue with using a hyphen in your URL, is it must be noted when *telling* someone your domain name. (Example: My author website is jcafesin.com. If the name was taken, though it was not, I'd have tried <u>author-</u>jcafesin.com, or jcafesin-author.com. To delineate my name from my keyword descriptor, I'd use a hyphen to separate my name from the word 'author.')

4. **BUY URLs.** If a name you like, **with a .com extension**, is available, **register the name** through your **webhost**, or **registrar**. For example, if you are using a webhost such as *Wix* to build and host your digital marketing efforts, purchase your URL through *Wix* (to avoid URL 'mapping' charges).

◆◆◆

-Tagline and Voice Conventions-

Taglines Are the Voice of Your Venture

Taglines, also called slogans, are often overlooked in the branding process. This is a mistake. The tagline, for your company *and* offerings, is as important, if not more important than the logo. There will be media you will market on in which no imagery, not even a logo, can be used, such as the **PPC** (**pay-per-click**) Text Only ads we see on *Google* at the top of search returns.

A tagline paints a story of what your company or offering does. They may be selling a perception, as in "Intel Inside," which infers the notion that *Intel* computer chips are a valuable component inside a computer. They may sell directly, as *Nokia's* "Connecting People," tagline, that tells us that Nokia devices, like their cellphones, connect people.

Your taglines, whether for your corporation or your offerings, are **implied CTAs** (**Calls-to-Action**). Don't forget, ALL marketing, from identities to ads, must have a direct or implied CTA, (or you've produced fine art, NOT marketing).

Taglines employ an implied CTA—a *suggestion* to act—i.e. *remember* the company by its brand. They utilize a limerick, like lyrics in a song, to tout a real or perceived benefit of your offering and company. Unlike corporate names, taglines sometimes change over time as the company's offerings evolve. They also change in response to competition, to distinguish your offering or company from a serious competitor. Your roll-out taglines, the taglines you use with your logo identity at the launch of your company and product, should project a specific image, and brand your offering and startup with a unique *voice*, that speaks to a specific, though broad target market.

Think of this voice as a sequence of notes in a piece of music. Is the note sequence rock 'n roll? Rap? Punk? Swing? Orchestral? Taglines are a sequence of two to five words, a short phrase that suggests, or brands your offering and company to who you're talking to—what unique benefit your company provides, what problem your offerings solves, or what desire your product, service or message fulfills.

Apple's tagline, "Think Different," implies if you buy and use their products you will become a unique thinker, more creative, more independent than those who use similar devices from their competitors.

Disneyland's tagline, The Happiest Place on Earth," invites guests with the promise they'll feel happy when they go to *Disneyland*. While it is a creative, engaging environment, as a parent who raised two kids, when they were toddlers they weren't so happy between 2:00 – 5:00pm, cranky and tired from over-stimulation at the theme park. And my husband and I were exhausted by then, trying to keep our kids entertained while standing in endless lines most of the day to get on the rides. Like *Apple*, *Disneyland's* tagline is selling the *perception* of benefit their company offers.

BMW's tagline, "the Ultimate Driving Machine," is branding the car company at a specific target audience. This group of buyers are in their early-30s to mid-60s, mostly men, mid-level management working in tech, finance, sales or marketing. They may be nouveau riche—recently made money on tech stock or sales (as old wealth never flaunts it). They are likely to be rock 'n roll, and/or rap music enthusiasts, but may occasionally listen to classical to feel intellectual, or worldly. They read the latest trending books on the New York Times Bestsellers list, and watch late night TV of popular talk hosts.

Words like 'ultimate,' or 'machine,' evoke imagery. 'Ultimate' implies *fast*, even reckless, *skating the edge*. These are feelings young people possess, as when we are young, we feel indestructible. We're looking for our experiences to be intense. 'Driving machine' implies high-tech, sophistication, smart. *BMW's* tagline effectively brands their vehicles to a tightly targeted market, which is almost exclusively mid to upper income *men*. These particular men are single/divorced, in their mid-30s, looking to display their success; to mid-60s, seeking to feel young while going through their mid-life crisis. *BMW's* target markets desire a status symbol.

Volvo, which offers vehicles at similar price-points to *BMW,* has a more conservative tagline. "For Life." Words like 'life' evoke longevity, loyality, timeless quality. *Volvo's* tagline also brands their offerings to a tightly targeted market. Their tagline is branding their cars to attract parents of toddlers to teens, even perhaps new grandparents. They are middle to upper income, educated, usually liberal/democrat, female over male (which is good because women yield more influence in purchasing expensive items than men). They listen to pop, or 80s rock, or easy listening. They are focused on taking care of their family beyond just themselves, are fairly conservative spenders except regarding the happiness and welfare of their children. To stand out from all the other car companies, *Volvo* brands themselves as the '*safe car*,' the kind of vehicle you can trust to hand down to your kids when they go off to college.

These two car companies, *BMW* and *Volvo*, are target branding utilizing taglines. The tighter you target your marketing efforts to a specific group of people, even in your identity, the more likely you are to brand your company and sell your offering.

Taglines also distinguish your offerings from competitors to uniquely position your company in competitive markets. *McDonald's* and *Burger King* started around the same time in the mid-1950s. Though they offer virtually the exact same menu, to the same target markets, *McDonald's* became the Goliath of burgers in the 60s and 70s. So, how did *Burger King* go up against the Goliath of *McDonald's*?

McDonald's tagline has changed over time many times. "You Deserve a Break Today," was their most widely used, beginning in 1971, but in the 1960s they used taglines that touted home cooking, with, "Go For Goodness," and "The Closest Thing to Home." Their current tagline, "I'm loving It," is still in the same vain as their past taglines, touting that whatever you get from McDonald's you ostensibly will like. The issue with this is, you can basically only get what *McDonald's* serves. If you want something else, like a burger with no sauce or pickles, you have to wait ten minutes for somebody to get your *custom* order together, and then they're screaming your name above the din in the restaurant for you to come to the front desk and pick up your "special order." You'd *better* love it their way, because it sure is a hassle to get a burger *your* way.

Burger King's marketing exploited this issue with their biggest competitor. BK's tagline, *"Have It Your Way,"* from 1974 forward, claims BK solves this custom order problem with *McDonald's* by providing you with a simple way to get the exact burger you want. In this way, they branded themselves differently than the Goliath of burgers, and earned some of *McDonald's* market share. They updated their tagline in 2014 to *"Be Your Way,"* inferring if you eat at BK you can get your burger your way, which makes you unique, independent, *better* than the hordes at *McDonald's*.

Taglines are a powerful marketing tool. They help communicate a real or perceived benefit of your offering, and uniquely position your product and company for launch and beyond. Taglines can also revitalize a company's brand. Instead of rebranding the corporation—creating a new identity, new brand standards, and new business collateral—which can be extremely expensive, simply changing the tagline can re-position your offering and/or company to encapsulate its uniqueness, and differentiate your venture from competitors.

Product Taglines

Taglines, or **slogans** for offerings, follow the same paradigm as taglines for a company. The difference is that product taglines are transient, short-lived. Though they may be employed over several campaigns, slogans don't last as long as corporate taglines.

Apple used "iThink, Therefore iMac," and "Blows Minds, Not Budgets," slogans to market the iMac in 1998. "The iMac to Go," was used to introduce iBooks in 1999. "The Plot Thins," also in 1999, was used to market the "thinner" PowerBook G3. And "Less is More" was used to introduce the PowerBook G4s in 2003. Their *iPhone* 10, released 2018, uses, "Say Hello to the Future."

The tagline, "The One and Only Wonderbra," is obviously for the bra, *Wonderbra*. It is one of many apparel products of the *HanesBrand* Corporation.

Bounty paper towels, a product of *Procter & Gamble* uses, "The Quicker Picker Upper," to tout their offering's greatest benefit—that it picks up spills fast.

M & M's candy, a product of the *Mars Corp.* used, "Melts in Your Mouth, Not in Your Hands," to market to parents who were sick of cleaning up melted chocolate bars.

While it isn't strictly necessary to create taglines for your offerings, it will help your launch marketing efforts in several ways. Tagline/slogans for your offering

aligns your campaign messaging with real or perceived benefits of the product or service you are trying to brand and sell. It also gives each offering you produce a unique identifier that helps concertize your company's overall brand image.
-
-

STOP! Do LSB PROJECT #1b before moving on.

◆◆◆

LSB Workbook 2: PROJECT #1b
Corporate and Product TAGLINES

1. **Write a TAGLINE for your startup** that broadly reflect a real or implied **feature** and/or **benefit**/solution representing your **offering/s**, and/or **industry**.

Corporate taglines should follow the 'umbrella' naming convention, and be a real, or, more likely, a *perceived* value that brands your offerings and company to an industry or concept. The athletic shoe maker *Nike's* tagline, *"Just Do It,"* tackles the voices of laziness in most of us. The tagline challenges us to exercise, and implies, or *suggests*, we use *Nike's* shoes to get out there and *'just do it.'*

2. **Write a TAGLINE for each offering your startup is projected to produce** (or has already produced), reflecting a real or implied **feature** and/or **benefit/solution** representing the **offering itself. PRODUCT taglines** should be *the* **differentiator**, the defining feature and/or benefit of your offering. Example: *"Kills Bugs Dead,"* reflects a real benefit, *the* **UVP** of *Raid* bug spray, a product of *SC Johnson Corp*.

Corporate *and* **product taglines** should be **no longer than seven (7) words**. Five (5) or less is optimal.

◆◆◆

◆◆◆◆◆

MODULE 14: DESIGN FUNDAMENTALS

Is it Art, or Graphic Design

When I attended university, the Marketing building was a quarter mile away from the Art building, where the graphic design students, myself among them, blithely put together advertising campaigns without any understanding of marketing.

I was fired from my first job out of college a year into working as an art director for a global publishing firm, partly *because* of my university education. "Design an album cover," was a typical assignment in one of my advertising design classes. There were no perimeters given to create a design directed at a target audience. There was no instruction on touting the UVP of the band, what made them different from every other rock bank out there. There was no information given on how to actually *reproduce* the artwork we created, so that the album cover was affordable to print, and would look good when printed. The professors had no knowledge of marketing, and gave no instruction as to what type of cover could help *sell* the music inside. We created "art." So, my first job out of college, I designed 'art,' instead of creating marketing.

"You are an artist," my sweet boss, Alex, said the day he fired me from the publishing company I was working for. "Your book covers have leveled-up Windsor's image, to be sure, but you're costing us a fortune in lithography (this was before the Macintosh and desktop publishing). "Regardless of the obvious quality of the work under your direction, the ROI just isn't there." He was very apologetic, though he shouldn't have been. It wasn't like the first time he'd told me to come up with simpler design solutions instead keeping their lithography lab working almost exclusively for me.

Shortly after I was fired, I got a job art directing five international divisions of a popular jewelry manufacturer. The computer was just coming into play, and lithography was going away, but I understood from my first job experience that Alex was right. Advertising and marketing are all about making money, *not* 'art.'

Most businesses operate in much the same way my university did. The Marketing department, and the Design department have little to no communication. Yet, **graphic design is based on marketing**. It shouldn't have mattered that *I liked* my album cover design, or my teacher did, as I was taught to believe. All that matters in creating *any* marketing material, is if the design gets attention, communicates a message, and subsequently motivates conversion (buy; try; subscribe). The marketing effort should help brand and *sell* the offering.

Branding an offering and company requires any business to *continually produce* advertising and marketing material, from corporate and product identities, to integrated marketing campaigns. This is how to build brand awareness of your products and services, but also garner awareness of your company.

So, now that we are all on the same page about the difference between creating 'art,' and branded 'marketing' material, before you design an identity, or even direct those you hire to do it for you, you must understand a bit about working within the perimeters of design itself.

-The Design Process-

Everything you use, and everything you see, has been designed, even if just by Mother Nature. Physics is essentially design *rules*, or perimeters of physical laws, as in, we can't walk through [most] walls.

Graphic Design is marketing through visual communication. In design terms, graffiti written on a wall in spray paint is no different than hieroglyphics from ancient Egypt. They are both visual design written on walls, meant to communicate *something*. From the lamp that gives you light to read by, to the books themselves, whether digital ebooks, or print, someone *designed* these products. Even if the book is all text, a graphic designer likely created the pages to read as effectively on your cellphone as on your laptop (**responsive design**).

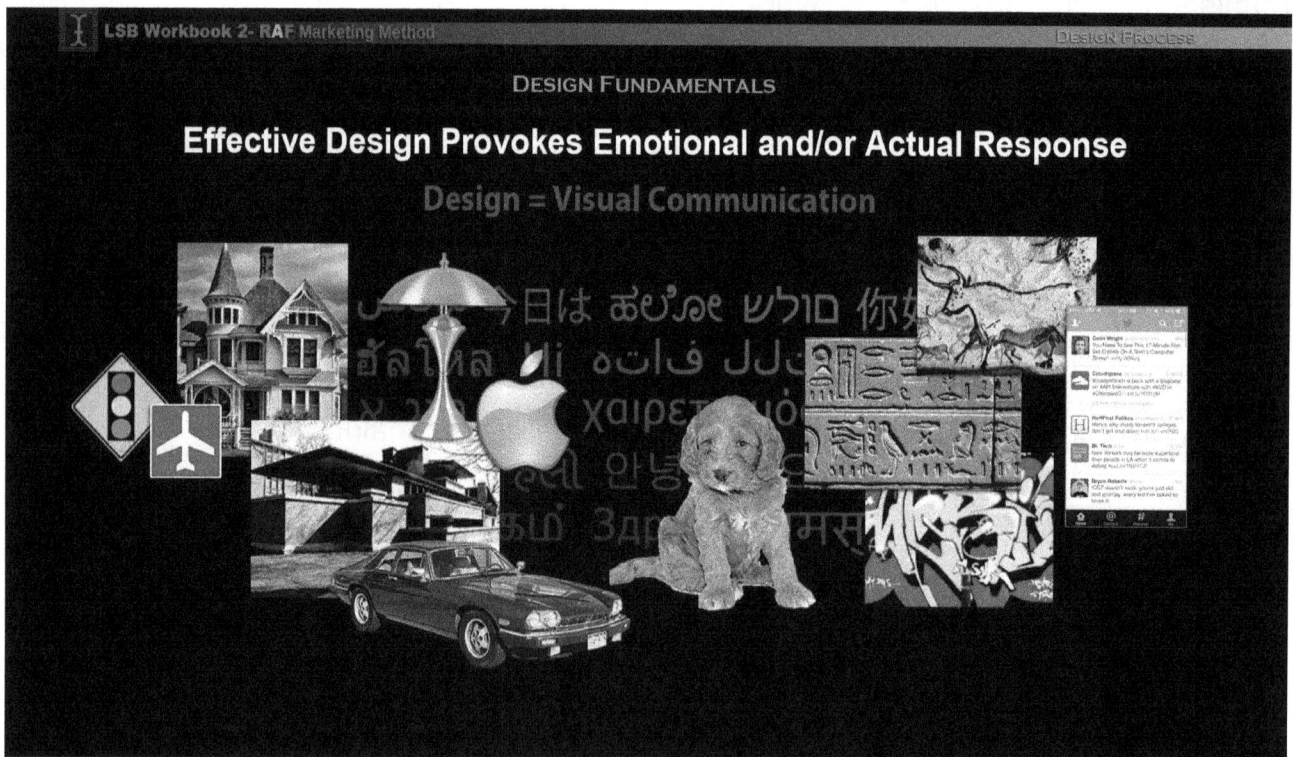

Your apartment or house, to the clothes you wear, to the sidewalk you walk on, to the street signs you read while behind the wheel of the car you drive, someone, somewhere, designed it all. We design food with GMOs (genetically modified organisms). We even design dogs now. Labradoodles, are a combination of a

Labrador and a Poodle. We design all types of animals, from horses to cattle through the process of cloning.

Graphic design is NOT product design. While both employ the elements of design, and adhere to design perimeters, **graphic design is visual marketing**. Graphic designers create visual communications to market/sell a potential, or completely developed, product, service, or nonprofit message.

In this module we'll explore how to create effective **graphic design—visual marketing**—across all media. You'll discover the perimeters of design, and how to apply these rules, not just to identities, but all advertising and marketing material to effectively execute the branding process, and build brand awareness of your products and company with every campaign.

The Three Components of Design
To create design, *any* design, fine art or marketing, requires [at least] these three components:

- **Space**—what space is required to produce the design? Are you designing within a **two-dimensional** (**2D**) space, like a magazine ad campaign, or a direct mail campaign on specific sizes of paper? Are you designing in 2D virtual space, perhaps creating a website, or CPC (cost-per-click) social media marketing (SMM) campaign? The size of your advert—the *space* it takes on the timeline of the social media platform—will be different on *Pinterest* than *Facebook*.

  Volume and **Mass** exist in **3D space**, as in designing buildings, or a physical product, or a trade-show booth.

- **Materials**—what materials are required to create and produce the design? Digital (virtual), or physical (print), both require materials to actualize the design.

  Creating print media, such as a brochure, billboard, display, trade-show booth graphics, a physical product or packaging for a product, generally requires working with a personal computer (PC) or laptop today. Required programs to create and produce the job range from *Photoshop*, to *Illustrator*, to a page layout application like *InDesign*, to a word program for the copy decks. To *print* the design you create requires a digital, or offset printing press, as well as inks, paper, maybe plastics, and many other physical materials to produce the marketing effort.

  Are you designing an online video marketing campaign? To create and produce the video, materials like a camera and video editing software will be required. Additional materials will be needed such as stable internet access, a webhost to serve up the campaign...etc. To produce *any* design requires some sort of materials, even if just programs and/or applications.

- **Time**—to develop, create and produce anything, including graphic design, takes *time*. It may seem obvious, but step back for a second and think about this. To produce design takes time, and you, the CEO of your productize offering, have to determine how much time you want to invest in design, in order that it pays off with the ROI—return on investment—of your time down the line.

Time is money isn't just a colloquialism. In business, your time is costing you money. If you invest it into your company without initial monetary compensation, as most startup partners do, you don't want to waste your time, aka your money.

Before beginning any marketing effort, first determine how to apply these three perimeters of design, *any* design—SPACE, MATERIAL, and TIME—to produce effective marketing campaigns that will yield a healthy ROI, even if that ROI is to build brand awareness of your offering and new venture.

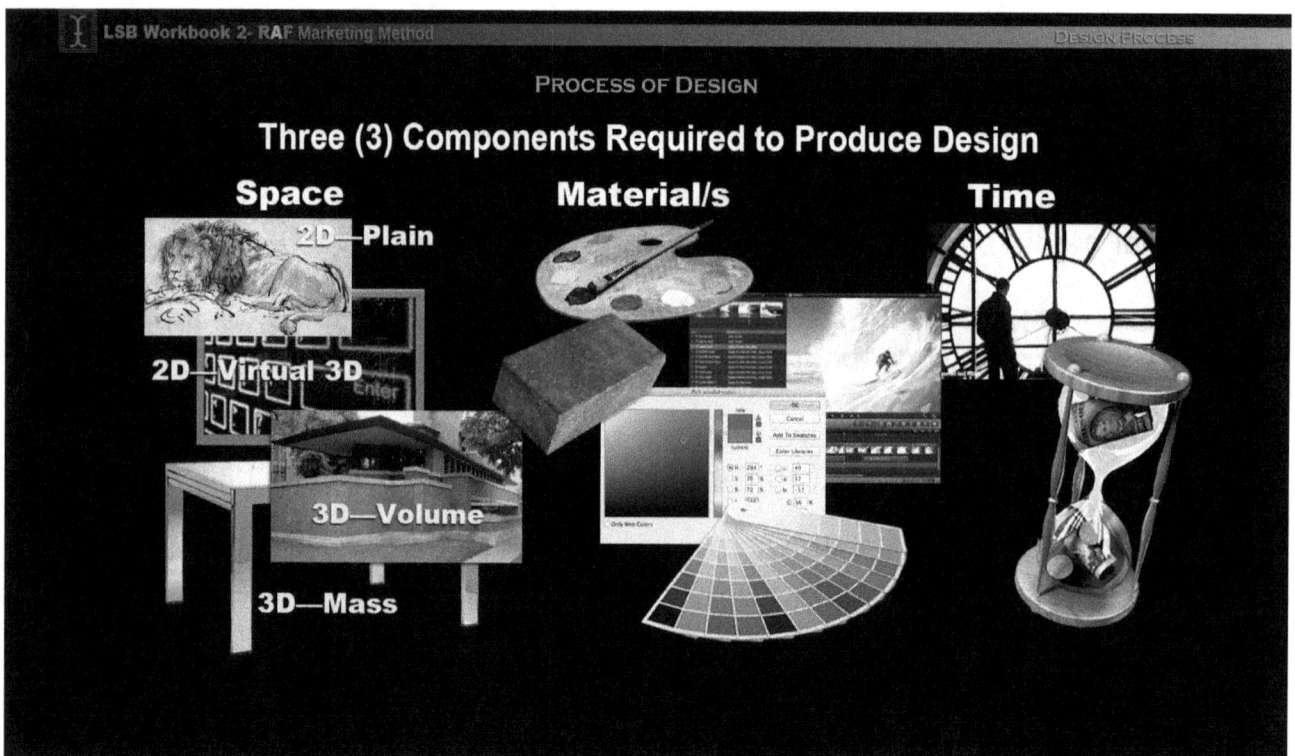

Design as Visceral Telepathy
Design is visual (sometimes *visceral*, or unconscious) **communication**. We all respond to what we see. Sometimes we interact with design, like road signs, or the road itself, but we also have an unconscious response, like the red of a STOP sign causes tension, enough for us to be cautious, and stop. We all have *feelings*

about the design of vehicles, including those we choose to buy. Whether we get them for fuel economy, luxury, or a status symbol, most of us like the design—the lines, the shape, the form, and color—of the cars we choose to purchase.

Design elements are the basic units of a visual design that form its structure and/or convey a visual message. There are four basic **design elements**:
- **LINE**
- **SHAPE**
- **FORM**
- **COLOR**

These design elements occur in nature, and generate similar [subconscious] feelings in most people. These elements are reflected in man-made design, whether fine art or visual marketing (aka 'graphic design').

[Good] graphic designers use the elements of design like LINE, or SHAPE, or FORM, to evoke a feeling from the viewer, whether the viewer knows it, or not. Most of us are programmed over eons to a respond a certain way to certain imagery. Blue is, by far, the favorite color of most people globally. The reason is obvious. Blue sky. Blue water. Both are rather calming natural phenomenons.

Designing With Line

Technically, there is no such thing, in nature, as a **LINE**. Weird, right? It's true, though. LINE is a *perception*, a delineation between foreground and background. Even when we draw a line, or multiple lines to create an illustration, or print words on paper, it is merely the difference between the ink and the paper, or the pixels in black on a white computer screen, that distinguish the LINES that make up the letters.

Along with our perception of what we characterize as LINES, comes a long lineage of *feelings* associated with them. We unconsciously associate specific images with, or by, their line quality. Softer images, with flowing lines, like rose petals, or gentle waves of water, are calming. The thorns on the rose stem, however, with their sharp, pointing lines are threatening, unnerving.

Remember, the foundation of marketing is our psychology. Marketing is selling, to *people* (not markets). We must get behind how people feel, to motivate them to take the action of remembering or brand, and/or buying into our messaging. In branding our offering and company, we must pay attention to the known primers and triggers that motivate people to feel, and therefore, to *act*.

Some known feelings, whether conscious, or not, associated with the quality of LINE:

- **Soft, Curvy lines** ($\approx$) typically generate a calm, relaxing response from the viewer.

The *Princess Cruise Line's* logo is a stylized silhouette of a woman's profile. Her thick, blue hair is blowing in soft, curvy, rippling lines to the right of her face. *Princess Cruises'* corporate identity marries classic design, with marketing their message of relaxing vacations, to their #1 target market—*women.*

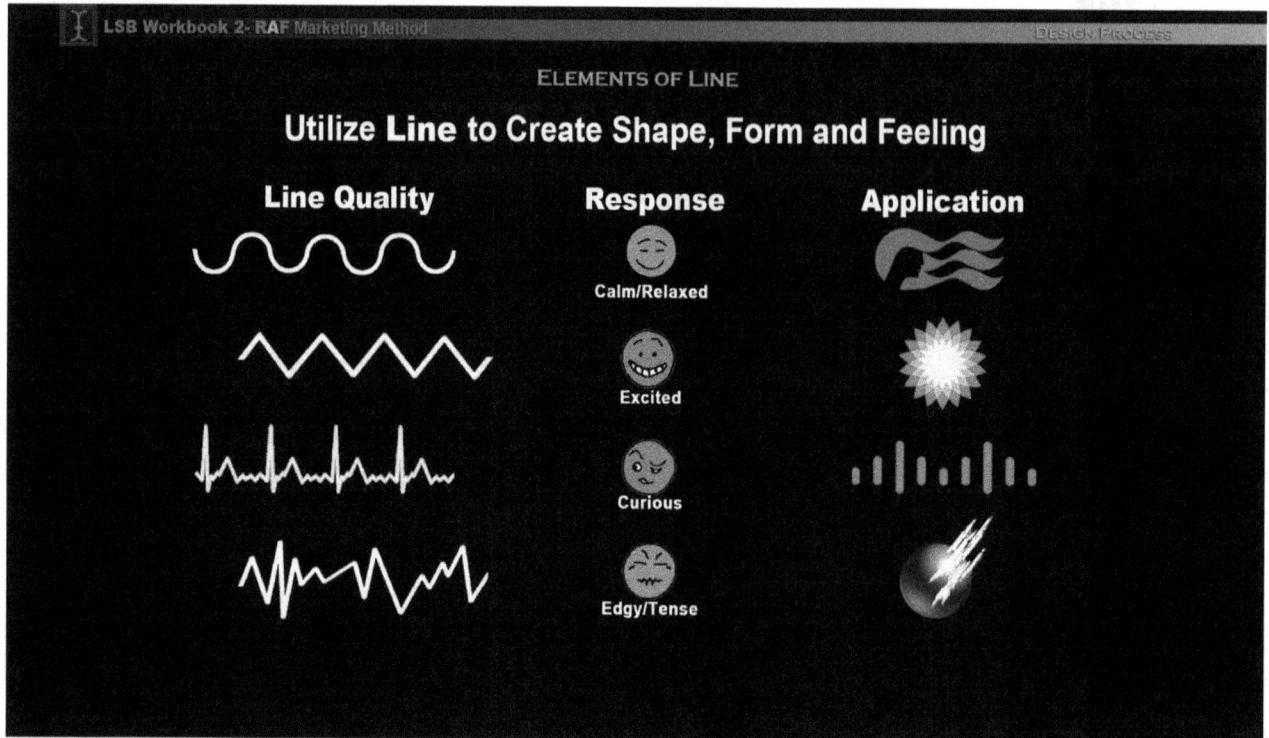

- **Sharp-edge lines**, like a zigzag, (⌒⌒) evoke a feeling of mild tension, excitement, and therefore piques interest.

BP Oil Company rebranded their logo in 1997 to a stylized sunflower, with an analogous color scheme—colors that are next to each other on the color wheel. Zigzag-edged concentric circles of white in the center then yellow then green subliminally suggested their new 'green' logo made them an environmentally responsible company. But *BP* is an *oil company*, and drilling and fracking the earth is not good for our planet. Be this as it may, graphic design is visual *marketing*, i.e. *selling*, reality, or not. Marketing, branding, even rebranding (which we'll review in the Logo Design module), is about creating a positive *perception*, a likable brand image.

- **Repeated** (even complex) **patterns in line**, like those of an EEG heart monitor, evoke strength, confidence. Our brains are pattern-making machines, which is why repeated patterns in line also evoke curiosity, as our brains search for structure that the line renders. We recognize and rely on patterns in behavior to give us foundation. We count on most of our interactions with each other to be peaceful exchanges. We rely on the weather changing with the

Cisco Systems company logo uses repeated line pattern particularly well with their stylized rendition of the Golden Gate Bridge. Using teal vertical lines in a repeated pattern that arch to a peak on two distinct sides, illustrates their strength, and suggests their software's stability, power, and complexity by the design of their identity.

- **Erratic lines**, like a scribble, especially with sharp edges, the feeling evoked is edgy, tense, unpredictable. *Touchstone Pictures* is a movie production and distribution company, owned by *Disney Studios*. They typically release films for adults, with mature, darker themes than those released under the *Disney* identity. The *Touchstone Pictures* logo is a dark blue ball, with an erratic glittering gold scribble, almost like a lightning strike, floating in front of the blue ball. Their logo gives the feelings of dramatic tension, and dark, chaotic excitement.

It is obvious the feelings that these companies are hoping to generate by the line quality they chose in their logos. Identity design is the *beginning* of branding. While rebranding is necessary sometimes, it is expensive, and complex, requiring many marketing campaigns to change the association from your old logo to your new one. It's better to get your logo design right the first time, and use it out of the gate at launch to begin the brand building process. We'll engage in the process of designing your logo, step-by-step, in Module 15 of this workbook.

Designing with Shape
Similar to LINE, **SHAPE** plays a key role in our psyche. Most of us unconsciously respond to specific shapes with specific feelings. So, graphic designers use shapes in our identities and icons that reflect an implied feature or benefit of an offering and/or company.

Four (4) basic SHAPES evoke four different feelings in most people.
- **Circles/Ovals**
- **Squares/Rectangles**
- **Diamonds**
- **Triangles**

- **Circles** communicates global, connection, community, completeness. A circle is intrinsically female, with a soft-edged, flowing line quality, and therefore, calming.

AT&T uses a circle as the basic shape of their logo. *AT&T* sells connectivity and communication, globally. Their logo, a blue and white spiral-stripped sphere, subconsciously evokes this messaging.

©2019 J Cafesin   39

LG is a global electronics corporation. They sell appliances, and cellphones, among other devices. Their logo's basic shape is also a circle, a maroon one, with thin white lines that spell out the letters LG, with a dot for an eye to complete a smiling face integrated in the letters. More women purchase appliances, by far, then men, but most of us smile when we notice the subtle, stylized face in the logo. We all want to feel happy with our purchases.

Target is a mega-department store with locations worldwide. According to their Media Network, 70% of their guests are women. In my suburban, kid-friendly neighborhood, it's more like 80+%. Working, and domestic management moms are clearly *Target's* main market. Beyond their red circle identity being a stylized, simple bullseye, it is also inherently female. Women are inherently maternal—community oriented, communicative, and generally more social than men.

- **Squares** represent order, logic, reason, solid, strong, secure, contained, science, technology. Squares are intrinsically male.

Lego, the global corporation that sells plastic building blocks, has classically been branded to boys. Their corporate logo: a bright red square, with the text LEGO in all caps. Typeface is bold, cursive, i.e. playful, in white, with a bright yellow outline around the text, marketing directly to parents with kids.

LinkedIn uses a blue square with the bold white lowercase letters 'in' centered in the square as their corporate identity. According to their 2018 stats, 56% of their users are male. When the platform for upwardly mobile professionals first came online in 2003, it was predominantly male users.

Microsoft's logo is four squares, red, blue, green and yellow, stacked two over two, into one larger square. Order, logic, reason, science, are all symbols of computer technology, *Microsoft's* core business.

- **Diamonds** evoke luxury, strength, durability, precious, refinement, wealth, elegance, timeless quality.

Superman's logo, the diamond-shaped crest across his chest is an obvious choice to represent his strength, and longevity.

The corporate identity of the car maker, *Renault*, is a narrowed silver diamond, created from what looks like two strips, or ribbons of cast metal, one overlaying the other. Again, the association of luxury, durability, refinement, are precisely what the car maker was hoping to evoke with their logo.

The *Sun Systems* logo is not as obvious, but stunningly effective. The word SUN is repeated on all four sides of the diamond, the 'S' and 'N' alternating between acting as an 'S' or 'N' to start or end the word SUN. Why would a computer company use a diamond? Strength. Wealth. Quality. We all want the hardware and software we purchase to be quality products, that will help us be more efficient with our time, and/or make us money. Look it up. It really is a great corporate identity!

- **Triangles**, usually seen as pyramids or crests (an inverted pyramid) evoke authority, control, power, wealth, balance. Both pyramids and crests are distinctly male, and subliminally communicates ageless wisdom, law, philosophy, history.

Adobe Systems, makers of *Photoshop* and other image-editing software, combined two distinctly male shapes—a red square, with a stylized 'A' in bold white type, the legs of the 'A,' removed after the center bar, so it looks like a pyramid, against a deep red square. Software, until recently, was created and utilized mostly by men. Beyond this fact, using a pyramid concertizes Adobe's messaging that their products are powerful, and give the user control within the creative process.

Adidas, the athletic shoe maker, uses a triangle made of three black, bold slanted stripes as their corporate identity. The association is obvious, promoting balance, power, control, even the authority of a 'winner,' and slanting the lines is a great visual trick to evoke speed.

Mitsubishi Motors connects three narrow diamonds at the center to create a triangular logo. Control, power, elegance, balance, are all features most of us want in a car.

Universities, like *Harvard*, are famous for using crests, alone, or inside a circle of laurel leave. These learning institutions want to appear ageless, established, prestigious, making crests an obvious choice for an identity.

The shapes that you choose for your identities matter. They effectively communicate something about your offerings and company. Whether for a logo, or an icon, or other marketing effort, consider the response you're hoping to evoke, then design, or direct those you hire, to carefully consider the basic shape of your identity, to effectively brand your products and startup.

Designing Balance
Form, in visual design, is a **combination of shapes**.

So, let's examine some shapes to learn how to create dynamic, dimensional forms, especially when we are restricted the flat, two-dimensional space logos exist most often, as in an advert, or e-blast, or on the side of a building.

As previously reviewed, basic shapes, like squares and circles, evoke specific, unconscious feelings, but often don't have the impact we're looking for. We see circular or oval logos, or text against a square, or spelled out in a rectangular shape all the time. To design a striking logo or icon, we often combine shapes to create more dynamic imagery.

Gucci uses two merging circles to represent a highly stylized 'G' and 'C,' in their logo, to create a unique, and pleasing form. Circles are distinctly female, which is by far, their largest target market.

The *HP* logo knocks a circle out of a blue rectangle, and floats the italicized lowercase letters "hp" in the center of the circle. Combining both male and female shapes, creates a strong, but connected form. Italicizing the '*hp*' lettering suggests their company is forward thinking, creating the future, which is powerful messaging for the computer maker's corporate identity.

Toyota uses three interwoven ovals, two narrow ovals forming the letter "T", encircled by a larger oval for their corporate I.D. While their vehicles are purchased by both men and woman, women, by far, motivate costly purchases. Regardless of this fact, putting a vertical oval over a horizontal oval subtly suggests a joyous person with arms raised. Surrounding both ovals with a third creates a complex icon of soft wavy lines that evoke calm, smooth strength.

The *Olympic Games* logo uses five circles overlapping each other—three circles overlapping on top, overlapping two more on the bottom. Each circle is a primary color, blue, black, red, yellow and green. The messaging is obvious, as the games are international, global competitions meant to connect humanity in a common activity.

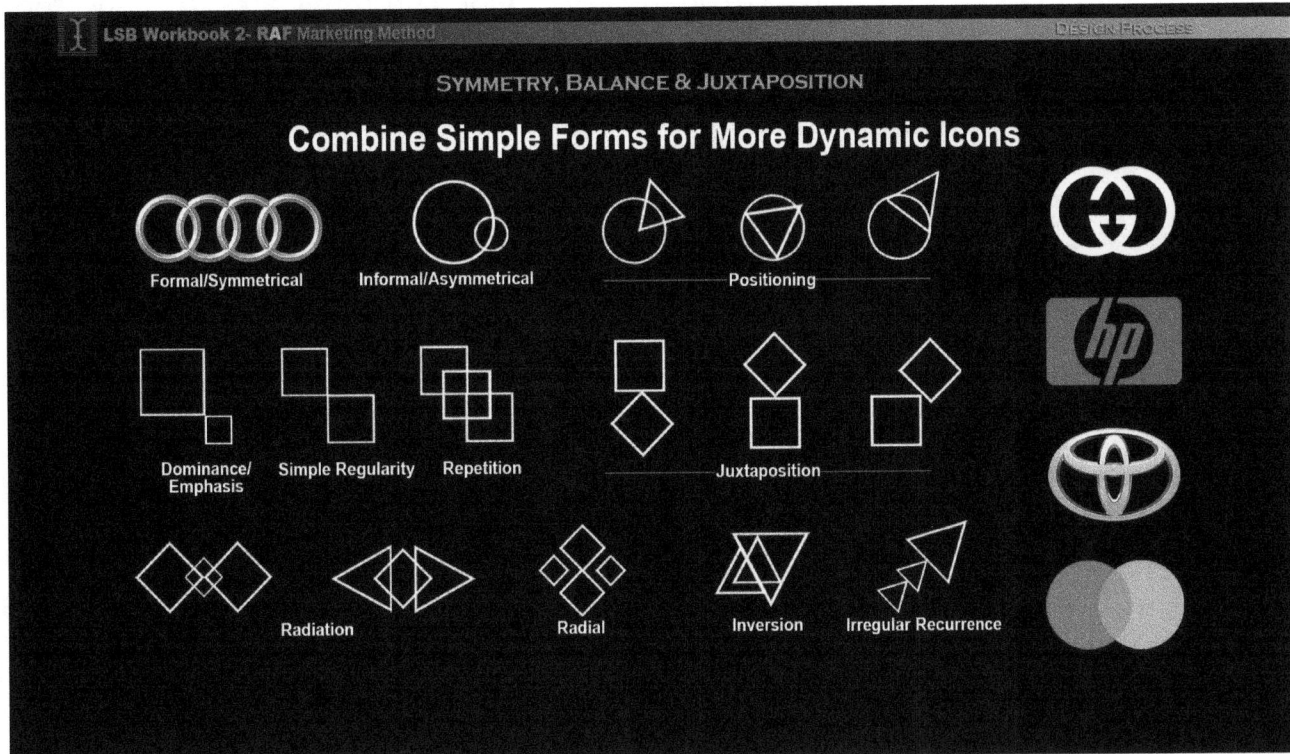

Forms creates feelings, consciously or unconsciously.
- A triangle piercing a circle creates [visual] tension.
- A triangle on top of a circle reminds us of a clown, or party hat, and evokes happy, and 'fun.'
- A triangle inside a circle, piercing the circle from the inside out, evokes a different type of tension, like *breaking out*—a release— instead of the *breaking in* tension from a triangle piercing a circle from the outside.
- A square on top of a diamond of the exact same size, is top heavy, and therefore feels unbalanced, unstable, with the box sitting on the tip of the diamond under it. Again, this form produces [visual] tension.
- A diamond, sitting on top of a square of the same size, creates balance, as the diamond is visually supported by the solid square box under it. This form projects balance, stability, foundation.

Combining line quality and shapes creates forms, or icons with impact. To design your offering and company identities, begin with line and shape. Use them alone, or combine them into forms that subliminally represent something about your new offering and venture.

Marketing With Color

We've explored branding basics, and reviewed design fundamentals and best practices for product and corporate identities. Color communicates feelings too. Next, we examine color's impact on our psyche, and how to choose colors that represents the look and feel you're hoping to communicate with your identities, and in all your marketing efforts.

-Basic Color Theory-

Branding with Color

Just like LINE, SHAPE, and FORM, **COLOR** has specific emotional responses too. These responses are typically the same for most of us. In other words, we all react to red as stop! We all reacted green as go, or nature.

What is your favorite color? Most people say some shade of blue. And we can understand why. As we've already reviewed, blue evokes all kinds of life affirming symbolism, from the sky, to water. It's relaxing. Peaceful. Probably half of all logos are some shade or shades of blue. Close to the other half of all logos out there are in some shade of red. The reason for this is obvious. Red screams for our attention. *Stop! Look!* Remember the **conversion funnel** in LSM Workbook 1? To brand, or sell anything, first, we must get people's attention, and make them aware our offering and company exists.

Pure colors, like saturated blue and hot red are striking, and therefore will generally get attention. The implied CTA with red is 'stop and look.' See radiant blue, and its likely to generate a calm, relaxed feeling.

Green is often associated with natural, health, growth, energy-efficient. Bright green demands our attention with its radiance, its implied CTA is 'go forward.' Deeper shades of emerald evoke tranquility, like looking at a languid pond.

Oranges to yellows are often associated with sunshine, summer, gold, and therefore evoke feelings of happiness, optimism, energy.

Bright pinks are children's colors, party colors, and emanate joy, happiness, and the high-energy of youth.

Deep purple is generally associated with old wealth, or royalty, and evokes satisfaction, stability.

Browns often get muddled online, and look more like shades of warm gray, which is why we avoid using them in our digital marketing campaigns. We can retain rich brown in quality *printing*, however. Browns are warm, cozy, and often used to evoke age, well-worn, like a favorite leather couch.

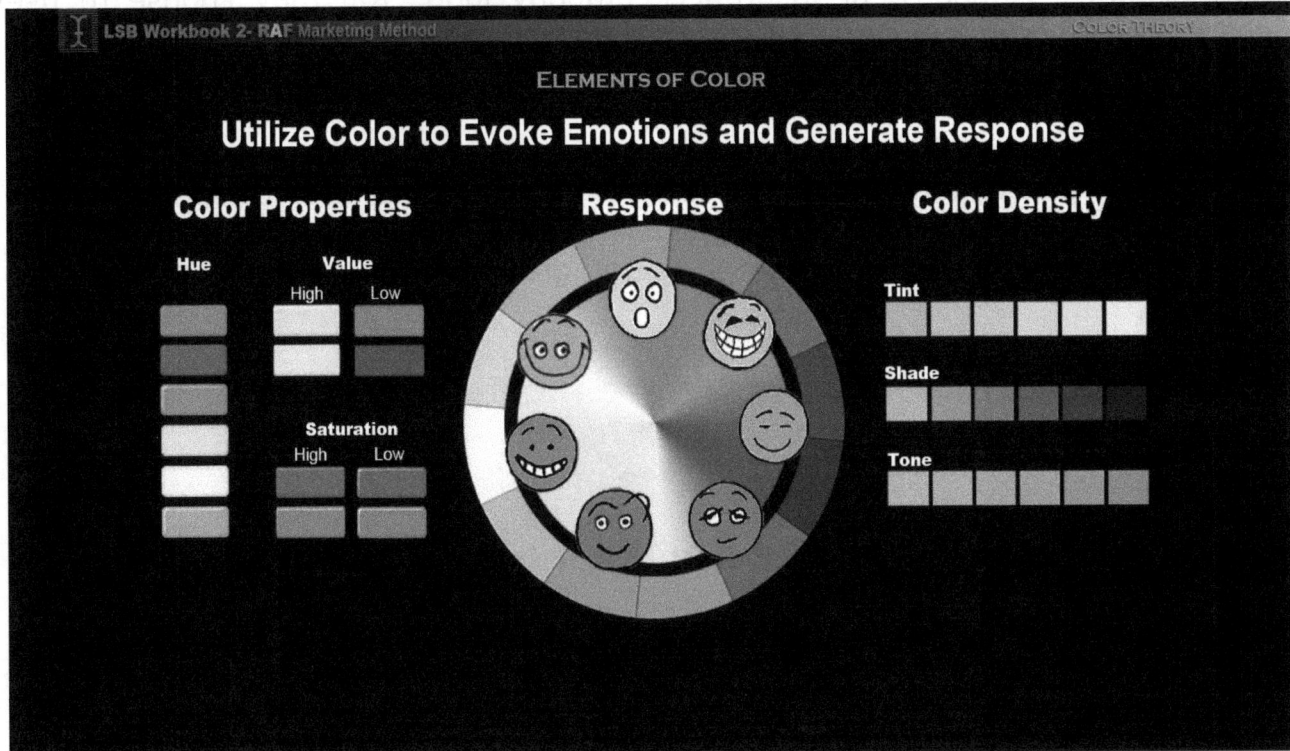

PROPERTIES of color also evoke feelings. In designing your identity, or any of your marketing material, you want to choose colors that reflect the feelings you want to communicate about the campaign, as well as your offering and company. There are six (6) basic properties of color:

- **HUE**: The hue of any color refers to its name, i.e. the color turquoise has hues of blue and green.

- **VALUE**: Color with a HIGH VALUE will be lighter. Color with a LOW VALUE will be darker.

- **SATURATION**: Color with a HIGH SATURATION will be intense. Color with a LOW SATURATION will be dull—**desaturate**.

- **TINT**: is pure HUE + WHITE. (Red becomes lighter and lighter shades of pink by continually adding white).

- **SHADE**: is pure HUE + GRAY. (Colors dull, become desaturated by continually adding gray.)

• **TONE**: is pure HUE + BLACK. (Light blue becomes midnight blue by continually adding black).

You don't want to use high value or intense colors for a funeral parlor, pharmaceutical company, or insurance company logo. You may choose to use desaturated color in a circle or square background, and tinted, saturated color for the identity symbol and text, so they visually 'pop.'

Color will reproduce differently online than in print. We'll review why this is, next, but for now, just understanding the response most of us have to specific colors will help you design identities, advertising and marketing material that will communicate more effectively, as well as get greater response and conversion.
-
-

STOP! Take CHALLENGE #2 before moving on.

◆◆◆

CHALLENGE #2: Color in the Dark

Take a pad and pen (NOT an electronic device) into your closet at home or at work and close the door, shutting yourself in with a light on. Write down [at least] 5 items in the closet, and **note their color in detail**.

Specifically describe the exact color of each item. Do NOT put RED for your red shoes. Describe the **type of red**, i.e. **low value**, and **high saturation**, with a hint of **shade**, so, it's a *deep, saturated, earth-toned red.* Note how the curve of your earth-toned red shoes creates certain parts of the shoes to be brighter red than others, depending on how the light is hitting the shoes. Describe the many tints, shades and tones of red that are reflecting back at you as you examine your red shoes.

Now, turn off the light. Make sure all the shades are drawn on any windows, and there is little to no light coming into the closet. Wait a minute to let your eyes adjust to the dim light inside.

What color are each of the five items you described earlier with the lights out? Odds are, any one of them is some dark **shade** of gray, or black, depending on how dim it is inside the closet, because without light there is no color. Color is created by light.

◆◆◆

-Designing with Color-

Branding is a form of marketing. Designing identities to ad campaigns, color will be used throughout your marketing efforts to effectively brand your venture with a specific look and feel. The colors your choose for your logos and icons will be used as part of your **brand standards** across all media, since an identity should appear on most all of your marketing efforts.

Much like line, color is an illusion, created by light. More precisely, our perception of color comes from how our brains interpret wavelengths of photons (the partials that make up light).

When we design an identity, or marketing effort, in a hand drawn sketch or on a computer, we must **reproduce** the design *concept* into a printed or digital campaign. Our logos will likely be in color. And we'll likely use photography or other imagery in most of our marketing efforts. But even just black and white must be reproduced and delivered on some type of media. So, how do we turn our sketch, or even computer-generated concept into a print or digital campaign?

We begin the process of reproducing our marketing efforts in two ways: **PIGMENT** color, and **LIGHT** color.

PIGMENT Color
PIGMEMT is physical color. Inks (for printing), or dyes (for plastics), paints

(for painting), colored pencils (for illustration), stains (for wood), are all PIGMENT color—real, actual, *physical* color products. **Print media** is created with PIGMENT color, usually with inks, specifically developed for paper, or plastics for packaging, or other physical material. We use these coloring materials for brochures, to print ads in magazines, to trade-show booths, to packaging, to signage, to the color of your car, and even your clothes.

There are three (3) primary PIGMENT colors:
- RED
- YELLOW
- BLUE

Combine all primary PIGMENT colors, and you'll get black. (Think of a child doing finger painting, overlapping colors until they've created a black blob.) Most PIGMENT colors, such as the inks we use for printing, are transparent. Only enamel-based colors are opaque, like those we use on plastics, or vehicles. This is important to remember, as we can not print white over other colors on paper. The other colors will come through, and the white won't be pure white, but tinted by the color/s under it. Because printer's ink's are transparent, we use the white of the paper in which the campaign is printed on to achieve pure white for our print marketing efforts.

Four Color Process

Brochures, billboards, ads and photos or illustrations in magazines, in-store product display units, postcards, direct mail (snail mail) campaigns, most product packaging and labels, are printed on an **offset printing press**, using the **four-color (4/C) process**. Also known as **CMYK**, after the four colors used in the process—Cyan (a tint of blue), Magenta (a shade of red), Yellow (primary), and Black (K)—when you combine these four colors, each in a unique pattern, or 'plate' of tiny dots, they align to reproduce what we perceive as a full-color image (using just the four CMYK colors).

Johannes Gutenberg invented the printing press in the 1400s, but his press could only reproduce in black ink. Asian cultures invented color printing with wood blocks as far back as the 1300s. Lithographic stones, then zinc plates were used for each color to reproduce a color image in print, until the early 1900s.

The **CMYK process,** also known as **color separation process**, begins by separating the original artwork, such as a photo or illustration, into red, blue and green. These three colors are then converted into cyan, magenta, yellow and black (for depth and shadow) plates of tiny dots, that when aligned and printed recreate an exact print of the original artwork. *Sort of.* CMYK **color reproduction** is not precise. Printing a photo full of midnight blues will look more like dull blue/gray depending on the printing press and the quality of paper it's printed on.

CMYK printing process reproduces **continuous tone**. This means it can print the soft, gradient blending of color and light in an original photograph, painting, or illustration. But, as noted, CMYK colors get muddied, dulled, with their mixing during printing.

Your identities should look the same across all media, from the typeface you choose, to the colors you use, they should look the same in your print and online campaigns to build your brand awareness. To assure the particular blue of your logo will appear the same color across print and digital media, you must add a **solid color** of your *particular* blue to your 4/C (four CMYK color) printed campaigns.

Pantone® [color] **Matching System (PMS)** is well known in the printing industry, and by educated graphic designers, as a palette of solid colors. In other words, each distinct color of ink they offer is only one (1) solid color of PIGMENT. It may be turquoise, or orange, or ultraviolet, or any one of the almost 2,000 single colors Pantone offers, but each distinct color will enhance the printed piece to assure your logo is the same color online as it is in print.

Print campaigns often require adding solid colors to the CMYK 4/C process to assure your identity is consistent across media. A five or more color campaign (5/C; 6/C) is often required to make sure your twilight blue and golden yellow identity looks as radiant on your printed brochure as it does on your website.

Adding solid colors to a print job adds cost to the printing process. You can mitigate these costs by choosing colors for your identities that reproduce well across digital and print media. Highly saturated colors, like radiant blue, or intense colors, like day-glow pink, get muddled, dull in print. *Facebook* uses a dull blue behind their white 'f,' making it easy to reproduce anywhere. *LinkedIn, HP,* and many other blue logos have purposefully dulled the intensity of blue in their identities so they reproduce the same across media. Red, and yellow reproduce particularly well across media. *McDonald's* bright yellow 'M' against the hot red square, or the *Target* department store logo look (reproduce) the same online as in print.

Identities that look identical in digital or print media help build brand awareness. When we even *think* about *Facebook*, many of us picture the particular dull blue of their logo. Remembering an identity is at the foundation of building any brand.

Logos with many colors that blend softly (continuous tone), like in a photograph or realistic illustration, also reproduce poorly in print. Aligning all those tiny dots from each of the four CMYK screens will often muddle and dull, even blur the identity once its reproduced on to the paper, or other substrate material that it's printed on.

We'll drill down on **continuous tone vs. solid color** as key components in icon and logo design next. For now, let's explore what you see on your 'black mirrors'—your cellphone, monitors, laptops, and tablets, i.e. the *screens* on your electronic devices.

LIGHT Color

LIGHT gives us the perception of color. Waves of photon particles from the sun, and from man-made light, come at our eyes from our TV, and our computer monitors, and the light bulbs that illuminate our home. We can't touch light color. There is no pigment to it. It is not *physical* color, but *perceived* color, a response to how our eyes and brain experience light.

There are three (3) primary LIGHT colors (RGB):
- RED
- GREEN
- BLUE

Combine all primary LIGHT colors, and you'll get white. When you see white on your screen it means the RED pixels, and the GREEN pixels, and the BLUE pixels of your monitor are all ON at 100% of their intensity. Black text against a white screen mean the letters have 0% light, or the pixels are OFF where each letter exists on the screen.

Regardless that photographs, videos, and everything else on our devices appear in their full color spectrum, we are only seeing three colors when we look at our monitors and screens—RED, GREEN, and BLUE. Like offset printing, that employs the CMYK process of dot screens combining each color to reproduce full color, LIGHT color, or RGB, does virtually the same thing. RED, GREEN, and BLUE dots of LIGHT are aligned to reproduce full color imagery.

LIGHT is pure color, the intensity undiluted or muddled by the printing process, or what a campaign is printed on. Remember this when designing your company's identities! Your radiant blue logo online, will *not* look radiant in print, unless you use a solid color blue, like a Pantone® blue, in addition to CMYK during the printing process.

It is imperative you understand how to reproduce your marketing concepts when designing your campaigns and corporate or product identities. This knowledge provides perimeters during the design process that will assure our campaigns are cost effective, as well as present the same colors, look and feel across all media to establish and build brand awareness.

-Color Reproduction-

Line Art, Solid Color vs. Continuous Tone
Why does understand the difference between PIGMENT color and LIGHT color matter?

You have to reproduce the designs you, or those you hire, create on the computer into a print, and/or digital marketing campaign.

- **PRINT media = PIGMENT color.**
- **DIGITAL media = LIGHT color.**

Logos for your offerings and your company will appear all over your marketing material, both in print, and online. Putting your identity on most of your marketing efforts, externally with campaigns, as well as within your organization on your company's collateral materials, helps you build your brand. You'll have to reproduce your identity on your print efforts, from your business cards and stationery, to your sales kits, brochures, trade show booths, and direct mail campaigns. Your company's identity will appear on your digital efforts—on your website, landing pages, PPC (pay-per-click) ads, as well as your social media marketing campaigns on *Facebook, Instagram, LinkedIn*...etc.

Since your identities need to appear in so many places, across so many mediums, in so many different sizes, and against dark and light backgrounds, logos and icons needs to be flexible to reproduce well on your company's *Twitter* feed, or on the side of your corporate headquarters building. Your logos need to look great huge, or tiny; in black and white, or in color. And as we discussed, the colors you choose for your identities must reproduce the same across all mediums to help build your brand awareness.

Sound like a tall task for any graphic designer? Not so much, when you know what you are doing.

Line Art and Solid Color

To assure our identities reproduce clearly, and appear in the same colors in both print and digital media, we **design logos and icons in LINE ART**, essentially **an outline**. We fill in the outline with **SOLID COLORS** to create color logos.

Picture the white 'f' inside the blue box of the *Facebook* logo: . Two specific components make up the *Facebook* identity. The lowercase 'f,' in white, and the blue box surrounding it. Their logo is only one color, dull blue. We would not need

CMYK process to print it on a business card (assuming it is the only image on the card). We need only one (1) **solid color (1/C)**, the particular Pantone blue they use for the box in which the white 'f' resides. We can *not* print white, so the pure white of the 'f' is the color of the paper the logo is printed on, and the 'f' is essentially an outline, or *knocked out* of the blue box.

Now, imagine changing *Facebook's* blue box to green, or pink, or any solid color. Easy, right. Just change the color of the box. The logo would still take only one color (1/C) to print, whatever one solid color you choose.

Imagine changing the 'f' from white to blue, and the background box to light gray, so the logo stands out against a black background or dark photo. Still easy, right. Just change the font color, and the color in the box. In this example, however, we've added another color, and the logo has now become a two color (2/C)—blue and gray—print job.

The *Facebook* logo is simple, *flexible* design. Large or small, dark or light, in color, or black and white, the logo translates across media and mediums without losing any quality because it was created in **line art** with **solid color**.

Imagine the *Facebook* 'f' as an outline, as well as the box it sits in. Picture the entire logo as *just* an outline, black lines against white paper. Now imagine filling any part of the line (outline) art with any one solid color you want, like a kid's coloring book. Designing logos and icons in just outlines makes them *flexible*. **Line art solid color** logos also insure the identity will reproduce clearly across all media.

Identities and icons should be designed in LINE ART and SOLID COLORS. They should be produced in a **vector** file format (*not* raster format like jpg, png, pdf, gif, which we'll review in Module 16—Visual Content). Remember, LINE ART IS AN OUTLINE of your logo, which you fill in with SOLID COLORS.

Yes, there are exceptions to this rule, which we'll review next, however, it is smart design to create logos and icons in line art, solid color, for clean and consistent quality reproduction across all media.

Continuous Tone

CONTINUOUS TONE, also known as **Graduated Tone**, is a **soft blend of color** from one to another. Imagine a photograph of a person's face. The shadows from the curves of their facial features blend softly into the highlights on their cheeks, nose, or chin.

Unlike solid color, which is solid blocks of color that do *not* blend, continuous tone gradually blends color and light to create a realistic image, instead of the stylized or illustrative quality of images produced in solid colors.

Using a continuous tone image for a logo identity is a bad move. First, it's harder to reproduce soft, blended colors in quite a few mediums, like newsprint, or even online, without getting *banding*—bands of solid color instead of a smooth, soft blend. Additionally, as discussed, it's difficult to reproduce a small, clear continuous tone image, especially in print, and your identity will have to appear small in a lot of your marketing efforts.

In solid color reproduction, the computer only has to account for one solid color of blue, and/or red, green, yellow...etc. Beyond the clarity and color banding issues with continuous tone, the computer has to account for the thousands of shades between the dark shadows to the soft highlights, making continuous tone file sizes a lot larger than the solid color format.

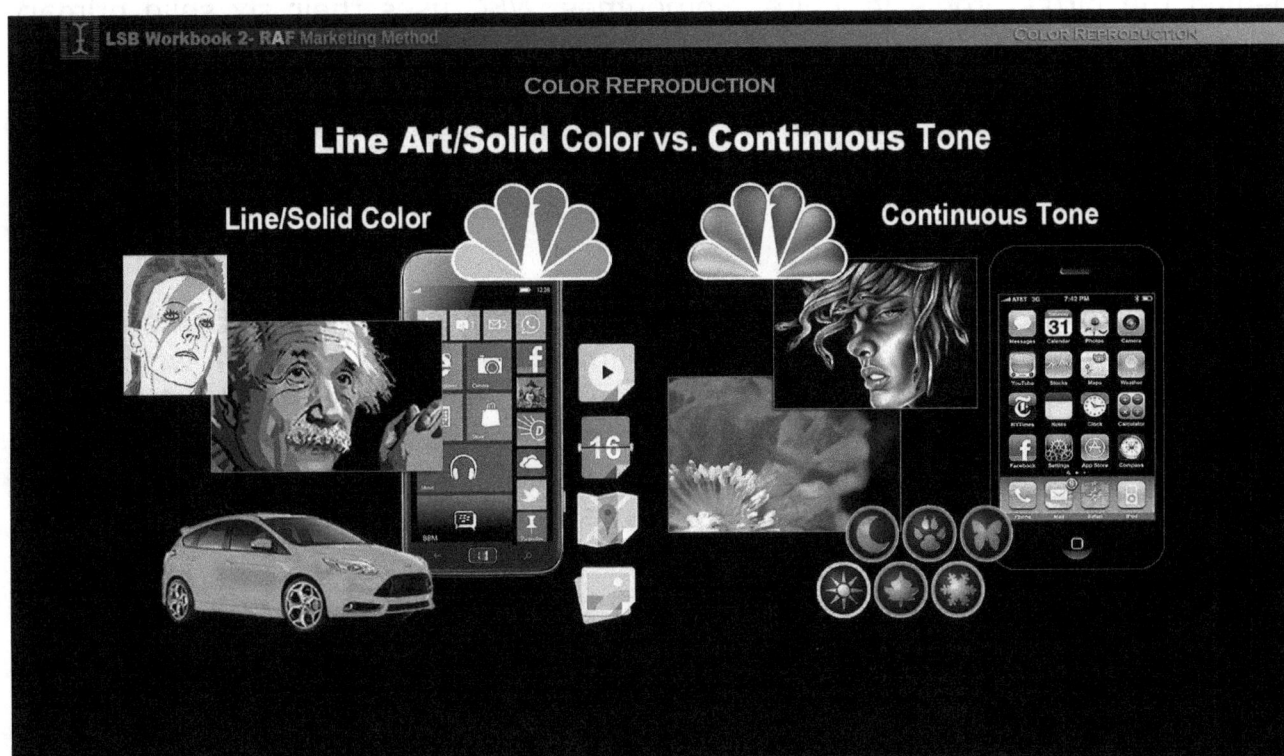

Remember, your logos will appear everywhere, on most all of your marketing material. In digital reproduction, your logo file size should stay small, because other, high file size imagery, like picture galleries and video content will be used in your marketing campaigns along with your identity. Make sure that your logo file sizes are small to keep the file size of your online campaigns as minimal as possible, so your websites and landing pages load fast—appear quickly on device screens.

Exceptions to Every Rule

There are times when you will want to use continuous tone in your identities. You may want to 'color in' part of your line art logo in a blend of your corporate colors, or a blend from light to dark of the same color to add dimension to your identity.

No problem. If you design a logo in line art, it becomes a stenciled palette for you to play with. Just know what medium you'll be publishing on, and how continuous tone, i.e. soft blends translate in that particular medium.

Regardless of the marketing effort on which your company I.D. appears, you are always designing within the limited palette of your corporate colors. You do, however, have virtually endless creative possibilities in how you apply them.

The *NBC* logo is a stylized peacock with six broad feathers, in six primary colors behind the bird's profile in white. Sometimes, *NBC* uses their six solid primary colors, when the other images in a campaign have a lot of dimension, like detailed pictures or video clips. But when they run a station I.D. Campaign, with mostly simple imagery, with flashes of color or animated swirls of light, they use a soft blend of their primary colors in each feather of their logo. This continuous tone effect makes their logo look dimensional, and helps it 'pop' against the other imagery used in the campaign.

Using solid color or continuous tone for your company's identities within any given campaign is fine, as long as you know the limitations of the media on which it will reproduce. Additionally, you, or those you hire must stick to the palette of corporate colors. Remember to design and produce your principle corporate and offering logo identities in LINE ART, SOLID COLOR, so you have a flexible, low-resolution identity that will look great in any size, and across all media.

-Harmonic Color Theory-

Choose Your Identity Color Palette

Once Productization is complete, and you've named your offering and company, you're ready to design, (or direct those you hire to design) and produce your identities. You'll develop them in LINE ART, SOLID color, and produce them in a vector format, in *Adobe Illustrator* or some other vector program, so in reproduction they can be enlarged and reduced without any quality loss, across any medium.

But *which* combination of solid colors should you choose, out of the millions of colors out there, to create striking, pleasing identities that represent, and support the brand image you're trying to generate?

Harmonic colors are known combinations of colors that are pleasing to the eye. We use harmonic color principles and practices to determine a color palette that will be pleasing to most who view our identities.

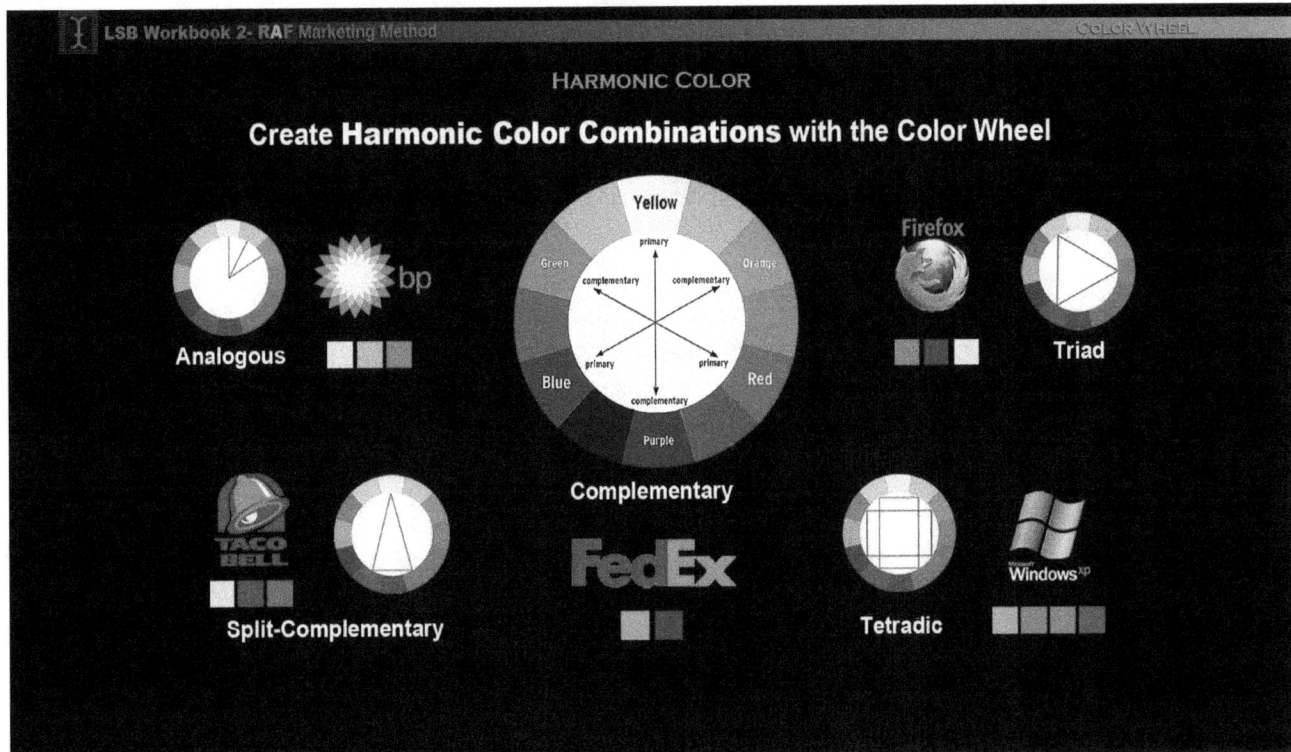

Begin with the color wheel, the one that most of us learned in grade school art. This is the circular rainbow spectrum of colors from yellow to red to blue to green, and back to yellow to create a complete circle of colors. Working with the color wheel, we can create a virtually endless palette of pleasing color combinations.

COMPLEMENTARY colors are opposite each other on the color wheel, such as yellow orange and deep purple, like the *FedEx* (*Federal Express*) corporate identity. Complementary colors are high contrast, which is great for logo design, as they visually 'pops.'

An ANALGOUS color scheme—colors next to each other on the wheel—often provide a soft, blended color combination, without having to use continuous tone. As previously mentioned, *BP Corp.* uses white, then yellow, then light green and then middle green concentric circles for their 'sunflower' logo.

You can create a SPLIT-COMPLEMENTARY color scheme by using a narrow (isosceles) triangle inside the color wheel, so each point of the triangle 'points' to a specific color on the wheel. Rotate the triangle to find a split-complementary color palette that works for your offerings and company. *Taco Bell* did this particularly well with their choice of yellow, purple, and magenta, giving the fast food chain a Mexican fiesta look and feel.

The *Firefox* logo uses a TRIAD color scheme of three primary colors: Red, Blue and Yellow. Create triad color schemes by rotating an equilateral triangle—a triangle with three equal sides—inside the wheel, so each tip of the triangle 'points' to a different color on the color wheel.

Microsoft uses a TETRADIC color scheme for a large palette of brand colors to choose from when designing their marketing material. Tetradic color combinations are achieved by rotating a rectangle inside the color wheel. The four 'points' of the rectangle identify two sets of complementary colors (for a total of four) that visually harmonize.

The more colors you choose for your identities, the harder it is to brand your organization with a particular color, like *Facebook* does with their dull blue box, and white 'f.' The larger your color palette, the more expensive it will be to reproduce your identities when printing your company stationery, and much of your corporate collateral material. Additionally, the file size of the identity will be higher in logos with many colors. However, choosing a color palette with multiple colors also provides you with an array of colors to choose from within any given marketing effort, such as product packaging, in-store signage, and even in digital campaigns. Using three or four colors in your identities will give you greater design choice with the navigation buttons for your websites, or background colors for your landing pages, or colored headers for your social media profile pages that will help build brand awareness of your startup.

Building a Brand

Understanding our emotional response to color, basic color theory, and color reproduction across media and mediums, is vital to creating effective identity designs. Utilizing the color wheel as described, you will generate harmonic combinations of colors for your logos and icons that will brand your new venture with a specific look and feel. Your corporate colors will be used as **brand elements** across most all of your marketing efforts, to help concertize your brand image.

We'll review brand elements and setting up brand standards in detail at the end of Module 15: Identity Design. You'll learn how to apply your product and corporate **brand standards** across all your marketing efforts. You'll discover how to use the same line quality, shapes, forms, and colors of your product and company identities across all your campaigns. Presenting the same look and feel with each marketing effort is an important part of building your company's brand.

Applied Branding

By now, you've likely productized your offering into eight (8) Productization lists.

You know some features and benefits of your product or service, and have some likely target markets and potential users in mind who will find value in your offering. There is no inherent value in your startup before the launch of your product, service, or nonprofit message. Companies are branded by the utility of their offerings, not the other way around.

If you've completed projects 1 and 2, you've chosen a name for your startup, *and* your new offering. And you've written taglines for each as well, or, at least, you've donned your new venture with a tagline that entices and reveals a unique value that your company offers.

You now have a good understanding of design best practices, and basic color theory, as well as print and digital reproduction.

You're ready to TAKE <u>A</u>IM, and design identities for *your* new venture.

◆◆◆◆◆

MODULE 15: IDENTITY DESIGN

Corporate Identity Development

We now have an understanding of what effective design *is*, and how it triggers our thoughts and feelings, both consciously and unconsciously. We've examined design elements, and our response to line quality, shape, form, and color. We've reviewed how we use LIGHT and PIGMENT color in reproducing our campaigns on print and digital mediums. Additionally, we now understand that effective logo and icon design begins in LINE ART, and SOLID COLORS, for quality reproduction across all media.

You're now ready to put what you've learned into practice, and design a **corporate identity** for *your* new venture. Company logos differ from product logos, in that your corporate I.D.'s should have *broad* appeal, just like your company name. Your new venture's visual identity should capture the essences of what your business plans to sell at launch, as well as the many offerings you'll add to your product line in the future. The symbol you create for your business should suggest the heart and soul of your organization.

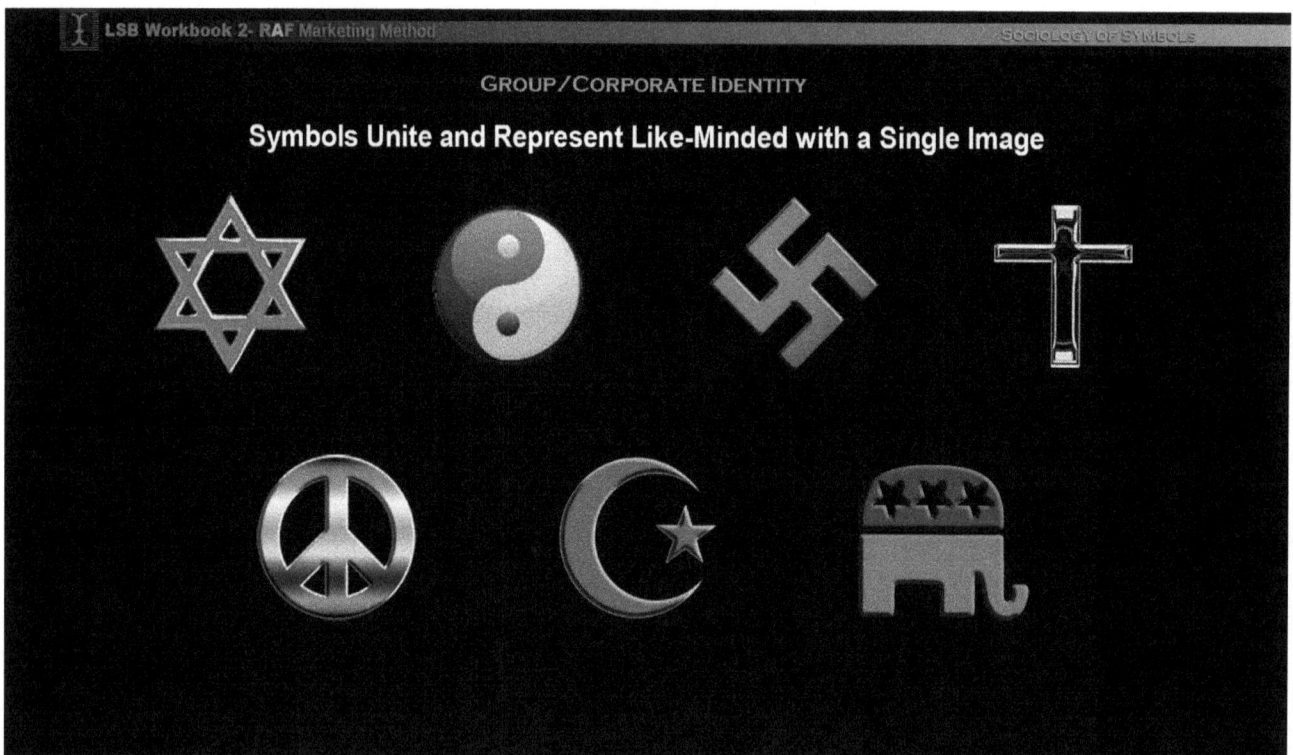

Symbols—visual icons—unite like-minded groups of people under a moniker, but also under an idea, or even an ideal. Corporate identities do the same, not only for their employees, but for their brand advocates as well. Most who purchase *Apple* devices are proud of their logo glowing on top of their laptops, or on the back of their cellphones.

Once branded, symbols, logos, icons, communicate a feeling about the company or culture who unite under that symbol. We are all familiar with the Peace symbol, or the Yin Yang symbol. Most companies hope to achieve the brand recognition that these timeless icons have.

Feelings associated with symbols may change over time. The swastika (卐 or 卍) is an ancient religious icon, a sacred symbol of morality in Hinduism, Buddhism and Jainism. In the 1930s, the Nazi party adopted it as their Nationalist icon. After the war, it became a symbol of fear, and hate, which it remains today for most Westerners.

The Republican Party symbol may evoke pride in some. Others might feel anger when they see the blue and red elephant symbol of the GOP.

Symbols matter! They unite and represent groups of people. They give people an umbrella to gather under, join together, and brand their cause, or company.

Limitation, Tricks & Tips of 2D Design
Most of the time when developing and producing graphic design, we're creating within a two-dimensional space. Logos and icons are created in line art, or outline, and by default are 2D. So, how do we design bold, memorable, dimensional images when we only have two-dimensional space to work with?

The following design applications are techniques for creating dynamic imagery in two-dimensional space, while adhering to LINE ART, and SOLID COLORS perimeters of effective logo design.

• **Positive/Negative space**—create an image utilizing **Positive** *against* **Negative** space.

The *Yin Yang* ☯ symbol is probably the most recognized use of Positive/Negative space. A soft, curvy line divides a circle into two halves, one filled in with black, and the other white. Inside each side, is a small circle of the opposite color. The icon is a strikingly effective use of Positive/Negative space, regardless of the colors used, as long as they are opposites, aka **complementary** on the color wheel.

Another advantage to using the Positive/Negative space technique in design is that it creates **visual contrast**. The greater the contrast of light against dark, or the other way around, in logos, photos, or videos, the more dynamic, dramatic, attention-grabbing the imagery will be.

Showtime Entertainment utilizes a read circle, with the letters 'SHO' knocked out of the circle, while the rest of their name is in solid red—'WTIME.' The visual contrast works great to imply that the red circle is a spotlight, like a movie premier.

- **Solid Color Gradations**—utilize multiple solid colors, in an **analgous** color scheme to attract attention.

Sony's PlayStation logo uses an eye-catching rainbow of solid color stripes, filling in the standing 'P' and the laying 'S' for *PlayStation*. Their full color spectrum can also be express as shades of gray, from black to white, in marketing efforts that don't allow for color, such as certain newsprint or some comic books.

When *Google* uses only their 'G' icon, they also employ a solid color **analgous** color scheme, beginning at the top of the 'G' with red, then to yellow, then green, then blue.

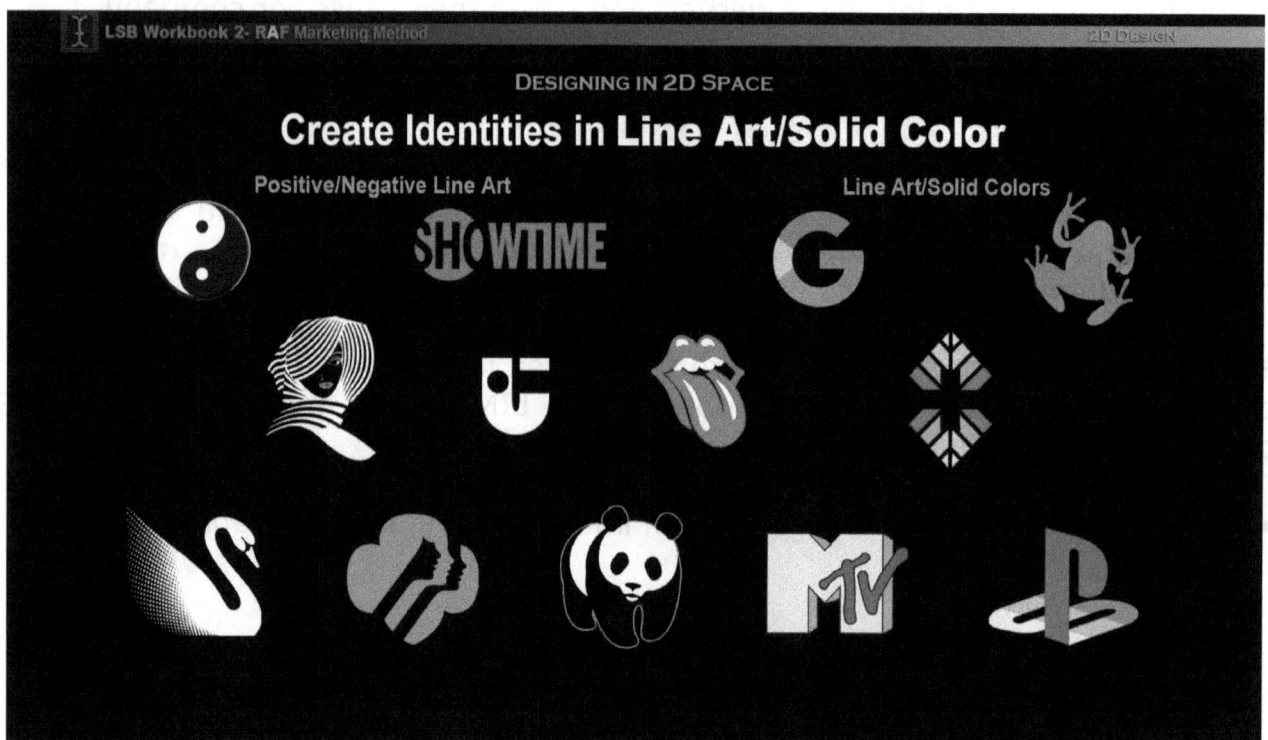

- **Solid Color Shading**—using color, line quality, tones, shades, and tints of a color can simulate highlights and shadows. This is quite common to add dimension to an icon, to make it look 3D.

White is most commonly used for highlight, as in the *Rolling Stones* rock band's red tongue sticking out of red lips. White highlights the upper part of the lips, and streaks down the tongue as well.

Gray, a tint of black, is often used to shadow icons, but altering the line quality will achieve gray, or shadows. *Swarovski Jewelers* uses a white swan, that turns to a series of fewer and fewer dots for the swans feathers.

- **Create Forms**—combining shapes, and merging them, like the edges of circles overlapping (think *MasterCard*, or the *Olympic Games* logos). As previously discussed, using one shape to pierce the other, or breaking out of the other, adds tension, and therefore garners attention.

MTV (music video cable channel) does this particularly well, using a bold, wide, capitalized 'M' as a square background, with the letters 'TV' in graffiti script partially overlaying, and partially *breaking out* of the visual square created by the width of the massive 'M' behind it.

Identity Design Made Easy

To fully grasp how to design attention-grabbing logos and icons, research effective identity designs by googling, "Logos," then clicking on IMAGES (instead of the ALL page *Google* defaults to). Quickly scan the pages of identities, and note the ones that catch your attention. Even if you already know the brand, examine each logo as if for the first time. Note the techniques they've used to create the look and feel that garnered your notice. Imitate what you like—the positive/negative style, a complementary, or triad color scheme, the basic form— then create identities with the look and feel you want *your* offering and company to reflect.

Perimeters of Identity Design

To design *anything*, you are limited by the SPACE you have to work in, as well as the MATERIALS and TIME it takes to produce whatever you've designed. **LOGO DESIGN** has strict perimeters too.

As previously noted, corporate and product identities must appear on a wide variety of marketing material. In fact, your companies logos should be on most every piece of marketing you produce, to build awareness of your brand. To ensure your identities look fantastic across all your marketing efforts, designers use three (3) fundamental perimeters in logo design:

1. **Identities must be able to scale without losing any quality.** Our identities must look great on cellphones, social media feeds, and the side of our buildings. We achieve this in two ways:
   - We develop *flexible* identities and icons in line art (outline), and solid colors.
   - We produce our logo designs in *Adobe Illustrator*®, or another **vector** drawing program, so they reproduce in most any size without losing quality.

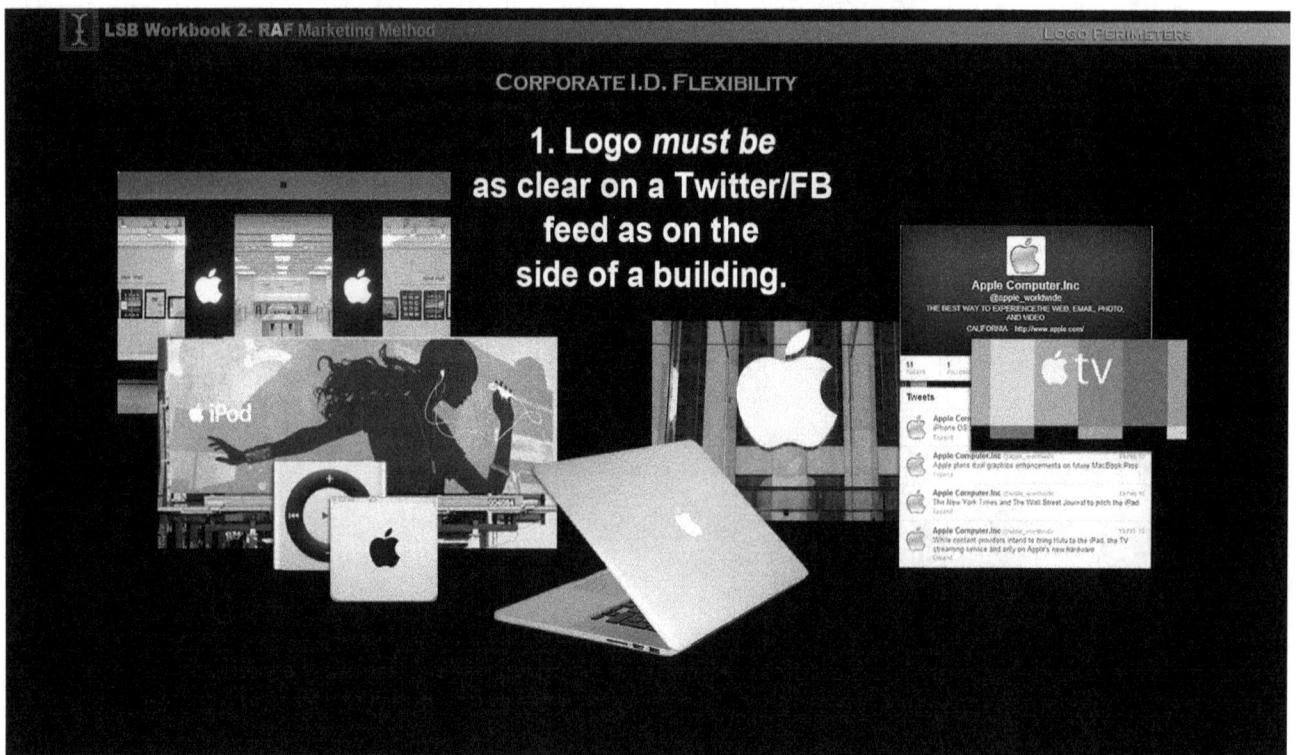

Apple Corp. is a great example of a flexible, versatile logo identity. It looks virtually identical on their storefront in the mall, on a billboard, on a *Twitter* feed, or lit up on their laptop covers. It is line art, a simple outline of an apple with a bite taken out on the right side. Designers creating campaigns for *Apple* products can 'fill in' any color, or blend of colors, or generate shadows, or even light inside the apple's outline, without losing, but, in fact, enhancing, *Apple's* 'creative' brand image.

2. **Identities must communicate** *somethin* **about the offering and/or company.** We achieve this by using design principles of response, and carefully choosing which line quality, shapes, and colors that best express what our company IS, what our offering DOES, and for WHO.

As previously mentioned, *Target, Inc.,* the global retail warehouse chain, carries a huge inventory of consumer items, from clothing to food. While they've chosen the obvious target symbol, they've used only one circle filled in hot red, and one thick band, also in hot red, surrounding it.

Some of our innate, unconscious associations to circles are global; female; completeness; wellness. *Target, Inc.* could have used cross-hairs, like those on a gun-sight, as their symbol, instead of concentric circles, but those would *not* have communicated effectively to over 80% of their customer base—female shoppers.

These are *broad* visual associations, not specific imagery like with product identities. Remember, your corporate identity should be a wide umbrella to cover all the offerings the company produces, or will likely produce in the future.

The Home Depot uses an orange square to house the words, "The Home Depot," in an angled, stenciled white typeface, inside the square. The orange is the color of construction cones. *The Home Depot* sells building supplies, and 70% or more of all their customers are male. Building is ordered, mathematical, structured, and in using the square, *Home Depot* is visually associating their identity with what they do, *and* the target audience to which they are communication.

3. Identities must REPRODUCE the same, retain the same color/s and clarity across all campaigns and mediums.

Beyond just variations in size, logos must look and feel the same across all mediums, whether it's a digital or a print campaign; in full color, or in black-and-white; or it's against a dark or a light background.

We achieve this in three ways:
- We develop *flexible* identities and icons in line art (outline), and solid colors.
- We produce the final identity for reproduction across all campaigns and mediums in *Adobe Illustrator*, or another vector drawing program, so they reproduce in most any size, and on any medium— online; print; packaging; display—without losing quality.
- We use solid Pantone colors when printing our logos, in addition to four color (4/C) process printing full color campaigns, to assure the colors of our identities look the same online and in print.

Follow these simple guidelines, these three (3) logo design perimeters, to create and produce effective logos and icons for your offerings and your company, that you'll use on most all of your marketing efforts for the life-cycle of your products, services, and business.

Put a Face on Your New Venture

Let's begin with designing your **corporate identity**. You'll design and produce your **product identity** using the exact same perimeters and best practices as developing your company logo.

As with naming your company, develop your corporate logo design utilizing one of these three common graphic design conventions:
- **Symbol only**
- **Text/Type only**
- **Symbol and Text combined**

Symbol only breaks down into two (2) distinct categories:
- **Initial Cap**, or the first initial of the company name, as in *McDonald's* and *Facebook* and *Acura*.
- **Symbol only**, like the Christian cross, or the *Java* programming language logo of the the steaming cup of coffee, or the four colored squares of *Microsoft Corp*.

Text/Type only breaks down into two (2) distinct categories:
- **Company Initials**, as in *HBO*, or *NASA*.
- **Full Company Name**, as in *Oracle*, or *Kellogg's*, or *Google*.

Symbol and Type identities use both a symbol *and* initials, or the full name of the company. *Nike* uses the swish under their name spelled out in italics. *Starbucks Coffee* uses a green circle with their name in white, surrounding a twin-tailed mermaid. (*Starbucks* is living proof it is not the name or identity that makes a company, but the quality of their offerings that created their brand.)

The Power of the Initial Cap
An INITIAL CAP is the first letter of any word.

It is common to see identity designs using initials as symbols. It is common because it's a quick and easy way to design identities that adhere to all three logo design perimeters. Remember, it isn't the logo that makes the company, the quality and value of the company's products and services that will brand them.

Wordpress, the rather complex **CMS** (**content management system**) software that a third of all websites are built on, uses an elegant white 'W' in a blue circle. *Dairy Queen* uses their initial caps, 'DQ' in white, simple italics typeface, inside a bright red oval that looks like stylized lips (they sell ice cream). Both these identities use just the initial cap or caps of their name, inside a shape, and in specific colors, that communicate *something* about their offerings and/or companies.

The initials, or initial cap does not need to be centered in a shape. In fact, images get more interesting when the text is *not* centered. *Facebook's* lowercase 'f,' inside the blue square, is much more to the right side of the square than centered, walking our eyes into the image. *HP* uses the stems of the lowercase 'h' and 'p' to break out of the circle surrounding the letters.

Using the initials of your company name, or the initial cap—the first letter/s of your company name—and putting it into a shape, and then choosing color schemes that reflects the nature of your offerings, is a simple way to design and produce an effective corporate identity while staying within the required logo design perimeters.

-Typography 101-

Designing with Type
Whether using the initial cap of your company name, or spelling out your entire company name, as with *Google* or *Amazon,* the text, also known as type, must be readable, regardless of the medium the campaign appears. In fact, the #1 rule of typography, is the type must be *readable*. If it is not, there is simply no reason to use type. If you choose to use text only for your I.D., make sure the type is readable. If you'd prefer *not* to have readable type, stick to symbol only, and use visual imagery, like the *Java* (programming language) line art logo of a steaming cup of coffee, or *Microsoft's* four colored squares.

All corporate identities require *some* text. Even the *Apple* logo has the company name spelled out under their icon of the bitten apple on some of their marketing efforts. You won't always show the text with the icon, assuming you design them as separate elements. However, it is *smart* marketing to show them together across most of your marketing efforts in the startup phase of your business (the first couple of years or more). Doing so, helps associate your icon with your company's name, and establish your new venture's brand.

Stylized initial caps as your logo design, as the *Gucci* logo does, or *LG's* logo making a happy face with the 'L' and the 'G,' are not [necessarily] readable, or even recognizable text. While a logo icon created with only initial caps does not need to be readable, in fact, all corporate I.D.s must have the company name spelled out *somewhere*, either as the I.D. itself (type only), or under, on top, or to the side of the company icon, and this text must be readable to build brand awareness.

In the old days, when typographers used a separate block of metal for each letter, and then put them in a line to create words and sentences for print, they established a measuring paradigm called the '**points**' (**pt**) system. The number of points measured the size of the metal block in which each letter fit.

Today, we use the DTP (desktop publishing point) system, as the standard to measure the size of the text we choose, *and* the space between the lines in a block of text. A one inch letter is [generally] 72 points (25.4mm). Different typefaces set at the same font size won't necessarily appear the same size on the page. The variations in type size is rather staggering depending on the font. Most serif typefaces usually look smaller than sans-serif typefaces.

Headlines in a full page magazine ad typically run between 18 – 60 points (18pt – 60pt) depending on the size of the ad. Subheads, the secondary messaging to the headline, run between 14pt – 20pt type. Bodycopy, the blocks of text detailing the headline and subheads, generally run between 9pt – 12pt type.

Serif vs. San Serif Fonts

Before the internet, when most marketing was in print, designers had a more extensive palette, with many more styles of typefaces (aka **fonts**) to chose from for our identities and marketing efforts. The reason for this simply readability. It's hard to read complex letter forms, like the *Old English* typeface of the *New York Times* identity, on a 3" cellphone screen, or the 1/4" space allocated for icons on our social media feeds.

Most of our reading and viewing of marketing these days is done on our cellphones, or laptops, or tablets, or other electronic devices. In the old days of only print media, the size of the text in a magazine or newspaper was fixed. There are no variations in text size with print, like there is with digital, i.e. **responsive** media. A 72-point (1") headline, printed on paper or other substrate, will remain 72pt, unlike with our electronic devices today. A 72pt headline on your laptop might be close to 1", but on your cellphone reads more like 18pt type.

Since digital media became predominate for marketing in the early 2000s, we've learned a few things along the way about typography. We've discovered what is readable, and what isn't, on specific mediums.

There are two (2) basic types of fonts:
- Serif
- **Sans-Serif**

Serif

A SERIF typeface has tiny flags, or wingtips on the ends of each letter. It also means the font will have thick and thin components.

This is the serif font, BASKERVILLE. Notice the thick and thin stems of the 'A' and 'K.' Even the 'E' has a thick vertical stem, while the horizontal stems are thinner.

Serif fonts are generally used in print, as headlines and subheads, and even bodycopy if it's 10-12pt type. Anything under 10pt type, and serif fonts get hard to read. The thin lines of most serif letter forms disappear, leaving only the thick lines remain, making readability more difficult. Additionally, the tiny wingtips at the end of each letter are often lost, making the letter form look ragged at the ends, instead of creating a clean, crisp line of text.

Sometimes serif fonts are used in identities. Serif fonts can be used for the initial cap or initials of your company name. If you want the letters in your icon to be readable, just be sure the thicks and thins of the letter form you choose are *not* extreme, as in *Egyptian* or *Slab* typefaces, like *IBM* uses for their identity. On a *Twitter* feed, through a cellphone screen, your logo will likely be harder to read in serif fonts.

The *VOGUE* (magazine) identity was designed for their print publication, back in 1905. They customized the serif typeface *Bodoni*, to create their logo identity. It works beautifully in print. The severe thicks and thins of their letter forms add elegance and refinement to their I.D., their logo effectively communicating to their primary target market—women.

Online, however, the *VOGUE* logo is hard to read, especially small. The thin lines disappear, drop out in digital reproduction. You'll have to use your identities across all media, both in print and online. The names of your offering/s, and your company should be a readable component in your identities regardless of the medium of delivery.

Sans-Serif

To avoid poor quality reproduction of our advertising and marketing material, we now generally use **SANS-SERIF** fonts in our identities and campaigns. 'Sans' means "without" in Latin. In other words, *without Serifs*—no wingtips—just clean letter forms, generally with little to no variation in thicks and thins.

The entire Lean Startup Marketing series, all three workbooks, use the sans-serif typeface *Verdana*, in 12pt type. This typeface has no thick or thin stems in their letter forms. It will be as readable on your cellphone in ebook form, as each workbook will be in print.

Since your identities must appear tiny, like on your social media feeds, or huge, like on the side of your building, you'll mostly use sans-serif fonts in your marketing efforts, as they tend to reproduce better than serif across mediums. Most campaigns today are designed for digital media. These campaigns are also being simultaneously utilized as print campaigns, to build brand awareness with the same look, feel, and messaging across multiple marketing channels.

Most sans-serif typefaces can be used large, as headlines, or tiny, as with your identity in a social media post, without losing quality. Sans-serif bodycopy can run as small as 5-point type and still be readable, even online, where we can enlarge our **UIs** (**user interface**) with a quick spread of our fingers on the screen.

Choose fonts wisely throughout all your marketing efforts (or hire designers with knowledge of typography). Sans-Serif fonts are used for online media, but also for print, and identity design. Avoid using serif fonts in digital media, since they reproduce poorly online. Utilize serif typefaces only when working exclusively in print media, in which the font size remains fixed.

Exceptions to Every Rule

Transitional Serif, and similar 'safe' serif typefaces have small serifs, barely noticeable 'wingtips' at the ends of most letters, with little variation in thickness within the letter forms. *Egyptian* (aka *Slab*, aka *Blockletter*) serif typefaces have thick serifs, also with little variation within the letter form. These fonts are generally fine to use online, as they mitigate the reproduction problems that occur with traditional serif typefaces. 'Safe' serif typefaces are a great alternative when designing identities to full campaigns, for a unique presentation, instead of adding to the excessive use of sans-serif fonts currently online.

Apply Typography to Marketing

Readability is the primary reason we use text (aka 'copy') in our marketing efforts. If it isn't readable, there is no need for the copy, and the imagery alone must communicate your entire campaign messaging.

There are a wide variety of readable typefaces out there to create unique campaigns and express your messaging to your target audiences. Let's review some font categories, and their real world applications:

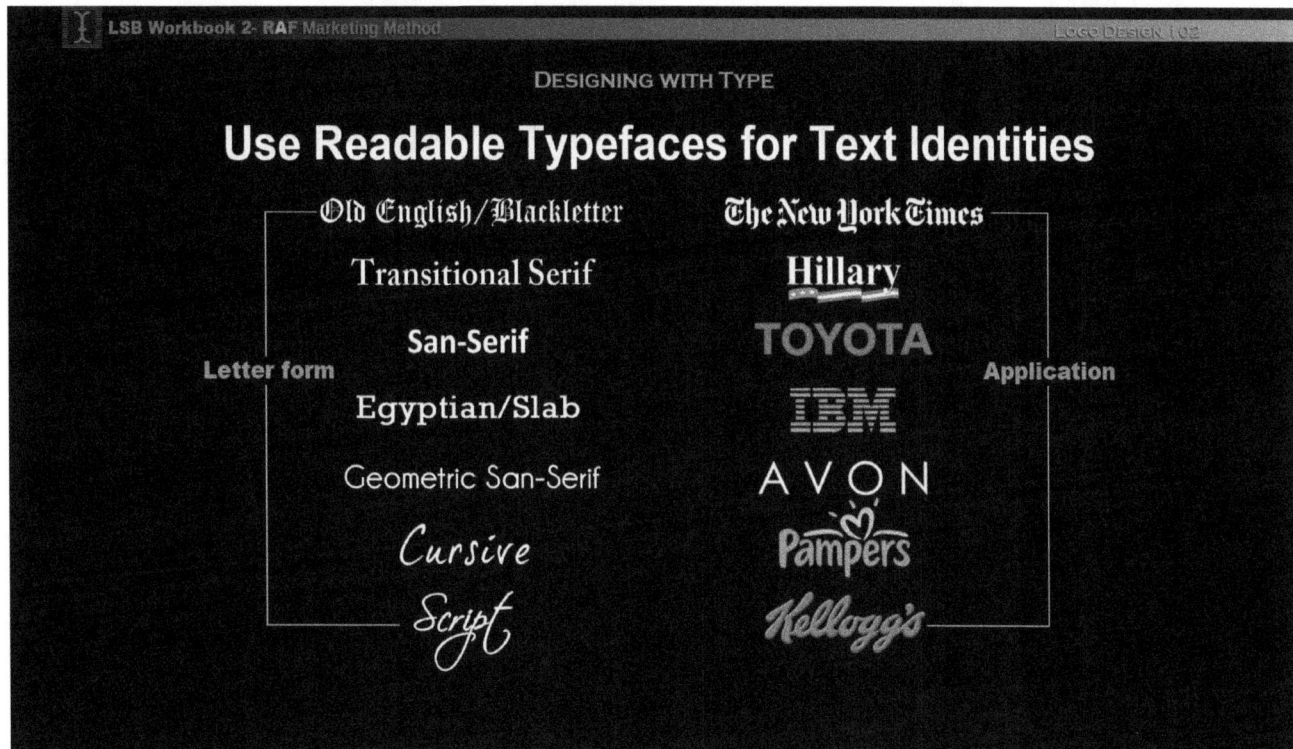

- **Blackletter**, also known as *Old-English* is used by the *New York Times* as their masthead. They also employ the letter 'T' in *Blackletter* as their initial cap icon on social media. Until 1996, the *New York Times* was a print publication only. Using a complex, serif face like *Blackletter* was typical when the newspaper began in 1851. And while it's impossible to see the complexity of thick and thin lines in their *Blackletter* 'T' icon online, they have sufficiently branded their I.D. so most of us now recognize the *Old-English* 'T' as the *NY Times* identity.

- **Transitional Serif**, as discussed above, is actually a category of modern serif fonts usable across all mediums because it has small serifs, without a lot of variation in thickness within each letter form. Since *Transitional Serif* reproduces well across media, but looks softer, more feminine than a sans-serif face, Hillary Clinton used it as her identity in her 2016 marketing efforts for President of the United States, against Donald Trump. Trump used *Akzidenz Grotesk* Bold Extended, a loud, block typeface, in all caps. Very male.

- **Egyptian** (aka **Slab**) serif fonts also work well across all mediums. Again, it doesn't have a lot of variation in thickness within the letter form, however, unlike *Transitional serif* faces, it has very thick serifs. The serifs are so thick, in fact, they don't drop out, or disappear in reproduction.

Egyptian or *Slab* typefaces are bold, even brash, depending on their application, and typically masculine. As mentioned, *IBM's* corporate identity uses a *slab* font for their initials (International Business Machines), similar to the typeface *Rockwell* to communicate to their mostly male target audience.

- **Sans-Serif**—We already know that we'll use a lot of sans-serif typefaces in our marketing efforts, because it reproduces large or small, in black or white, against dark or light, and across all media while remaining readable.

  Toyota uses a typeface similar to the famous font, *Helvetica*, in bold, for their corporate I.D. Their logo must appear on everything from their car parts to their vehicles, to all their collateral material, from their intranet (office) communications, to their technician training manuals. The simplicity of *Helvetica* makes it a great choice for a corporate identity that employs text only —spelling out the company name—as it will be readable in as small as 4pt type.

- **Geometric Sans-Serif** has no serifs, obviously, or variation in thickness in each letter, but its letter forms are geometric—perfectly round, or exact squares, or equilateral triangles. *Geometric Sans-Serif* is an elegant category of typeface, and is often used for a female audience, such as the *AVON* logo identity, the cosmetics company that targets their marketing almost exclusively to women.

- **Script** and cursive can be serif or sans-serif, but communicate different feelings. Script is similar to handwriting, like the corporate I.D. of the cereal maker, *Kellogg's.* Script communicates a more 'mature' feeling than cursive, and is often used to market family-oriented, or personally branded consumer products, like *Ford Motors,* or *Disney*, or the soda, *Coke-Cola*.

- **Cursive** is playful, childlike, but can be angry, almost violent, depending on the design application. *Pampers* uses a custom designed, fun, cursive typeface to sell their diapers to moms. The TV cartoon, *The Simpsons,* uses a playfully cursive font as well. The cursive typeface of the *Virgin Airlines* I.D. skates a thin line between graffiti and logo identity, and comes off more aggressive than friendly, especially in the blood red in which the company name appears.

Use Typography Wisely
New typefaces are released all the time. You can search online for new fonts, or, you can create your own by altering an existing typeface to suit the particular look and feel you'd like for your identity. Thing is, you don't need to take the time and energy to invent new typefaces. Be aware of the many fonts already available, and utilize them to create identities, advertising and marketing efforts that effectively express your messaging, offerings *and* your company brand.

Make sure when designing your product and corporate I.D.s, you adhere to LOGO DESIGN best practices to produce cost-effective, flexible, responsive (sizes to the device screen) identities, that retain their quality across all mediums and media.

Apply Identity Standards to Corporate Signature

Once you've designed and *produced* (in a **vector file**) your corporate logo identity, you've also (consciously or unconsciously) created inherent **brand elements**. The typeface you use, to the colors you choose, to the line quality and shapes that make up your I.D., are *elements*, or components, of your identity. You'll use these elements for your corporate signature—your stationery and business collateral materials—but also to help you build brand recognition of your company.

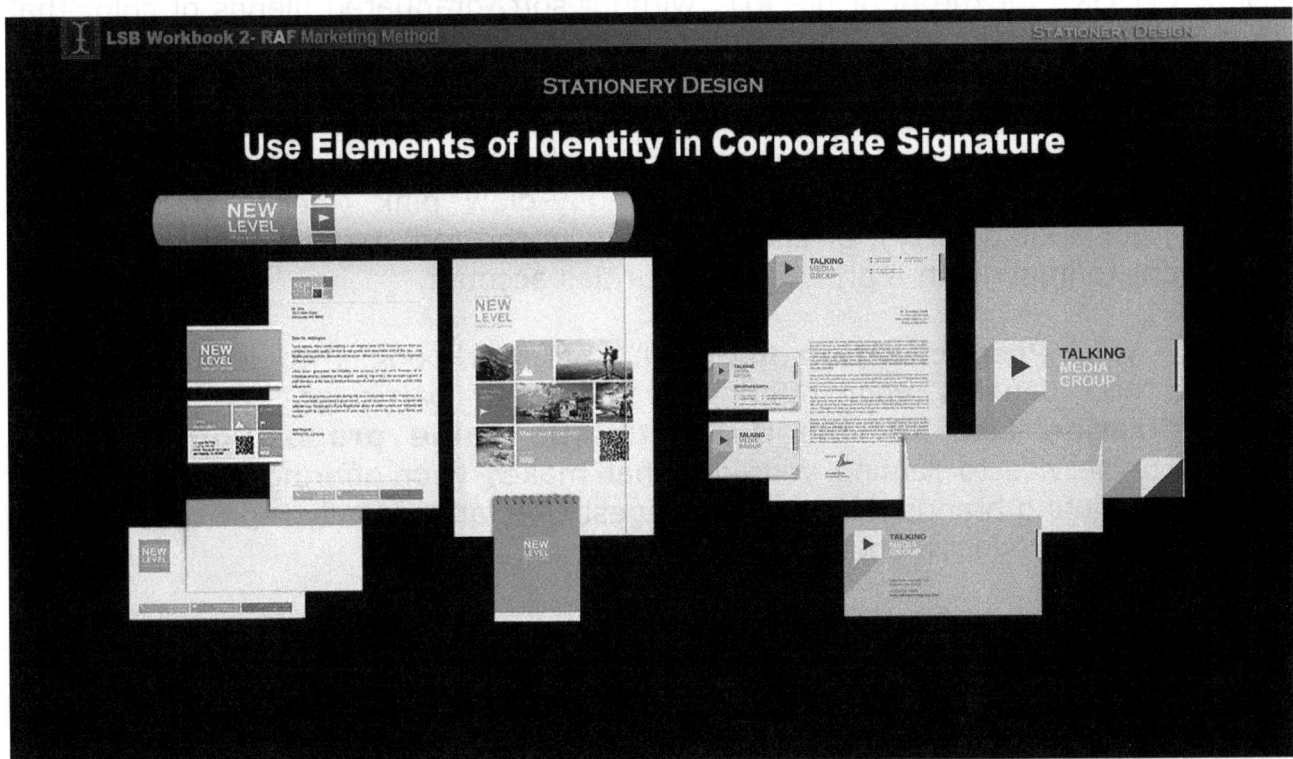

The components of your corporate identity become part of your **brand standards**, which we'll examine next. Brand standards guide you, or those you hire to utilize the elements that make up your identity throughout your marketing efforts. Adhering to these standards helps build brand awareness of your offerings and new venture. Your stationery, and much of your corporate collateral will use the exact same colors and fonts that appear in your identities. They'll incorporate the same line quality, forms, as well as your logo icon, as design elements for your branding and advertising campaigns.

Once we have an identity for our startup, that is as beautiful on our *Twitter* feeds as on the side of our building, that can be reproduced across mediums without losing quality, and that communicates *something* about our company, we are ready to begin creating our offering's identity.

Product Logos

Similar to product names, **product logos** should be designed to communicate something about the offering itself. Unlike the umbrella branding of your corporate I.D., product logos more specifically suggest *something* (real or not) that our offering *does*. They generally focus on a key feature the offering has, or a unique benefit or solution the offering delivers.

Product logos follow the exact same rules and best practices of graphic design that corporate identity's do. They should be designs as LINE ART, and using SOLID COLORS for the principle I.D., without soft, graduated blends of color that often don't reproduce well. The same paradigms of line quality, shape, form, and color combinations should be considered when designing product logos, to be sure the offering's identity communicates what the offering does in the proper tone and manner. A new financial product, such as a brokerage account attached to your savings account should not be day-glow pink (stocks should imply stability, not a kid's party), or cherry red, as 'in the red' means 'debt,' which you don't want to imply with a brokerage/securities account.

Refer to your **Productization list** from LSM Workbook 1 to identify specific features and benefits your offering provides. In particular, carefully review **Productization List 3B**: the **UVPs** (**unique value propositions**) of your product or service to remind yourself what makes your offering special, unique among competing brands. Pick your strongest UVP, and visually represent it in the design of your product identity.

STOP! Do PROJECT #1c before moving on.

◆◆◆

LSB Workbook 2: PROJECT #1c
Corporate and Product LOGOS

CORPORATE Identity
1. **HAND-DRAW** [at least] five (5), **LINE ART (outline) LOGO designs** of an **ICON** for your new company. **Fill in each LINE ART** (outline) logo with one (1/C) to four (4/C) **SOLID COLORS,** using Color Theory and Harmonic Colors best practices.

- When starting up, your company name MUST BE spelled out *somewhere* with your logo icon. THINK about how your startup's name and tagline will fit with your logo designs, even if your company name *is* your icon, like *Amazon*. Regardless if you choose to use your company name spelled out for your **corporate logo**, you'll still want to design a simple **icon**, such as an **INITIAL CAP** for your social media pages and your digital marketing campaigns.

- Make sure your logo sketches meet all three (3) design standards *required* of effective identity design.

- Take a picture of your sketches with your cellphone, then show them to as many as possible, hopefully people in your target markets (market research), to help you determine best design fit.

2. Pick one (1) CORPORATE LOGO identity, and **digitally reproduce it.**
- Refine your company logo in the digital landscape, and produce a **computer generated corporate identity** for your startup. Three elements are required for a startup corporate I.D.:
  - **Logo/icon**
  - **Company name in text**
  - **Tagline**

Create your **corporate logo** in a **VECTOR program**, preferred for logo and icon reproduction across all media. You can hire a graphic designer (from your local digital printer) to turn your sketch into a **vector file**. Have the designer save several **file types** of your **corporate I.D.**, to use in your marketing efforts across all mediums (digital and print):
- **jpg**: opaque background (generally white)
- **png**: transparent background (for putting your logo over imagery)
- **gif**: opaque background (generally white)
- **pdf**: opaque background (to use in Word documents)

PRODUCT Identities
3. Design and produce (computer generated) **PRODUCT logo/s** for your startup's offering/s by following steps 1 and 2 above.

Corporate and Product Identities
4. Digitally produce the following IMAGE FILES for your final Corporate and Product Identities:
- Logo alone, *without* product/company name
- Logo *with* product/company company name in text
- Logo with product/company name *and* tagline

Be sure to put all identities in their proper folders in your **Startup Hierarchy** (LSM Workbook 1), for easy access by all stakeholders developing and producing your marketing efforts.

❖❖❖

-Brand Standards-

Elements of an Identity

Building **brand awareness**, and subsequently a brand, begins with the real or perceived value of the products and services your company sells. Beyond the reception of your offerings, you corporate and product identities are visual cues that help us remember your company name.

A corporate identity is way more than just a logo and tagline. An *effective* brand identity encompasses the entire look and feel of a company. The design of the logo—the colors, the typeface, the layout, and the language used for the tagline—young, hip, serious, formal, are all considered **elements** of your corporate I.D.

We use the elements of our identity in the same, or in similar ways across all marketing efforts to create brand awareness. Doing so eventually brands a company with a memorable uniqueness within a specific industry segment.

First, let's review some of the required elements, aka **components** of any corporate identity package:
- **Name**
- **Logo**
- **Tagline**
- **Brand Standards**

Remember, building your brand should happen *simultaneously* with developing your offering. Branding begins when you adorn your new babies—your product and startup—with names, faces (logos), and voices (taglines). To build brand awareness with your first, and every subsequent marketing effort, all required identity components should be produced *before* launching any campaigns for your offering and/or startup. Your social media profile pages require an identity that will appear on the feeds of your SMM (social media marketing) posts.

Your corporate and/or product identities should appear on most all your marketing efforts. Before launching your new venture, you must have a complete identity package for each offering, *and* your new company. Once you've branded your company, your logo will act as an implied CTA, as *Apple*, or *Disney's* identities do. *Apple* user or not, most everyone thinks 'cool electronics,' when they see an *Apple* logo. *Disney's* I.D. evokes 'family-friendly fun.'

We've already established that the name of a company does not define its potential success. A startup's success is defined by the combination of a product or service that fulfills a desire for a specific group of people, *and* reaching these people with effective marketing that brands our offering and company as valuable.

Generally, we begin branding a startup with one corporate logo and tagline, and a logo and tagline for our first offering. We use these identities across all our pre-launch, and launch campaigns. As our company grows, we add new products, updates, and business divisions under our corporate umbrella. We use the elements in our corporate I.D.—logo icon; colors; typefaces, and position to logo icon—to create logos for these new offerings and divisions with the same look, voice, and *feel* as our original corporate identity.

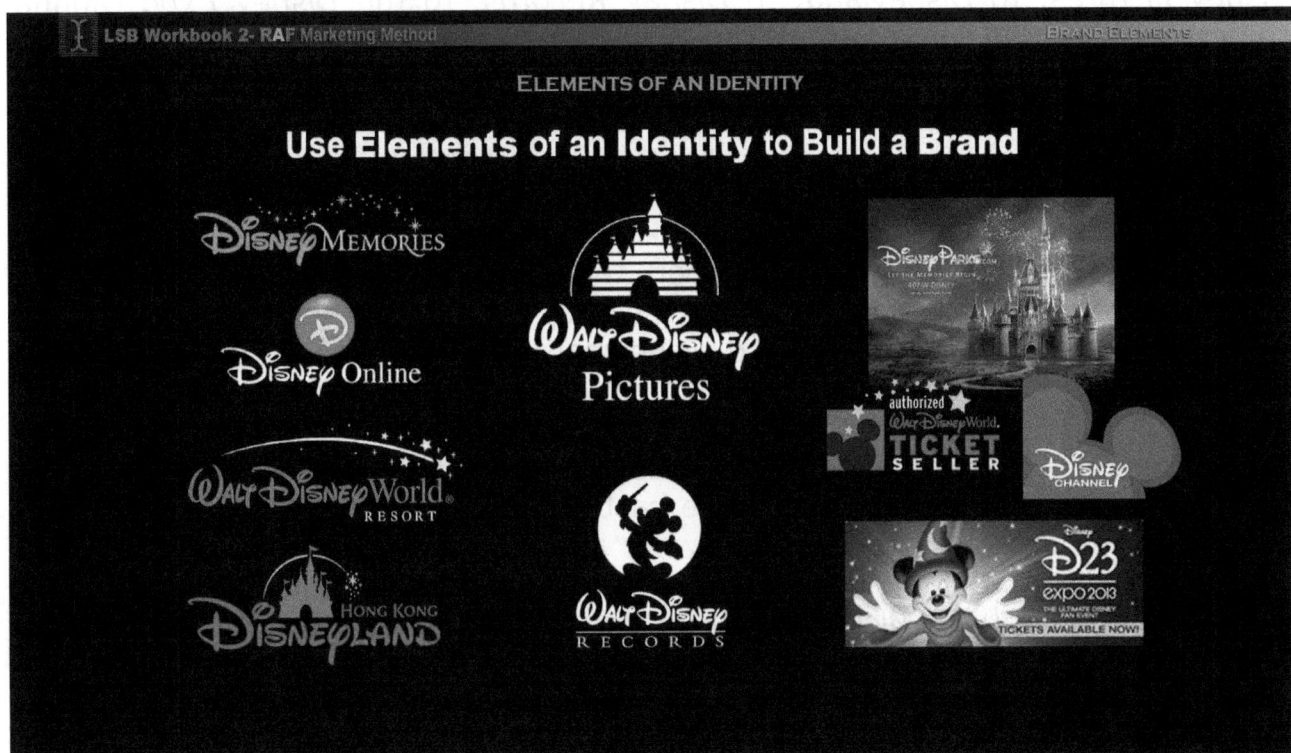

The *Walt Disney Company* is a great example of an effective corporate identity package that builds a unified brand image across all its subsidiaries. The signature of *Walt Disney* isn't Walt's real signature. It isn't even a stylized version of his signature. It's a graphic designer's version of a signature, produced many years after Mr. Disney died. It is easily one of the most recognized, i.e. *branded* logos of all time. And whether we think about *Disneyland*, or *Disney Pictures*, or *Disney Online*, we all have the same perception of family entertainment. *Disney* movies, shows, theme parks, ocean cruises, and traveling experiences are targeted at families, as the *Walt Disney Company* sells 'good, clean, family fun.'

Disney Memories, is a photo album application, that also uses the *Disney* signature as the first word in the logo.

Disney Online uses the cursive *'D'* (from the original *Disney* signature) inside a bright red ball. It floats above the word *Disney,* in their signature cursive typeface. The word *Online* is in a Transitional (modern) serif font, and follows the *Disney* signature to brand their online division with the original *Disney* identity.

Walt Disney World is, of course, a resort to take family vacations. In this case, they used the full *Walt Disney* signature, and added on the word *'World,'* using the same Transitional serif font as they did with *Disney Online*. The Transitional serif reads well across mediums because the serifs on the ends of the letters are small, and there is little variation within each letter form.

Disney Pictures, to *Disneyland*, to *Disney Records,* to the *Disney Expo* (annual conference), all use some form of the *Walt Disney* signature logo. But there are a *lot* more elements of the *Disney* identity that are common among all of their products, divisions, and marketing efforts.

The *Walt Disney* signature is unique, with elements of design, such as swirling curves and cartoon flourishes that evoke childlike fun. These design elements within their logo can be used to support their brand awareness in both off and online marketing campaigns. The cursive *Disney* 'D' in bright yellow, against a hot red ball brands *Disney Online* as a division that will likely produce online offerings for kids that are non-offensive, entertaining, uncomplicated entertainment.

Brand elements go way beyond logo icons. Stars are everywhere in *Disney* I.D.s. One star streaks in an arc behind the castle above the *Disney Pictures* logo. A main star with many little stars following appears across the top of their *Walt Disney World* logo. *Disney* logos often have a stylized or realistic illustration of the castle from *Disneyland*. Mickey Mouse, or his stylized ears, adorn the identities of quite a few *Disney's* offerings, as in *Disney Records*, or *Disney Channel*.

The *Disney* brand is target marketing to parents of young children. Obviously. While this is a very broad market, there are some things likely common to most all parents *and* their offspring. As a parent, I can say without question, it is simply awe-inspiring having the privilege of participating in my children's experience of youth—the newness of it all. Growing up, they were consistently blown away by that which I'd ceased to notice day to day. Symbols that evoke the magic, wonder, and amazement of youth are stars, the cosmos, castles, and bright red balls. And *Disney's* marketing uses these, and other elements in their identities, *and* throughout their advertising and marketing efforts to build their brand awareness.

Disney has branded their many divisions and subsidiary companies with these same elements of youth. The *Disney* 'D,' or the full *Walt Disney* signature is a part of any *Disney* related identity. Simple, high-contrast, or colorful illustrations of stars and castles, to magical airbrushed scenes appear in *Disney* marketing across all media. Their advertising campaigns consistently sell the *feelings* of youth—the ethereal, even supernatural way life appears when we are just starting out. In this way, *Disney* has, and continues to brand themselves as a *'fun, safe, family experience,'* generally targeting parents of young kids with their marketing efforts.

Applying Identity Elements to Brand

We apply **brand elements** of our identities across all media, and all marketing efforts to build brand awareness. Building awareness of your new venture occurs when a substantive group of people *remember* having heard of your product, your company name, or recognize your logos. Building a brand happens over time, with many iterations of advertising and marketing efforts, and viral messaging from customers talking about your offering to their associates, friends and family.

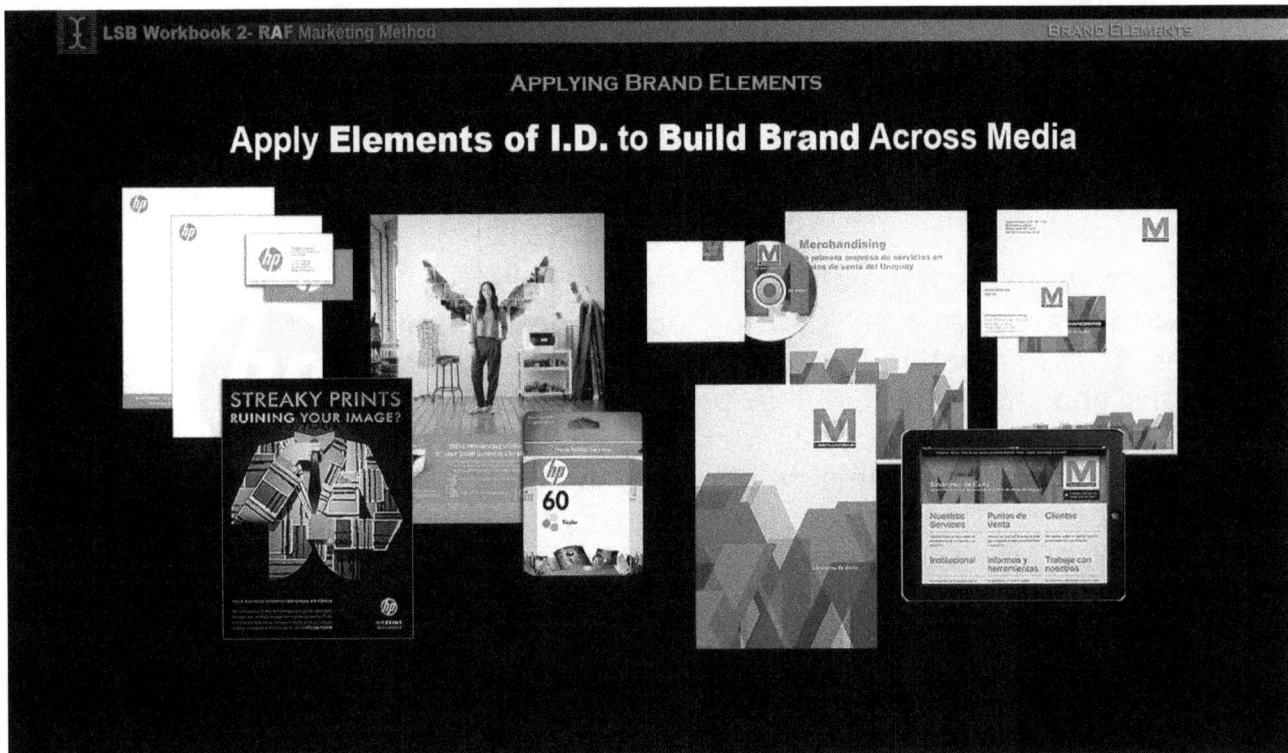

We already know a CTA (call-to-action) is require on all marketing efforts. Sometimes that CTA will be implied, using no headline or text at all, just your brand identity. *Apple* does this all the time. In a recent campaign, they show a silhouette of someone happily dancing while listening to an *iPod*, along with the *Apple* logo. That's it. The association is obvious—*Apple* delivers 'hip, slick, trending, cool'.

The line quality, the shapes, forms, the color palette—muted or bright—the combination of colors, and the typeface of the identity, should be applied across all your marketing efforts to support building your company's brand awareness.

The technology company, *Hewlett-Packard (HP),* uses the initials *'hp'* in lower case italics, inside a circle, which is inside a rectangle, as their corporate logo. Whether the letters *'hp'* are teal blue, or the circle is teal and the two letters are white, the particular shade of teal blue on their logo appears somewhere in most all of their marketing efforts. As the company grew, and became even a modest brand name, people become aware of their identity. Now, when we see that particular teal blue brand element of *HP's* corporate identity, we associate that unique color with *HP*, generally unconsciously.

The streaming entertainment service *Netflix* does the same thing *HP* does. It uses the particular blood red in their corporate identity throughout much of their marketing efforts. *Netflix's* logo is text only, all caps, in a very narrow, thin sans-serif typeface. Similar narrow sans-serif fonts are used in all capital letters in many of their advertising campaigns.

Brand elements of your corporate identity should be used on everything from your company's stationery to your corporate website. They are powerful visual cues you can use across all your marketing efforts to build brand awareness of your offerings and company over time.

Brand Standards for All Your Identities
Brand Standards are a 'catalog' of brand elements for each of your identities. It is imperative that each I.D. is represented the same way across all campaigns and media, whether in print or online, to build brand awareness. To build a memory of a particular identity in people's minds, both the logo and tagline must appear the same on all your marketing material. Use the same logo in its correct proportions, the same line quality, shapes, forms, colors, and overall tone, but also the same typeface for your text I.D., *and* your tagline. The elements and components that make up your identity must look the same across all media to spark awareness of your brand.

Cataloging brand standards can take several forms. In the old days, like 30 years ago, before cloud computing, we used to produce notebooks that included the identity *and* the elements of each identity. Some graphic designers still prefer this approach. **Brand Standard notebooks** have images of an offering or corporate identity, with, and without, their text identifier, or tagline, in several sizes, and file types—jpgs; pngs; gifs...etc., against a white background, and against a black background. This shows anyone working on your company's marketing efforts exactly what these logos should look like if the background imagery is dark, or light.

Let's assume you are producing an SMM campaign. If the campaign is horizontal, like a banner ad, or vertical, like a skyscraper ad, the Brand Standards notebook shows how the logos should be represented with their text identifier *and* taglines to fit effectively in the space of each digital ad. The logos are also represented without text, or the tagline, for social media feeds and other platforms where they will appear very small.

The elements of your I.D.'s, to the type of imagery to use, to the language you choose, to framing a layout for a campaign, are all part of an identity's Brand Standards. These Brand Standards should be available to all appropriate stakeholders, from in-house marketing, to those you hire—graphic designers, to ad agencies—to assure your identities, as well as the look and feel of your organization, appear the same across all mediums. Doing so, builds brand awareness!

Today, Brand Standard notebooks often take the form of **Brand Standard videos**. Like notebooks, these videos catalog elements and components in our identities, and communicate how to utilize them throughout our multi-channel (various media) campaigns.

DriveClub is a *Sony Play Station*, (*PS4*) video game. *Sony* utilizes a Brand Standard's video to keep their marketing efforts for *DriveClub* consistent across various media. (Search: "DriveClub Brand Guidelines Video," to view the video.) The *DriveClub* Brand Standards video (like a Brand Standard's notebook) shows how to use their logo, in vertical and horizontal layouts, and against dark or light. It shows what typefaces to use, and the PMS number of each solid color used in their logo, so the product's identity appears the same colors across digital and print campaigns.

DriveClub goes way beyond the typical Brand Standards notebook to direct the look and feel of every campaign produced, regardless if one is being developed in India, simultaneously with another campaign from an ad agency in the U.S. Unlike a notebook, the video is visual communication, and makes it clear in any language, with our without subtitles, how to brand the game.

The game's Brand Standards video *shows* how to use color overall, throughout all campaigns. Hot red and hot yellow are their primary colors. All other colors are muted. Photos and video clips of the cars from the game are always partially off-screen, or tilted, or driving off the edge of an ad. *DriveClub's* marketing never has a still, straight shot of a car. Their brand standard's video syncs to loud, hard rock music, to set the in-yo-face, fast-paced, masculine tone of each campaign. From the cover of the game box, to their print, and digital ad campaigns, to their website, the look and feel of each of their marketing efforts appears the same. In fact, the video delivers design elements and approaches that give all stakeholders marketing *DriveClub* a framework of imagery *and* tone that create a memorable brand impression.

Brand standards, whether a notebook or video, gives all marketing stakeholders a catalog of reproducible logos, taglines, *and* visual elements, as well as a framework to develop and design advertising and marketing within the brand perimeters. Consistently producing print and digital campaigns with the same look (logo), voice (taglines, and copy language), and feel (design and layout), is an integral part of building a memorable brand.

-Rebranding-

Rebrand Only When Necessary

Sometimes we design and produce a product or corporate I.D., and it's working for us for several years, but then something changes with the perception of our industry, offering or company, and we have to **rebrand** the identity.

You do *not* want to rebrand your company unless it is absolutely necessary. You'll likely spent years branding your startup with its original identity. With a library of adverting and marketing material built over time, you'll build brand awareness of your company through your original corporate I.D., so why would you ever rebrand your identity?

There are several reason you may need to come up with a different identity than the one in which you originally launched your offering or company:

- **Your company merges with another company.** You got lucky, and *Amazon* just bought your fledgling software company for billions! Even better, you get to keep your business in tact, as a wholly-owned subsidiary. Your identity may change to reflect the purchase, and more closely adhere to the brand standards of the parent company, *Amazon*.

- **Your company consolidates divisions under one identity.** Your company has expanded over the years. Your original identity no longer reflects your current, more popular offerings, now better known under their division I.D.s, over your original corporate identity.

- **Disassociate your product or company with a bad image.** At the turn-of-the-millennia, in 2000, *British Petroleum (BP)* updated its logo from its authoritative badge, to a bright sunflower. They were looking to rebrand themselves, and shed their 'big oil,' status with a bad reputation, to an environmentally-aware, energy service provider.

  As mentioned, *BP* is an oil company, *not* a nature conservatory, as their new identity suggests, but that's what *BP wants* you to feel about them when you see their rebranded I.D.

- **Revitalize your company.** Your company has an old-style identity, and you want to update your look and feel to create a fresh appeal to a broader, or changing, target audience. Advances in technology, science, and public perception dictate design trends, and require our identities look 'up-to-date.'

  The original corporate I.D. of the delivery service, *UPS* (*United Parcel Service*), had a silhouette of an eagle over a gold shield. Their logo has been rebranded four times in their over 100 year history. While they've kept the shield as their basic form with every iteration, each identity has reflected the design trends of their particular time period. *UPS* rebranded their identity the fourth time in 2003, to a simplified version of the shield. Brown covers most of the gold shield, except for the bold, lowercase, sans-serif letters 'ups,' knocked out of the brown to appear in gold. The brown background falls short of the sides creating a thin golden frame. It also falls short at the top of the shield, creating a thick, sleek streak across the top of the identity. The implied messaging: *UPS* is a modern, professional (the shield, or *badge*), fast delivery service.

Remember, rebranding should only be done when it is strictly necessary. It is expensive to recreate a product or corporate I.D., reprint all the stationery, signage...etc. It also requires time, and many marketing campaigns to etch the new image in our memories. Think long and hard before rebranding an existing identity. It's likely not your only option to revitalize your company's brand. Sometimes a new tagline, or a series of branding campaigns with your original I.D. will effectively reposition your offering or corporate standing.

Rebranding in Well Known Companies
Microsoft

From 1985 to date, *Microsoft Corporation* rebranded their identity nine times. Oddly, *Window's* started with a logo that's pretty close to their re-branded version in 2016. In the 1980s simple, bold design was all the rage. The iterations of their identity every few years reflect not only the changes in trending design, but also the changes in technology on which their logo would be seen. Several complex identities, full of detail and continuous tone colors, were designed the years the logo was produced mostly in print campaigns. As we all went online, the identity had to become responsive, and therefore needed to be simple, so it would not lose quality if seen on a PC monitor, or a cellphone screen. Simple, bold design is trending again. Most design styles come back around over time.

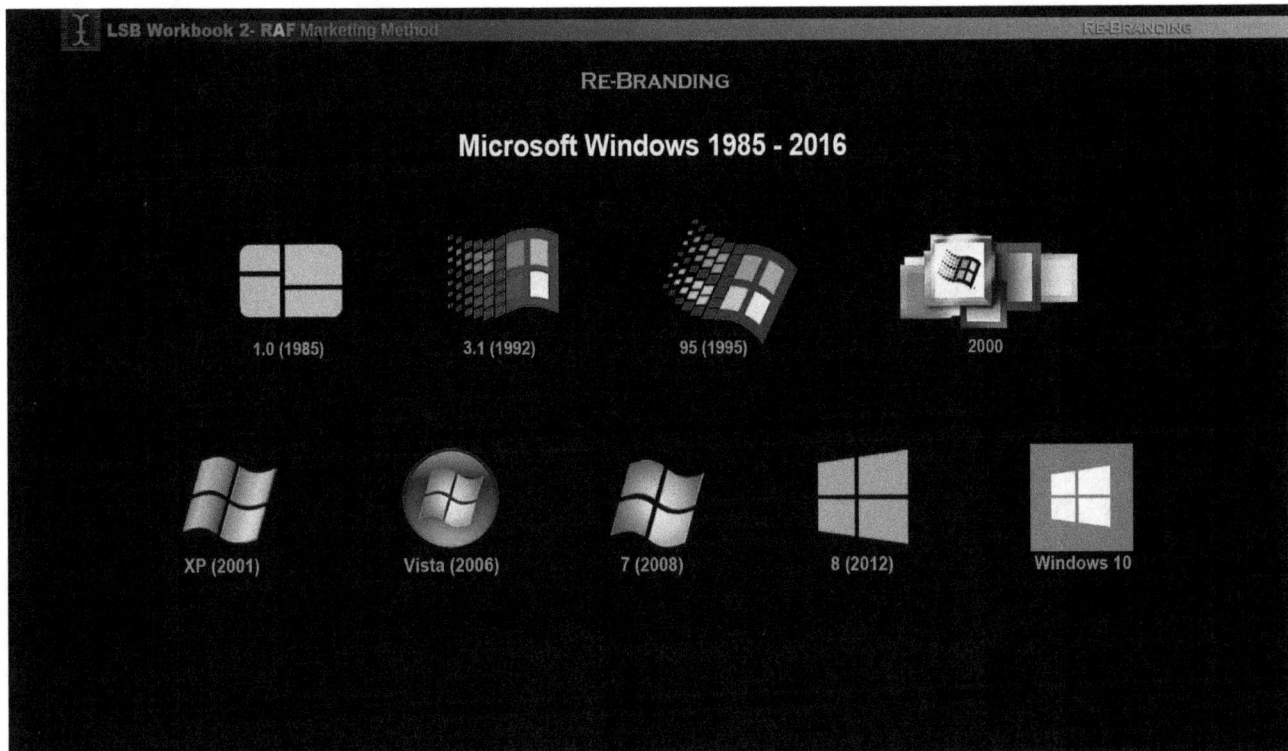

RE-BRANDING

Microsoft Windows 1985 - 2016

1.0 (1985)   3.1 (1992)   95 (1995)   2000

XP (2001)   Vista (2006)   7 (2008)   8 (2012)   Windows 10

NBC

NBC (National Broadcasting Company), has also rebranded their identity eight times from 1926 to date. *NBC* was a radio station when they began. As technology changed, so did *NBC's* platform. They became one of the first television networks. At first, TV was only black and white, so the color logo they used for their print marketing had to translate to black and white easily without losing quality. To accommodate this, they went with the three primary colors of red, green and blue, which translate with maximum contrast into black (red), medium gray (green) and light gray (blue).

When color television came along in 1956, *NBC* rebranded again, into a complex version of their now popular full color peacock logo. They dropped the peacock for simpler, more graphic versions of their I.D., which were tending styles of the times, then brought back the peacock in the late 1970s. They've gone through several iterations of the peacock, simplifying it over time for better quality reproduction online.

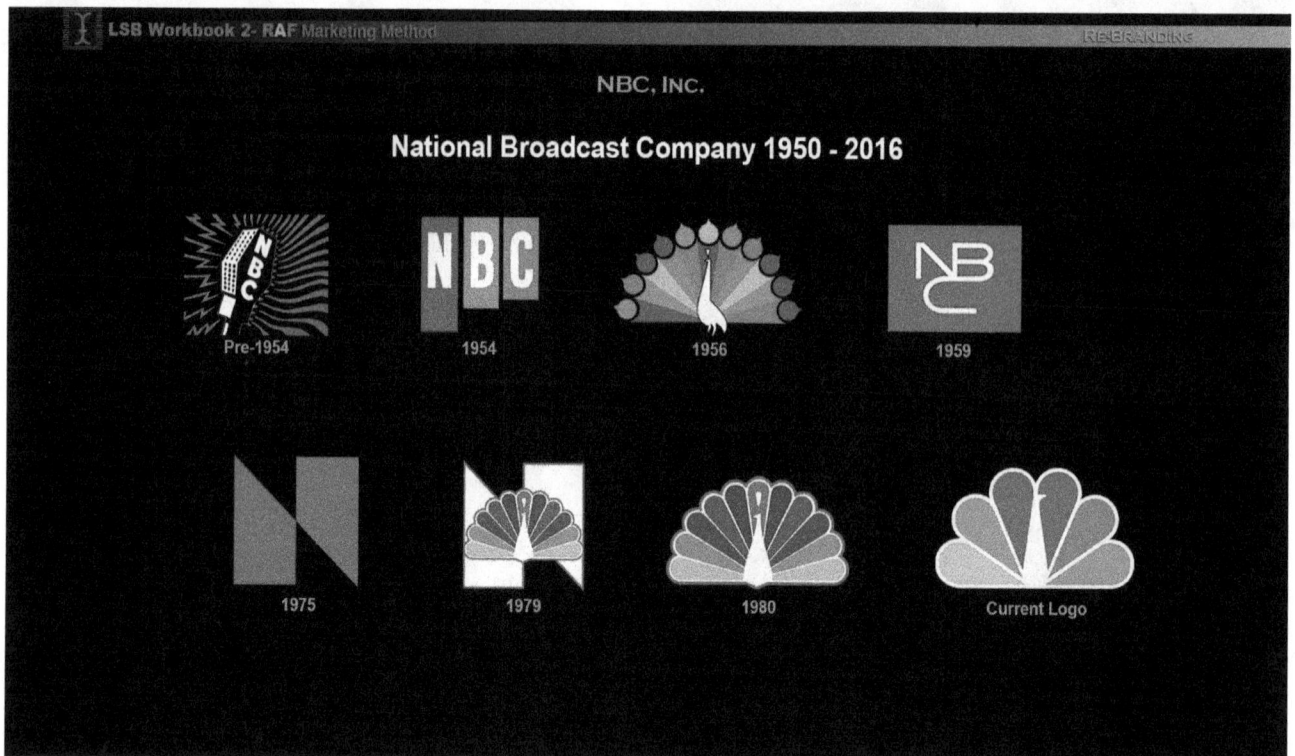

NBC, INC.

National Broadcast Company 1950 - 2016

Pre-1954   1954   1956   1959

1975   1979   1980   Current Logo

IBM

IBM has rebranded their identity numerous times since 1890 to revitalize, i.e. update their corporate look and feel as design trends, and their offerings, changed. Their original logo, under the name *ITR (International Time Recording Co)*, was in the Art Nouveau design style, popular at the turn of the century. Their original products were tabulating machines. Now, *IBM* is one of the largest information technology companies on the planet. Their identity was rebranded to its current clean, simple design of the letters 'I, B, M' in an Egyptian slab, serif font, with thin horizontal lines running through it (the barely perceptible scan lines on a computer monitor), to reflect the changes in their name, the times, and their offerings.

IBM's target audience is male. The thick, slab font is male. The logo is rectangular, bold, almost aggressive, with the center of the 'M' coming to a sharp point. Again, very male. *IBM's* identity is not only showing what they do, with the scan lines running through their lettering, but they are talking to their very male target buyer as well.

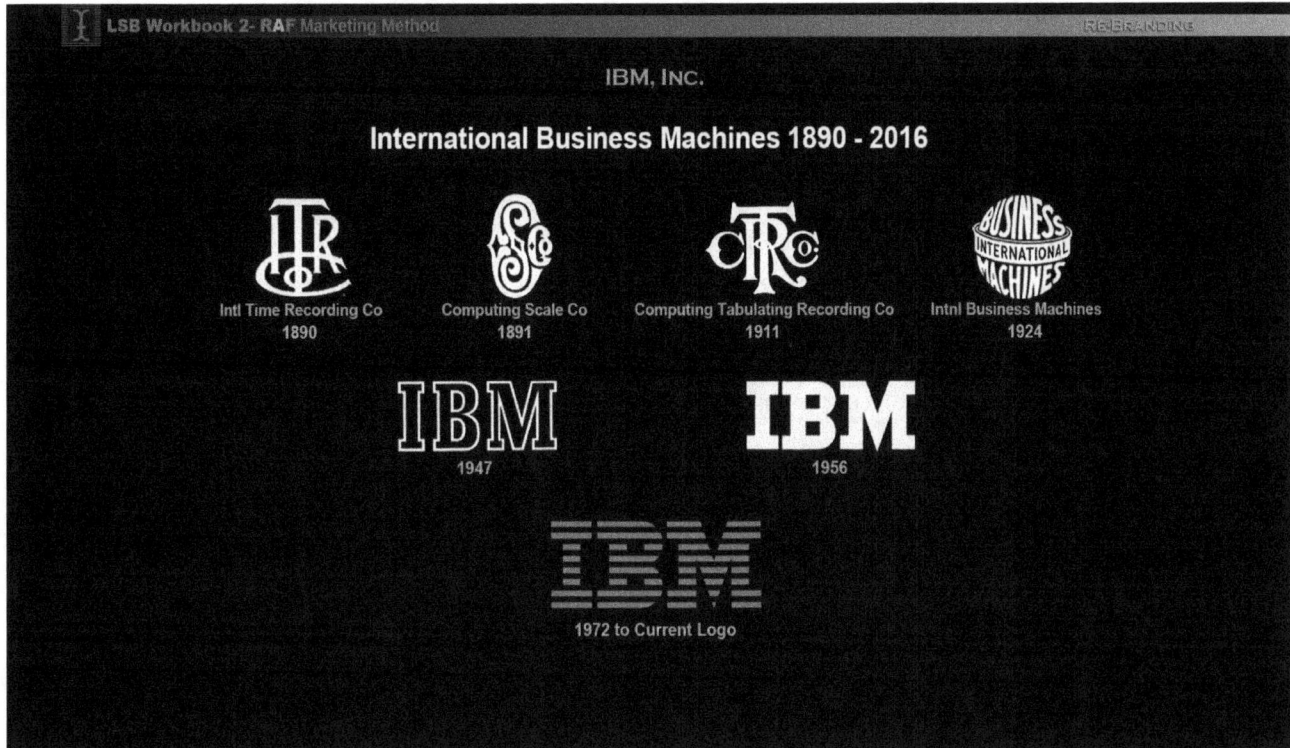

IBM, INC.

International Business Machines 1890 - 2016

Intl Time Recording Co
1890

Computing Scale Co
1891

Computing Tabulating Recording Co
1911

Intnl Business Machines
1924

IBM
1947

IBM
1956

IBM
1972 to Current Logo

Remember, rebranded is expensive, time consuming, and can take quite some time and many marketing campaigns to rebuild brand awareness of your product or company with your new identity. Be sure to utilize your rebranded identity as a marketing tool. Proudly promote your new image to vitalize the perception of your company, and eventually increase your overall brand awareness.

The larger your company grows, the longer you are in business, the more likely it is you'll have to rebrand at some point down the line. But for now, focus on the identities you (or someone you hire) must produce for your offering and startup before moving on to developing print and online marketing material. Remember, every campaign you create will require your corporate identity.

Beyond your product and corporate identities, your business must continually produce profession quality marketing tools, such as websites, landing pages, and digital and print advertising. Imagery gets attention, and you'll need a lot of pictures and video clips to use in your campaigns! Next, we drill down on visual content, from layout techniques that motivate response, to the qualities that make an image demand our interest. We'll explore methods of acquiring professional imagery, as well as building libraries of visual content to use in your marketing campaigns, at little to no cost, across all mediums. Visual Content is next.

◆◆◆◆◆

MODULE 16: VISUAL CONTENT

You know you need professional-quality marketing campaigns for your new venture. You have your corporate and product I.D.s, but right about now you may be wondering how to actually produce any of the other required marketing efforts. Sure, you can hire someone to create your websites and advertising campaigns for you, which is fine, but you better know how to direct them to get the most from your marketing budget. As the CEO of your idea, *you* are the most intimate with your offerings, and have a better notion of who will find benefits from the features of your product or service, especially if you've completed your Productization lists (LSM Workbook 1).

The **RAF Marketing Method** is a hands-on, step-by-step startup process. Creating and producing effective visual design, for both print, and online, begins with **layout**.

Quick reminder, you are not creating 'art' when designing websites, landing pages, SMM posts, CPC (cost-per-click) campaigns. You are creating *marketing*, and **marketing is selling**. Develop and design your marketing material to motivate an action (aka 'engagement') from the viewer.

The Price of Bad Layout

Let's pretend you have some fantastic pictures, and even videos, to use in your marketing material that concertizes the messaging of any given campaign. (We'll closely examine what makes an image effective in motivating response after Layout.) And say, you hire someone to create your website, and they reduce your great visual content to tiny imagery, and stick your pictures in the lower left corner of your website pages, if they use them at all.

Poor page layout, in a brochure, a billboard, or any given web page, usually leads to low response rates (engagement), and horrible conversion rates (buy; try; subscribe). It is the responsibility of the graphic designer to come up with layouts for all your marketing efforts that direct the viewer's attention in a *sequential order* to motivate an action, even if it's only to build your company's brand awareness.

We'll review what makes attention-grabbing visual content next. But right now, let's examine how to create an effective layout, and explore some tools, tips and tricks graphic designers use to maximize conversion.

Responsive Design

It is mandatory that every digital marketing effort is designed and produced to be **Responsive**, also known as **Adaptive**. Print marketing efforts, whether an ad in a magazine, or on a trade show booth, are *not* responsive, but fixed in the size the ink was printed onto the substrate.

Responsive **user interfaces** (**UIs**) are mandatory at this point, because we view marketing on a variety of digital media, from our mobile phones, to our tablets, laptops, computers, and TV monitors. We must make sure that our websites, our landing pages, our CPC ads looks great across every single one of these devices seamlessly.

Responsive UIs are <u>grid</u> [layout] systems, that adapt to the screen of the device. Look at most any website today on your computer monitor, and the web pages, from the homepage to all the interior pages of the site, will look different on your cellphone. You may see three boxes of images and text under the main picture on the homepage on your laptop screen, but only one of those boxes will appear on your mobile screen. You have to swipe the screen to see the rest of the boxes of information that are below what is known as the '**fold line.**'

The 'fold line' is the bottom of any device screen. It comes from an old newspaper term. The most important bits of news were put *above* the 'fold line' (newspapers were folded in half), to be seen first in newsstands.

Responsive layouts 'stack' content for smaller screens, so be sure to prioritize your content with this in mind. Headlines and CTAs must be *above* the 'fold line,' regardless of the device on which your marketing is viewed. We accomplish this by understanding that all device screens display imagery (including text) from their X, Y, coordinates. So, before your brain shuts down with complex math, this is simple. Just pay attention.

X, Y coordinates are respectively the horizontal and vertical location of any pixel on a digital display screen. Since screens are 2D, we only need two points to place any imagery. X, Y coordinates begin at 0;0 pixels in the *upper left corner* of any given device screen, then number each pixel along their respective axis to create a complete numerical grid of the location of every pixel on your screen. Images and text also have X, Y coordinates that begin at their upper left corner. When images appear on any given screen, the X, Y coordinates of the imagery are 'mapped' to the X, Y coordinates of your device screen, to appear in the location you see them.

So why is any of this important?

Responsive layouts *adapt* from a laptop screen to a mobile screen. To make sure we get the most relevant bits of our marketing campaign *seen* above the 'fold line' of any device it appears on, we must layout our images, headlines, text, and CTAs from the upper left corner *first*, or the 0;0 X, Y coordinates, so they stack properly when reduced from large to smaller screens.

Designing your own marketing, or directing those you hire, be sure to create responsive layouts for all your digital marketing efforts. Utilizing images and headlines, put the most important benefits—the *best bits*—of your offering and campaign first. Additional information should be prioritized and presented to appear in the order *you* direct.

The Grid System

Module 14: Design Fundamentals, began by introducing you to the design process, then examined tips and techniques to generate visual content that communicates specific tones and feelings. SPACE, MATERIALS, and TIME are the three components necessary to create any design. To begin the design process, whether creating art or marketing, we must first consider the SPACE we have to design in.

Designing a trade show booth is a very different space than designing a digital landing page to get sign-ups for your newsletter. To begin designing anything, you must first consider the space you need to fill.

Layout is the process of filling a specified space.

Most of your company's marketing material will utilize two-dimensional (2D) space. Print brochures, direct mail (snail mail) campaigns, email promotions, and web pages are all 2D. Layout for 2D space has some basic design principles, that, if followed, help us design more effective marketing, for the greatest possible response.

To design in 2D space for print or digital advertising, most graphic designers begin with a **grid system**. A grid of [generally] horizontal lines invisibly underlays a 2D space, breaking it up into manageable sections by restricting images, videos, headlines, subheads, texts, and CTAs, to the specified widths of these invisible lines.

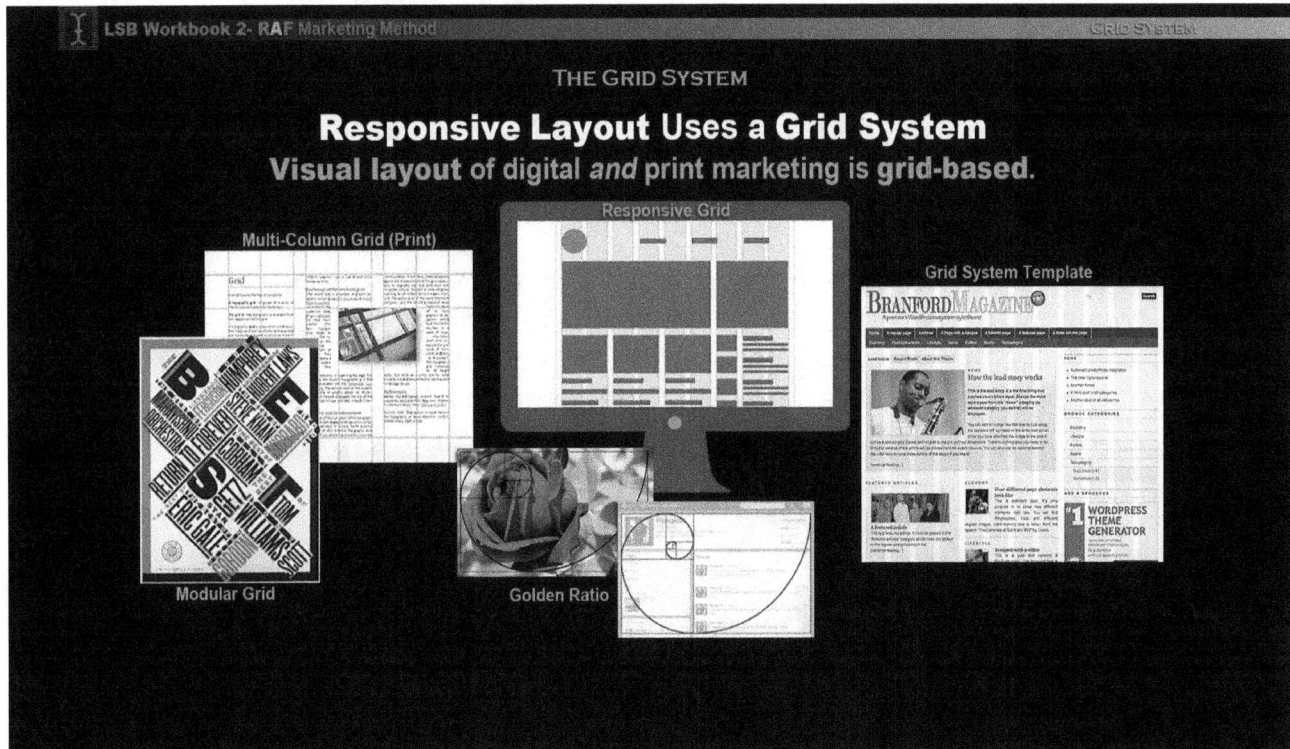

Responsive layouts *are* grid systems, which means if you design your digital marketing in a responsive grid, your campaign will adapt to fit the screen of the device it is viewed on.

Print campaigns do *not* require responsive grids, as they do not adapt, but remain fixed in size on the substrate the campaign is printed on. However, for creating effective print layouts, it is easier to design within a grid system.

Designing within a grid is a great layout tool to help you create a *sequential order* to the material in each campaign you want viewers to see first—usually the image and/or headline. The layout should then lead the eye to the second component you want viewers to see (subhead), then next (text/bodycopy), finally leading the viewer to your CTA, to motivate them to act.

It is important that your CTA is the last element seen on the campaign. Ever sent an email with two questions? You'll generally get only an answer to the last question. The first question is typically forgotten. It is the same with your marketing efforts. If your layout guides the eye to the CTA as the last component on the campaign, it is more likely the viewer will respond with the action your CTA directs.

There are free responsive grid templates online for websites, landing pages, and digital campaigns, or you can create your own grid system. Be sure when beginning any 2D marketing effort, print or digital, to layout the campaign components—image, headline, text, CTA—within a grid that provides single page layout. If you need to design multiple pages, as in a website, be sure the grid system allows for multiple page design on a page-for-page basis, to keep each page within the same guidelines, and also provide flexible, responsive layouts per page.

Eye-Tracking

While you begin the layout process with a grid, you still need to direct the viewer's focus with **eye-tracking**. Graphic Designers utilize visual cues, and prompts, to direct the viewer's attention in a *sequential order*—what they should notice *first*, then next, and then next, in any given marketing effort.

Let's examine a successful print ad campaign for the athletic shoe maker, *Reebok*, for their signature product, *Reetone*. On the right side of the ad, is a picture of the back of a woman from her waist down, walking her small dog down a city alleyway, shot from the ground up. The closest part of the image to camera are her feet, donned in running shoes as she walks. Her bear legs, and most of her butt cheeks peek out of her purple mini-shorts towards the top of the page, cutting off her image above her waist. Now, what do you suppose catches most people's attention in this ad? Clearly, the woman's butt, even though the shoes are closer in view.

The picture is shot in what is called, 1-point perspective, which we'll examine in a minute. Using this photo-framing technique walks the viewer's eye into the scene, or, into the ad. The woman's exposed butt is a visual cue, that demands our attention.

The next place the eye travels, or 'tracks,' is to their product logo, *Reetone*, large, like a headline, above the dog on the left side of the page. *Reetone's* I.D. is all text, in high contract colors against the dull background of the city street the woman is walking towards. In the lower right corner of the ad, and the last component on the page is the *Reebok* logo. This last 'thought' on the ad—the implied CTA—brands *Reetone* as an athletic shoe, in this particular campaign, for fashionable women. This ad campaign is boldly marketing *Reetone* shoes, *and* branding the company, *Reebok,* as sexy, stylish, cool.

The layout for this specific *Reetone* print campaign was designed to lead the viewers eyes through the advertisement in such a way that, first, gets our attention, next, communicates what the product is, and the name of the offering, then *directs* our eyes to the implied CTA—remember, i.e. brands, *Reebok* as a fashionable athletic shoe maker.

It is the graphic designer's responsibility to create marketing campaigns that grab and hold attention, and direct the viewer's eye through the information being delivered, then to the CTA, whether implied, for building brand awareness, or a direct CTA button to motivate an action.

Effective eye-tracking directs the viewers eyes to notice each of the campaign components in the order they *should* be seen. Generally, the imagery draws our attention first. Ideally, the headline is next, and touts the best bits about the campaign offer, *and* the UVPs (unique value propositions) of the product and brand. If there is bodycopy—a need for descriptive text—keep it short, and clear. (We'll thoroughly examine copywriting techniques and best practices in LSL Workbook 3.)

All marketing efforts require either an implied or direct CTA. Motivate brand awareness with an **implied CTA**, like the *Reebok* campaign above. Get the viewer to take an action with a **direct CTA**, in which you command the viewer to act with a verb, such as buy; try; subscribe. The entire point of any marketing effort is to lead viewers to the CTA, to motivate them to *act*, or *remember* your brand.

Combining effective layout, with eye-tracking techniques that guide the viewer through your campaign, and leads them to your CTA as the last thought, or component on the page, will typically increase your conversion rates substantially. Humans have 'goldfish memories' for information that is not relevant to us. Marketing pros have to make people aware of our products, services and company, but we also must get them to remember our offerings. Guiding the viewer to see the CTA *last*, you are increasing the odds they will remember, or *act* upon your CTAs.

-Image Reproduction-

DPI and PPI

You now understand responsive layout, and effective eye-tracking that direct viewers to notice your CTAs. And, you have produced your offering *and* startup, line art, solid color identities, in vector file format, so they will reproduce well large or small, and across various mediums.

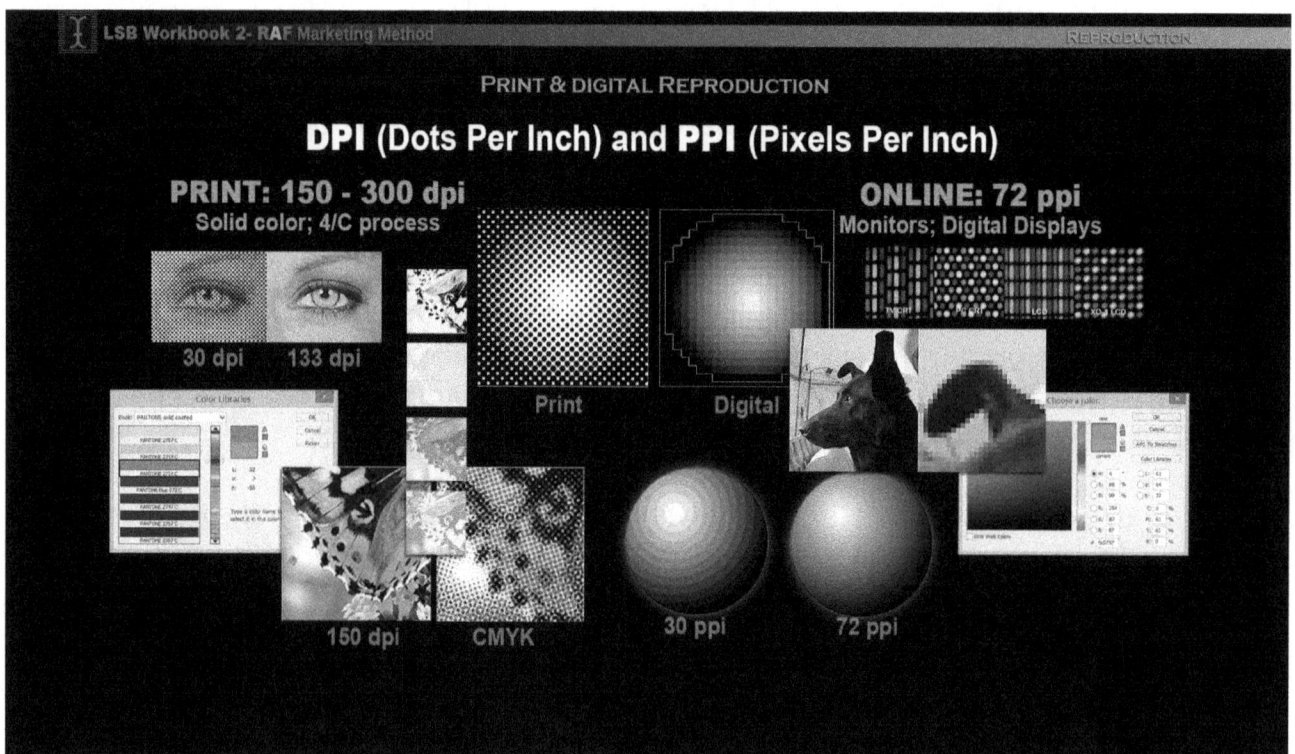

Your identities, and the layout of the first pre-launch campaign you've created, or your graphic designer has sent you, look fantastic on your computer screen! But how do you **reproduce** your campaigns to look as great across social media platforms and various mediums as it does on your computer screen?

PRINT and DIGITAL reproduction have two different paradigms for reproducing professional-quality marketing materials.

- **DPI—dots per inch**, refers to **PRINT reproduction**.

- **PPI—pixels per inch** refers to **DIGITAL reproduction**, on a computer monitor, on your mobile phone, or a TV screen.

And right about now you're probably wondering why you need to know any of this technical stuff. This is *Lean* Startup Marketing. To keep your initial out-of-pocket costs low, you'd better know how to create, produce, and publish most of the marketing you'll need to launch your new venture. Even if you hire someone to do the work for you, *you'd* better know that *they* know what they're doing, to get the most effective professional marketing campaigns for your money.

PRINT Reproduction

Print reproduction is any marketing effort we print onto paper or other substrate material. Brochures we hand to potential customers, packaging for our products, printed sales kits of our services we leave with, or mail to our target users, in-store displays, to trade show booths all have to be printed.

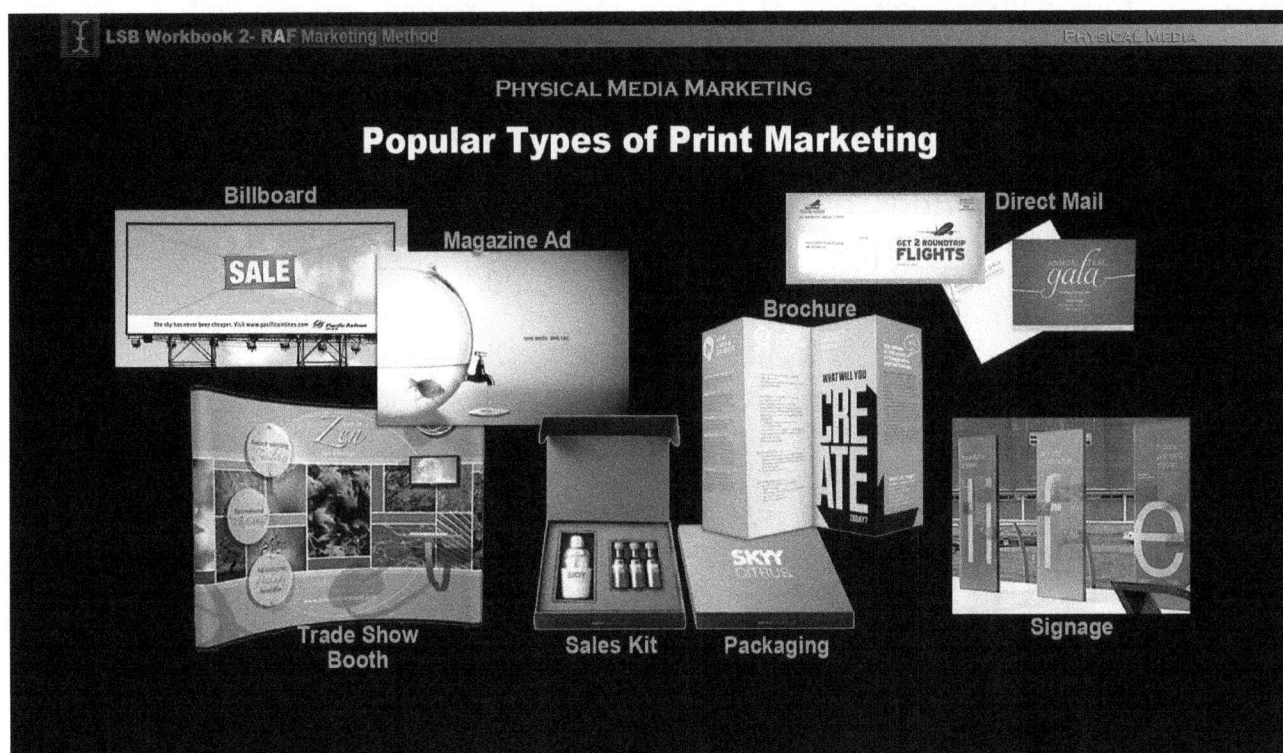

Let's say you, or someone you've hired, have created a brochure in the popular desktop publishing program, *InDesign*. You want to print, aka reproduce, several thousand of these brochures to hand out to potential clients. You'll give out these printed brochures at meetups, and other professional networking opportunities. You may also want to mail them in a direct [snail] mail campaign to your projected target markets. (And, of course, your brochure has CTAs of pertinent information, highlighting why your offering is valuable to your target audience, as well as links and phone numbers, that make the brochure worth keeping.)

What is the best, most cost effective way to reproduce, i.e. **print** your brochure, that has been digitally constructed in *Adobe InDesign*?

There are three basic types of print reproduction today.
- **Offset Lithography** (aka Offset Printer)
- **Digital Printing**
- **Silkscreen** (aka Screen Printing)

Offset Lithography

An **offset printing press** uses **halftone screens**, which transfer an image onto a rubber plate, and then rolls that image onto a sheet of paper, or other material (aka substrate), such as plastic, for signage or packaging. **DPI**, or **dots per inch**, is literally describing the *dots per inch* in a halftone screen, used on an offset printing press to reproduce an image. Known as **four color (4/C) process**, four halftone screens of Cyan, Magenta, Yellow and Black (CMYK), are *offset* at different angles on a printing press, to reproduce full color. For black and white printing only one halftone screen, black, is used. (Any *one* color can be used for 1/C printing.)

Offset printing provides the most accurate color reproduction, as well as crisp, clean, image reproduction, unlike digital printing. Offset is also the best choice for printing large quantities, 25,000 - 50,000 or more, as with mail-order catalogs, or direct mail campaigns.

In Module 14: Design Fundamentals earlier in this Workbook, we reviewed the difference between line art, and continuous tone. Line art is solid chunks of color, like in simple drawings or cartoons. Continuous tone, is full tonal gradation, as in photos, or realistic animation. This is particularly important to remember with print reproduction, to make sure our photos and illustrations have high enough **resolution**—enough DPI (dots per inch)—to reproduce clearly.

As a general rule, the higher the DPI—the more dots per inch that make up our images—the better the quality of our print reproductions.

Typical dpi of most printed material is between 133 – 300 DPI. Most consumer magazines; brochures; direct mail/mailers; packaging...etc, are printed at 133 dpi. *National Geographic* magazine, (and any ultra-high quality printing) is 300 dpi, which is the reason why their pictures look so vibrant. What this means for *National Geographic's* print magazine is for every inch of paper the photo is printed on, there are 300 dots per inch. Their text is also printed at 300 DPI, which makes it sharp, and clear. Their printing presses *print* (**output**) at 300 DPI.

It is unnecessary, in most cases, to output photography or illustrations over 300 dpi in print campaigns. Photographs must be taken in **high pixel density** to translate into 300 dpi for quality print reproduction. Using your cellphone pictures for your print campaigns is a bad idea, since cellphone photos generally interpolate pixel density poorly. And using photos off the internet in your print campaigns is also a bad idea, regardless of the legality of doing so, if you don't know how to lift images with high pixel density. (Luckily, I'm going to show you how to lift images to use in your marketing efforts off the net, after this Image Reproduction segment.)

Digital <u>**PRINT**</u> Reproduction

Digital Printing—creating a brochure to be printed on a digital printing press—begins the same way we set up a file for offset printing. We create a document on our computer, typically using a desktop publishing program, which outputs a **raster image** for printing. We'll review file types, such as vector and raster imagery next, but for now, it's important to understand that you must produce a **bitmap** that will guide the digital printer (usually laser or inkjet) to print the dots in the correct places. Unlike vector images, raster images are resolution dependent, meaning they exist in one size, so the flies saved in this format will be optimized for physical printing.

The placement of toner particles, or droplets of ink on a digital press, are not as precise as the placement of ink on an offset lithography press. Magnify a brochure printed on a digital press, and you'll see slightly blurry halftone dots (in contrast to the sharp printed dots of the offset printing process). Without magnification, today's digital printing will look [almost] as sharp as offset printing.

Digital printing is typically used for low quantity print runs of less than 25,000, to as low as 500 printed pieces through most commercial digital printers. Digital printing is generally cheaper than offset, and has the advantage of offering variable data capabilities. Digital can print each piece with a unique code, name or address, while offset printing can not, unless combined with a digital component, such as In-line Inkjet printing.

Two technologies dominate the digital printing process:
- **Inkjet printing**
- **Laser printing**

- **Inkjet**—the image is reproduced with minuscule droplets of ink sprayed, i.e. printed, onto the substrate. Inkjet printing technologies support a variety of substrates, including paper, plastic, canvas, even wood or ceramic. Economical for short runs, inkjet printing is typically used for signage, invitations, labels, large format posters, but generally not for high quality reproduction. Beware, only inkjet printers specifically designed for reproducing photography [ostensibly] yield high quality printed pictures.

- **Laser printers** use the pulses of light from a laser beam to reproduce images on a light-sensitive surface called a photoreceptor. The images are printed from dot matrix patterns, typically 300, 600, or 1200 DPI onto the substrate. Toner particles are attracted to the photoreceptor, then transferred to the paper. The toner is fused to the paper by passing the paper through hot rollers, the heat putting some limitations on the type of paper stock or substrate that can be used in a laser printer.

Pulses of light are more easily controlled than sprays of ink, which is one reason why laser printers generally print sharper imagery than inkjet. Text, especially small type, will print razor sharp, so laser printing is optimal for short to medium runs of books, stationery, catalogs, even brochures, and direct mail packages. You can print high density, vibrant photos from laser printers, which is why they're quite a bit more expensive than inkjet. However, laser printers are designed for speed, and yield higher volumes, so your print run can be as cheap with laser as with inkjet, depending on the quantity of the job.

Regardless of the software program used to create the marketing piece, or whether you're preparing files and documents for offset or digital print reproduction, **be sure each image in your document is 300 DPI**. Be sure the **output** on the entire doc file, with images and text in place, is 200 DPI *minimum* - 300 DPI, to assure quality print reproduction.

Offset lithography is clearly optimal for quality printing of your print marketing efforts. However, most startups don't need press runs of 1500 pieces or more, so digital printing becomes your best option. Below are two short lists of things to consider when choosing between an offset or digital printer for your print campaigns.

Digital Printing:
- Cost effective for short runs of 500 – 25,000 pieces.
- Print only the amount you need, *when* you need it.
- Variable data capability of printing names, addresses, codes...etc.
- Digital quality is continually improving, getting closer to the professional print quality that offset offers.

Offset Printing:
- Large quantities can be printed cost effectively. The more you print, the cheaper the price per piece.
- High-density (HD) print quality, with sharper imagery, and more vibrant color.
- Can print on a large variety of substrates.
- Custom inks, such as metallics, and additional Pantone solid colors can be added to 4/C process to enrich photos, logos and icons.

LSB Workbook 2- RAF Marketing Method   PRINT MEDIA

PRINT REPRODUCTION

Offset and Digital Print Reproduction

Digital Printing
- Cost effective for short runs.
- Print only amount you need.
- Can print variable data.
- Improving quality *close* to offset.

Offset Printing
- Excellent quality reproduction.
- Cost effective for large runs.
- Can print on many substrates.
- Add custom inks over 4/C process.

Screen Printing

Screen printing, aka **silkscreening**, is a process of creating fabric or synthetic screens for each layer of color required in the print reproduction. One color of ink is applied to each of the screens and then pushed with a squeegee through the tight screen onto the paper, canvas or substrate. We use silkscreening for a variety of substrates that offset and digital printing don't handle well.

We are all familiar with silkscreened T-shirts, that have a message, sports team or rock band logo emblazoned across it. Silkscreening is generally used for printing on clothing, because it's good for printing on most textile fabrics. Other substrates include balloons, physical devices from circuit boards to medical equipment. It is also used for printing on 3D products, like surfboards, or skiis. Metals, certain films and plastics used in signage are often printed with the silkscreening process.

Silkscreening is also used for fine art reproduction. Giclee, Gocco (Japan), and Serigraph are all silkscreening techniques for quality reproduction of fine art.

DIGITAL (online) Reproduction

As mentioned earlier, red, green and blue (RGB) are the three primary LIGHT colors that produce full color on your computer monitors and device screens. When you see white on your screen it means the red pixels, and the green pixels, and the blue pixels are all ON at 100% of their intensity. Black text against a white screen means the letters have 0% light, or the pixels are OFF where each letter exists on the screen. Variations in intensity of RGB produce variable colors, like the range of colors that display photos and even video content correctly.

All web pages, from websites, landing pages, digital advertising, SMM posts, to videos, and email—what you see on your screens—is displayed at the **PPI (pixels per inch)** of the imagery, in combination with resolution of the device screen, which will vary widely depending on the device, and the quality of its screen. Electronic screens display in a grid of tiny square pixels, that reproduce, aka *display* imagery on our screens.

The higher the screen resolution (display) of the electronic device, the clearer, sharper, more vibrant the quality of the display.

Monitors to cellphone screens are sold on the *diagonal* size of the screen. However, this is *not* how we measure the screen's pixel density. The monitor I use for my computer was sold as a 32" display. When I measure the width of my monitor, it is only 27.5". The height is only 15.4". The pixel resolution of my monitor's display is 2560 x 1440. To find the pixel density of my monitor, I divide the 2560 pixel density by the width, in inches, of my actual screen.

2560 pixels ÷ 27.4" = 93 ppi (approx.)
1440 pixels ÷ 15.4" = 93 ppi (approx.)

The pixel density of my monitor is approximately 93 ppi.

Regardless of the monitor's physical size, full **high density (HD)** monitors contain 1920 pixels from left to right, and 1080 pixels from top to bottom (1920 x 1080) of the screen. Cheap monitors may have lower resolution, such as 1366 x 768. Lower resolution means lower pixel density. Electronic screens with low resolution won't show near the detail as HD screens. Artists, graphic designers, and photographers typically use screens as high as 3840 x 2160 **ultra high density (ULD)** to display sharper imagery.

Apple's iPhoneX with the 6.5" (diagonal) display is 2688 x 1242 pixels, or 458 ppi. *Samsung's Galaxy S9* cellphone has a 6.2" (diagonal) display that is 2960 x 1440 pixels, or 529 ppi.

Imagery (pictures, video or text) **is displayed pixel-for-pixel.** Every single pixel in an image will take up exactly one pixel on your screen. If a picture is 660 pixels wide x 580 pixels high, the image would fill a 660 x 580 pixels of your screen. If I create a website on my computer monitor, and my site is viewed on *Samsung's S9* cellphone, the 660 x 580 image I use on my homepage will take up about 9% of the cellphone screen.

So, why does any of this matter?

First, you want your digital marketing efforts to look as good on a monitor as on a cellphone screen (responsive design). Second, you want your web pages to load on to any device screen *fast*. You want to keep the pixel density of your imagery as low as possible, so they will appear clearly and vibrantly on any screen virtually instantly.

Unlike print reproduction, your digital marketing efforts do not need to *output* any higher than 72 ppi. Anything less than 72 PPI and the imagery will appear very small. Enlarge it on the display, and it will be pixelated—the viewer will be able to see the pixels constructing the onscreen image, most noticeably around contrasting edges.

There is no need to output images to be displayed online with more than 72 ppi. Put the same 300 ppi picture next to its twin in 72 ppi, and they will look virtually identical on your computer monitor.

Sure, you want your online images to look fantastic, but you also want them to load onto our cellphone screen quickly. Don't make visitors to your website or landing pages wait for your web pages to load pixel data it does not need, to display the same quality image on a mobile phone, tablet, or laptop screen.

Optimally, images for any web page should be reproduced, i.e. **output** for online publishing at 72 ppi, for vibrant, photo-quality display. Doing so, will keep your online content looking professional, with the fastest possible load times onto our device screens.

Multi-Channel Marketing

Often, you'll create a digital campaign for your offering that runs simultaneously in print. Any given digital campaign may include CPC (cost per click) ads that link to landing pages, as well as a print campaign, maybe a poster display campaign or direct (snail) mail package to reach as many of your target users as possible. You'll want to use the same images, the same headlines and messaging, and similar layouts across these mediums to ensure your campaign messaging is converting viewers, and building your company's brand awareness.

Running campaigns across several **marketing channels** simultaneously is smart marketing. First, it builds product *and* brand awareness by extending your reach across multiple marketing landscapes. Repeating the same imagery and messaging of any given campaign across multiple touch-points that your target audience is likely to view will increase your conversion rates. Second, we're back to 'goldfish' memories when it comes to humans and advertising, especially now.

Ad blindness is real! If you want your marketing seen, and remembered, you need to show your campaigns multiple times, in a variety of ways, spaces and places.

OK...so I'm telling you that you need imagery that will look professional, clear, sharp, and full of vibrant color in your marketing material, whether you are running a print or digital campaign, or *both*, to cover multiple channels *simultaneously* with your campaign messaging. But how do you accomplish this with two distinctly different types of image reproduction required?

Depending on the size of the print campaign, whether it is a full page display ad for a magazine, or a billboard-sized poster for a subway station, the **dpi** (**dots per inch**) *output* of document could be very large, because you need to have 300 dots *per inch.* The larger the format of the printed marketing piece, and the high resolution required to reproduce vibrant images—the more dots required. For print press runs, the size of the doc file is of little consequence. The printer 'rips' the computer file into the 4/C process of CMYK halftone plates/screens, and prints the job.

Online, however, digital reproduction is critical to load time—the time it takes your digital marketing to appear on any given device screen. Digital file resolution for reproduction is the same all the time—72 ppi. The problem is, the digital doc file get particularly large by the visual elements—photos, video, slide shows, interactive media—we add to each web page. If you have a lot of pages on your website, with a lot of pictures, or videos, or interactive effects on each page, your file size becomes very large, even though you're only working in 72 ppi.

Beware of generating large file sizes for your web pages! It slows load time. And, basically, if I, or most anyyone else these days, have to wait more than, like, 1/8 of a second, I'm clicking off your web page, instead of waiting for it to load.

Listed below are a few best practices for designing effective **multi-channel** [print and digital] marketing campaigns.

- **Use large format, or high density (HD) imagery for quality reproduction across mediums.** In other words, use high-density (HD) cameras, *made* to shoot photography and video, that will produce picture sizes in **mega-pixels**, or **MP**, which stands for million pixels. Be sure the camera has an image sensor (photo receptor) that can handle processing all those pixels, unlike cellphones.

  Mega-pixel photos will easily garner 300 dpi when reduced for a print brochure or magazine ad. But, they can also reproduce clearly for billboards, or trade show booth displays. Sure, you'll have a huge file size for jobs like billboards, but for print, it doesn't really matter.

  But it does online! Don't forget about load-time...

- **Reduce load-time by reducing your image sizes.** Mega-pixel pictures are very large, depending on the capabilities of the camera. Reduce the image to the size you'd like it presented in your campaign, and reduce the document file *output* to 72 ppi to increase load-time of all your company's digital marketing.

- **Start out with large, clear, high-contrast images**, for any given marketing effort. Do NOT use small images with file sizes under 72 PPI, regardless of how great the pictures are. You can always reduce a large image. Image *reduction* is generally 'lossless,' meaning the picture does not lose quality when reduced.

  Enlarging photographs, however, you'll likely run into quality issues. We'll get into image types and formats next, but a photograph shot with a digital camera produces a pixel image. The more pixels in the image—the higher density (HD) of pixels—the better quality the image reproduction. But if you enlarge an image without high pixel density, it's likely you'll see individual pixels that make up the image, especially around the edges, making your marketing, and the perception of your company, look sloppy, and unprofessional.

  Additionally, you may only want to use a *part* of an image in any given marketing campaign. You'll want to pull in close on a particular subject or scene to communicate your messaging, and crop out what is unnecessary or distracting. Images with large file sizes, in the mega-pixels, allow us to do this. Enlarging an area of a picture is essentially the same thing as enlarging the entire photograph. We must begin with a HD photo or illustration. As we pull into a specific area of the photo, we are essentially reducing the number of pixels to just that specific area. If our photo is shot at 5,000,000 pixels (5MP), we have a lot of pixels we can shave off the full photograph to pull just the area we want, and still have well over the 300 dpi for vibrant print reproduction, or the 72 ppi required for clear, sharp imagery in our digital marketing campaigns.

-Image File Types-

Vector vs. Raster

Beyond the resolution required to reproduce and publish the document files for your various marketing efforts, to reproduce professional-quality logos, icons, text, photos and illustrations in your print *and* digital (even video) campaigns, there are two (2) basic types of **image files** you'll need to be aware of:

- **Vector**
- **Raster**

Vector Visual Content

Vector Images are mathematical constructs, usually created in *Adobe Illustrator*, or other vector program. A vector image is a numerical file that uses points on an X/Y, or 2D grid to construct a line.

Earlier in this workbook, in Module 14: Design Fundamentals—Color Reproduction, we reviewed 'LINE ART' (as opposed to continuous tone). Vector drawing programs create and produce 'LINE ART,' essentially an outline of the image, including all details. We then fill the areas inside the outlines with colors, or tonal gradations of colors, to create the complete image.

Vector files are **lossless**, meaning they do not loss quality regardless of how many times they are reproduced. Vector graphics are used for logos, icons, avatars, and other hard-edged graphics because they can be enlarged or reduce without any loss of quality. The only data that changes in a vector file is the distance between the points, that create the lines of the icon or drawing.

Your company I.D.s must be on most all of your marketing efforts, from those tiny icons on your SMM profile pages, to the 10' tall logo on the side of your corporate headquarters. As previously mentioned, product and corporate identities should be **produced** as vector graphic files, so your company's logos will consistently look professional across all mediums. When hiring a graphic designer to create your offering and corporate identities, be sure to *require* a vector file of your final I.D.s, for quality reproduction of your identities on all of your company's marketing efforts.

In most cases, vector files won't be the file format you use for printing, or even digital reproduction. Vector files, like those created in *Adobe Illustrator*, are used to create and edit the artwork. You will typically save vector files as jpeg or png for reproduction, as these file types compress the data to decrease the file size of the image. Additionally, you do not set the resolution of a vector file (like you do with raster content, like a *Photoshop* file). Working in vector format, the resolution is of no consequence, since the only changes when enlarging or reducing the artwork is the space between the points that generate the line image.

Raster Visual Content

Raster Imagery is rendered in pixels, also on an X/Y grid, but instead of points at grid intersections, the square pixels are fixed in a specific pattern of colors, *per pixel,* to reproduce the complete image.

Videos, photographs, and continuous tone illustrations, or soft blending of many colors, like a realistic rendering with soft edges (think wispy clouds), individual raster images, like photos, come in three **file formats** that graphic designers use for print and digital marketing:

- **jpg/jpeg**
- **png**
- **gif**

Make sure you are using the correct file format for the marketing effort you are developing, to achieve professional-quality reproduction across all mediums.

- **JPEG**—photographs, and illustrations with realistic imagery are typically reproduced as jpegs. In fact, jpeg is the most common image format. They are used for print marketing because jpegs have an opaque background, white, by default, which keeps the color vibrant.

  They are used for digital campaigns, because once reduced to fit most layouts, jpeg images compress to a lower resolution, so several small pictures, or even a full web page jpeg won't hinder your load time.

  The problem with jpegs is they are **lossy**, which means when the images are compressed, as most all images are for digital reproduction, jpeg permanently deletes data, unlike **gif** or **png** files. In other words, once compressed, the quality of the image suffers. In most cases, viewers won't notice because we begin with large original jpeg file sizes, shot in mega-pixels, to ensure quality reproduction.

Be sure to **keep your original [size] jpegs** in your **Image Library** folder inside your **Startup Hierarchy**. Use only copies of your original jpegs in your layouts, so you are able to utilize your jpeg images over multiple marketing channels and campaigns. (Next, you'll learn how to begin an image library for your new venture. We'll review how to lift the best possible quality images and video content from *Google*, and other content providers, to use in *your* company's marketing material, at little to no cost.)

- **PNG**—a **lossless** compression file format, supports 24-bit color (png-24), which gives you the full palette of subtle color variations that jpegs do. PNG is a good choice for reproducing small images, to retain the richness of color often lost in image reduction. PNG-24 captures all these colors by producing large file sizes, dense with pixels, so you wouldn't use png-24 for a billboard image. It is often used for line art, such as logos, graphs, or charts, and images with fewer colors than most photography, which is one reason why we don't reproduce most photographs, or complex illustrations, in png-24 format.

  The real advantage to using png images—**they are transparent**. Unlike jpegs, pngs have no background color—only the foreground image is opaque. This becomes particularly important for images like logos, as identities generally overlay other images in any given campaign. Because pngs are particularly high-resolution files, they can reproduce soft gradations of blended color, generally *better* than JPG can. Utilize the png-24 file format with small images that require 'pop,' as most logos on ad campaigns do.

- **GIF**—is a **lossless**, bitmap image file format, meaning it won't loose quality when compressed. However, gif is limited to 256 colors in reproduction, which kills the quality of most photography. GIF images are for relatively small file sizes. GIF is best suited for simple images, like line drawings, logos, and icons, with large areas of solid color.

- **Animated GIFs** are still images put together in one 'clip' to make it look like a video. It is virtually the same process as cartoon animation. We utilize animated (aka 'rotating') gifs in a variety of ways, such as memes, and slideshows, often seen on company homepages, in which the main header photos automatically 'play' when you land on the site.

  Some websites and social platforms don't accept video uploads, unless you pay for their 'Premium service.' Short, relatively small animated gifs are a good choice to bring motion onto your web pages, without the cost of Premium upgrades to support and deliver the huge file sizes of most videos. But beware, currently, *LinkedIn, Facebook*, and other sites, do not display animated gifs beyond the first image in the clip. Be sure when posting animated gifts that the site you post them on will play them through, typically in a repeating loop.

- **MPEG-4 or MP4**—standard video format. MP4 is the most common video format, and can be reproduced on most digital platforms. However, **mp4 is lossy**, and can not be enlarged without significant quality loss. Remember to save the original video in your **Video Library** folder inside your **Startup Hierarchy**. Use copies of the video, or copy video clips to use in your marketing efforts, as once you reduce the video size, the data is gone forever, and you can not enlarge it for another campaign later.

Image Reproduction Wrap Up

Well, *that* was tedious! All that math, and numbers, and resolutions, and file formats. Geez! How complicated. And for *what*, exactly?

Images are [generally] *so* much easier to understand than words. That's why marketing efforts with imagery typically get a *lot* more response than just text ads. At some point, you are going to have to come up with visual content for your advertising and branding campaigns, even if just to direct those you hire to produce effective marketing for your offerings and company. The images you choose must be of professional-quality, in the proper file format, with high enough resolution to reproduce them effectively.

Trust me, having to recreate marketing campaigns produced in the wrong file format and/or resolution *sucks!* Be sure the PDF file your designer sends for approval of your upcoming direct mail campaign, looks as beautiful on your computer screen as the printed version you'll send to your target customers. Additionally, you do not want to put up a website with pixelated images, or worse, images that don't show up at all, because they were constructed in file formats that don't translate well across the web.

Knowing how to set up your marketing efforts for reproduction will save you time, energy, frustration, and money. Contact your printer when developing your company's print campaigns, to help you (or to direct those your hire) to produce the right type of document and image files for the best quality print reproduction. Use smart layout, and eye-tracking techniques, to be sure your marketing efforts look professional on your computer screen when you're creating them, as well as when you print them, or publish them online in your digital campaigns.

Reproducing the visual marketing efforts you create on your computer across media channels is tricky, and, as you can now see, complex. If you still do not understand the basic image file formats and document resolutions required to produce your website, or multi-channel marketing campaigns at a professional-quality level, 1) Read **Image Reproduction** again. 2) Research the keywords introduced here, such as "Offset; Inkjet; Vector; Raster; jpeg; png"...etc, for a better understanding of what you need to know to produce quality, effective marketing material for your new venture.

Now that you have *some* knowledge of image resolutions, and the types of image file formats—jpeg; png-24; gif; mpeg-4—that you'll need to create effective marketing campaigns, in the following module we'll explore where and how to get quality visual content to use in your marketing efforts for little to no cost. You'll begin your company's **Image Libraries**, where you'll store your corporate identities, as well as visual and video content to use in your branding and advertising efforts. But first, you must understand what gives an image impact. Next, we'll examine what types of imagery grabs attention and invites viewers into the scene, for greater engagement, which typically translates into higher conversion rates.

-Effective Visual Content-

Ever visit *Instagram*, and you're scrolling through the pictures, and one catches your eye? Why? What about the image made you notice? Were the colors striking? What about the visual content drew you in? What was it about that image that caught your attention?

Let's explore the factors of what makes an image powerful, attention-grabbing, and draws you into a marketing campaign.

Following this section, you will learn how to rip and store copyright-free, high-resolution visual content from *Google*, *Vimeo*, *YouTube*, and other online sources. For now, let's explore what imagery to pull, or *create*, for your company's **Image Libraries**, and why.

Compelling visual content draws the viewer into the campaign. Effective graphic design directs their view of the content through layout techniques of eye-tracking, utilizing visual prompts that guide the eye to the CTA. Visual prompts, or elements within an image or campaign, direct our eyes to take notice, and enter the scene.

So, let's dive into techniques, tips and graphic tricks that will help you turn an ordinary image into an effective marketing tool. Visual content with impact increases viewer engagement—get more people to *notice* your company's marketing efforts—and likely get them to *act* on the CTAs in your campaigns.

Layering Techniques
How do you create dynamic, 3D images with impact, in 2D space?

Layering! You see layering in fine art—paint over paint to add real, physical dimension. You hear layering in music constantly—layering one rhythm over another (syncopation), or the harmonic layering of voices.

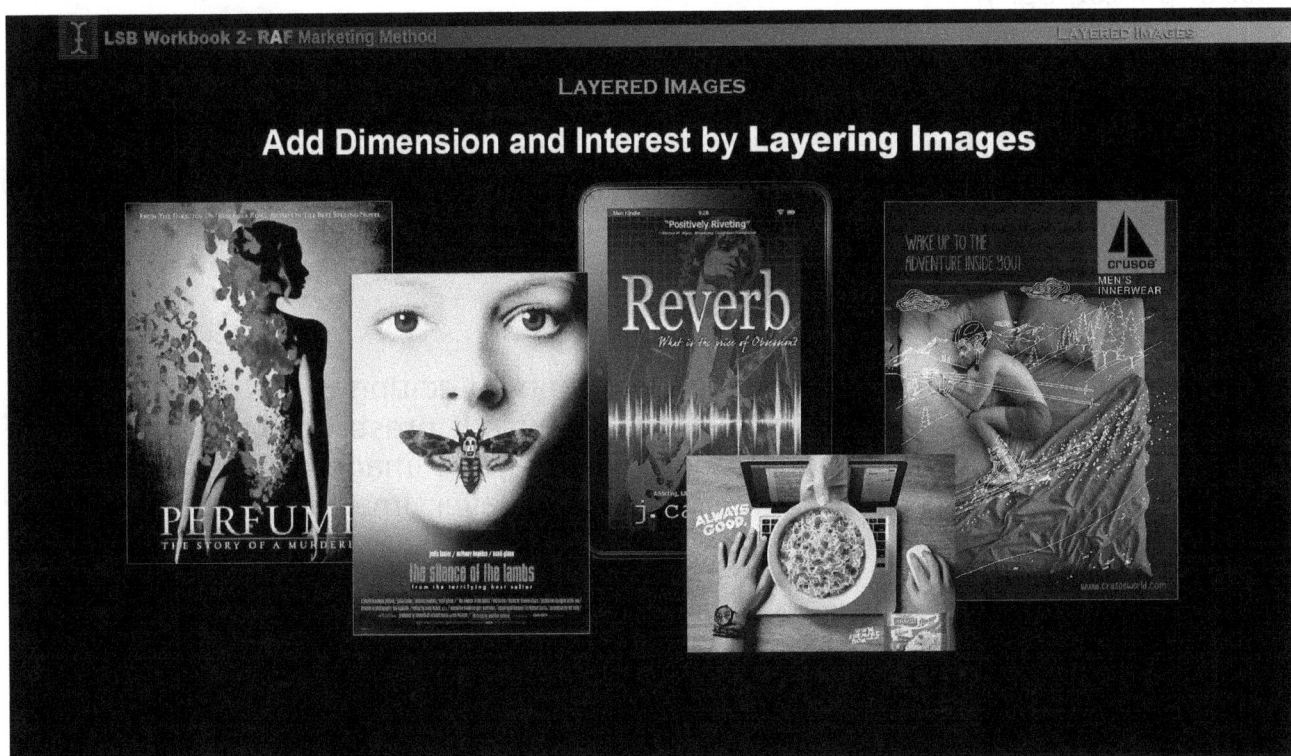

Most marketing material requires *some* layering. Your company logo, headline, tagline, and CTA are likely to appear over the image in your campaigns.

Image layering uses two or more images, generally with transparent backgrounds (png file format), and layers them, one over the other. You see it all the time in advertising and marketing campaigns. It's so common, you probably don't notice you are seeing multiple images at the same time.

We'll go over the legality of lifting and using images off *Google*, or any other site, and review image copyright law in the next section. For now, know that it is illegal to re-purpose images that have been copyrighted by the original creator in your company's marketing efforts.

Take any two or more copyright-free images off the net (from sites like *Pexels* and *Pixabay*) that communicate *something* about the offering you are selling, and the message of your campaign. Combine them into one coherent image that shows your campaign story.

An image of a Pina Coloda cocktail sitting on a pier at a tropical beach can be created without taking any photography at all. Find an image of a tropical beach, and another image of a Pina Coloda with a pineapple slice on the glass rim, and a tiny umbrella stuck in the pineapple, of course. Then layer the two images together! Place the Pina Coloda in the foreground on the pier, add a shadow, or not, to give it that high-noon surreal effect, and voilà! A *lean* solution to generating striking visual content for my travel agency ad campaigns without the cost of photography.

Photoshop, or most any image editing program, even easy to use, free online photo editing software such as *SumoPaint*, or the free *Photoshop* alternative, *GIMP*, have a **layering tool**. Look online for free and inexpensive photo editing software that works for you. Utilize *YouTube* for free training on almost any software out there.

The Layering Process

To layer images, bring any two pictures into a photo editing program. PNG image format is the best for layering techniques, because it preserves transparency. As mentioned, png has no background color, however, the image *content* is generally opaque. This is important to note, because to layer images, you *change the opacity* of one, or both images.

On the cover of my novel *Disconnected*, I began with a picture of my face. *Disconnected* is a 'novel memoir,' so showing my face is an obvious choice for the book cover. I show only half of my face on the cover to add **visual tension**. The half of my face takes up the entire right side of the cover, forehead to chin. I use this selfie at 100% opacity. I've layered some handwritten text over my face on the left side, where the image, beyond my face, fades to black. The text layer is set to only 30% opacity, so it blends with the fading background of the side of my face. I've added a layer of fuzzy lines, to break up my face to look...disconnected, like TV fuzz. I used this layer of lines at 20% opacity, so viewers can see 80% of my face through these lines.

All I'm doing is layering image on top of image, and playing with the opacity of each image to create an arresting book cover. I'll use this book cover in my pre-launch ('cover reveal') campaigns. And I'll utilize the cover of my book in most all of my marketing efforts as well, to brand my novel, regardless of the other visual elements I use in any given campaign. I'll save just my layered picture as a jpeg, and add it to my Image Libraries, to use all or part of the image in other campaigns down the line.

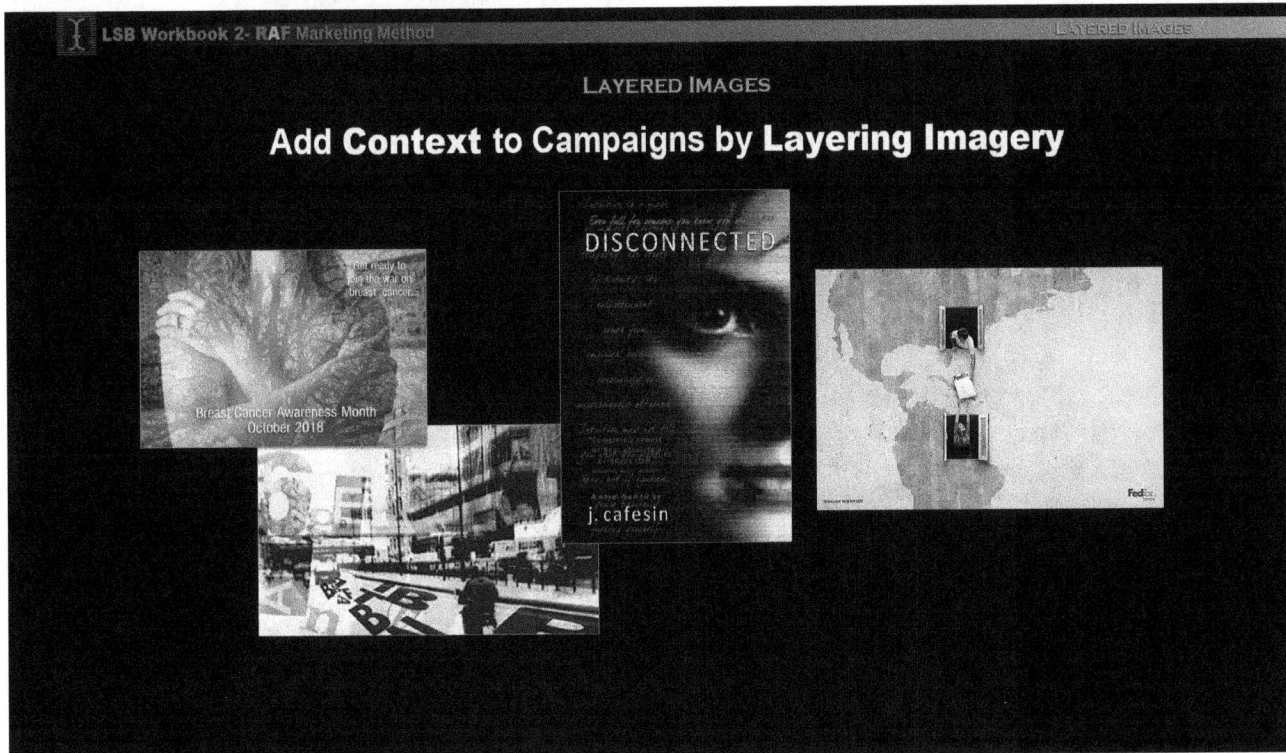

Layering 2D images creates context, dimension, interest, and therefore increases engagement, which builds brand awareness.

One Point Perspective

One-Point Perspective is a mathematical construct for representing three-dimensional objects on a two-dimensional space. It's likely you learned One-Point Perspective in your elementary art class, where you drew a horizontal line across your paper, put a dot in the center, and then drew a railroad track, or road converging towards the 'vanishing point' on the 'horizon' line.

One-Point Perspective images commands attention by pulling the viewer into the scene. They are used all the time in advertising and marketing because the image draws your eyes directly into the picture to the *one point* in the distance. Think of standing at the beginning of a pier, with crystalline turquoise water surrounding it and the ocean beyond. You're looking towards the end of pier, the point where it ends in the distance, where the width of the pier appears more narrow then where you are standing. This illusion of One-Point Perspective walks our eyes into the scene.

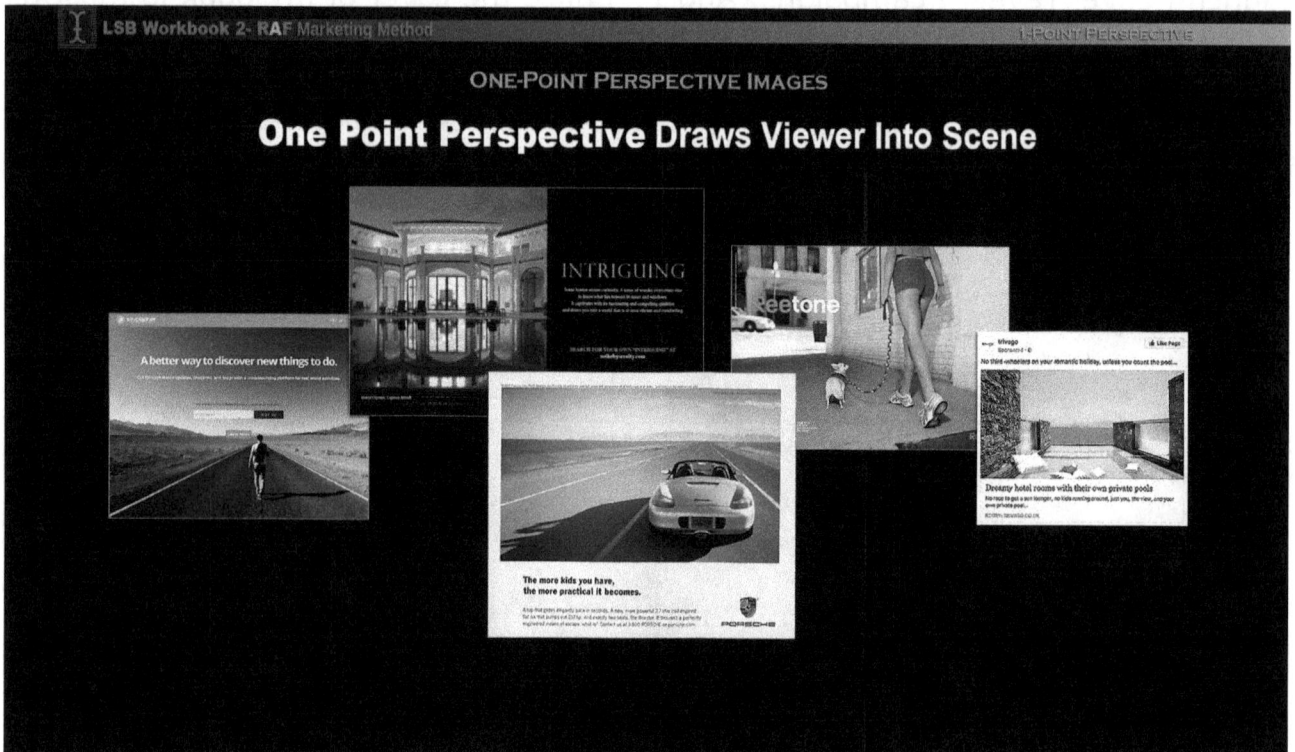

You can control the viewers focus by placing headlines at the end point, where the eye will naturally travel. With One-Point Perspective images, be sure there is a strong image up front, like that Pina Coloda with wedge of pineapple stuck on the glass rim, sitting on the pier a few feet onto the wooden deck. This will catch the viewers attention *first*, and lead the eye to the *one point* in the distance where the pier ends, close to where the headline should reside. If the headline is powerful, has distinct value to the viewer, they'll likely read on to the CTA, especially if placed in close proximity to vanishing point, like a bright button which reads, "Click for 15% Discount Booking Your Vacation Today!"

Popular Images

Using **trending** or **popular images** also increases engagement, as most of us are 'wired' to notice past or present famous people, or holiday symbolism.

We've all seen ads with pets in them. We are drawn into the scene because most of us like cats and dogs. We're likely to have one or more, of either, or both. The car company *Subaru* uses, "The Barkley dog family," with a mom and dad Golden Retriever, and their two pups in their print and video campaigns. These dogs are driving their cars, and sitting in front of their SUVs, as a humorous way to attract their target audience—family-oriented parents, with one or more kids, and a dog.

Exotic animals, like the baby tiger *Cartier* uses to sell their expensive jewelry, draws us into the scene with their adorable cub, and connects their brand to the offerings they sell. This is effective marketing in two ways. First, more women buy jewelry, and more jewelry is *bought* for women than men. Additionally, the baby tiger, or baby *anything*, will likely attract the attention of women, especially of a certain age—the [upper-income] older woman—that can afford expensive jewelry. She's likely a mom, most 'older' women are. Her kids are in their tweens, teens to adults, but all these stages work great for jewelry purchases, to help women feel more attractive, even desirable, with adornments through these life transitions.

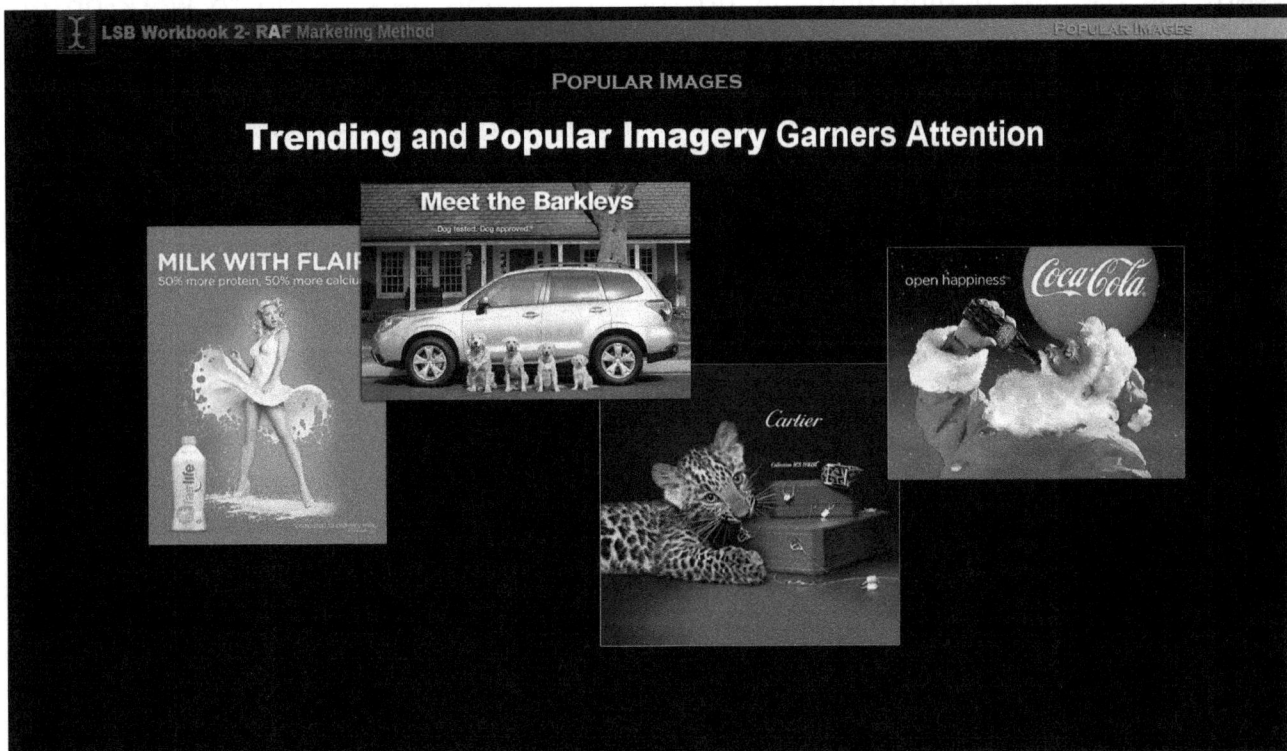

Celebrities, even dead ones, like James Dean or Marilyn Monroe, pull in viewer's attention. Why? A lot of people revere celebrities, think famous people are smarter, innately talented, even born gifted. Others admire the tenacity celebrities invest in achieving excellence. Still others envy their reportedly lavish lifestyle. This gives famous figures a certain cache. Fans are curious to know what their favorite celebrities have to say, what they stand for, what products they use and endorse. Imitation is the ultimate form of flattery!

Visual Tension

Images with motion, like someone running, or jumping over something, or papers flying everywhere, or coffee spilling, creates **visual tension**. Components of images close to the edge of the advert, or off the edge, like seeing only the back end of a car as it races beyond the visual space, creates visual tension.

Imagine an ad for *Chevron Oil Company* in the magazine *National Geographic*, a known advocate of environmental protections. This campaign will appear as a *'double truck,'* full page spread, but will also be used for online campaigns as well. Their message: *Cycle to work to save the environment.*

The irony of this message, being *Chevron* is an oil company, is lost on the viewer, who is more interested in the picture, most of which is of just blue sky and white, wispy clouds across the entire two page spread. The interesting bit is the cyclist, riding off the right edge of the page. Only the back of the man's head, donned in a bike helmet, and a bit of his shoulder clothed in a white-collar shirt, can be seen. His tie flies behind him, giving the impression he's racing to work on his bike, as if this is how *Chevron* employees get to their job, branding *Chevron* as an environmentally friendly company. The visual tension is not only in the flying tie, but also piques the viewer's curiosity as to who the the cyclist is, with his face cut off by the edge of the page.

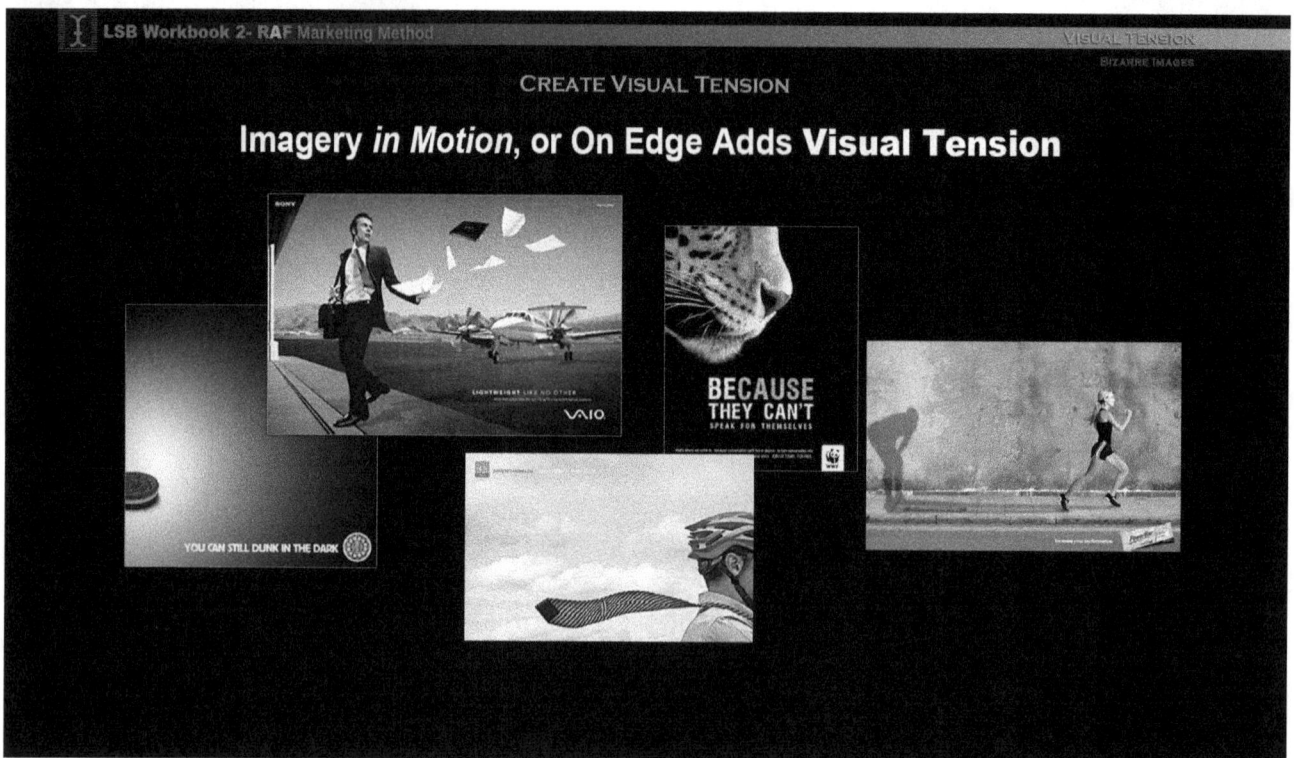

Whenever possible, use or create imagery with motion! Visual tension grabs attention, increases engagement and builds brand awareness.

Mixed-Media Images

Using graphic tricks to create bizarre visuals is often time-consuming, and therefore generally expensive. Simple layering of several photographs can create some spectacular imagery, as previously mentioned, without going to the expense of hiring graphic designers with an in-depth knowledge of *Photoshop*. For *lean* marketing solutions, don't waste a lot of time and money creating **mixed-media** visual content, unless you have a large advertising budget.

Creating an image that requires complex graphic programs, and computer illustrators or animators, often cost a lot of money to produce. While special effects enhance a photograph of a simple *Nike* running shoe with sparks, sparkles of light, swashes of colors, as if the shoe is in motion, *Nike* can afford to hire not only the photographer to shoot the shoe, but a computer illustrator to add these special effect to their campaign.

Most statups don't have *Nike's* marketing budget. There is a *long* learning curve to effectively utilizing complex image editing software, like *Photoshop*. Unless you are already proficient at using these programs, or have a friend who'll enhance your images for low to no cost, design your branding and initial launch campaigns without expensive multi-media effects.

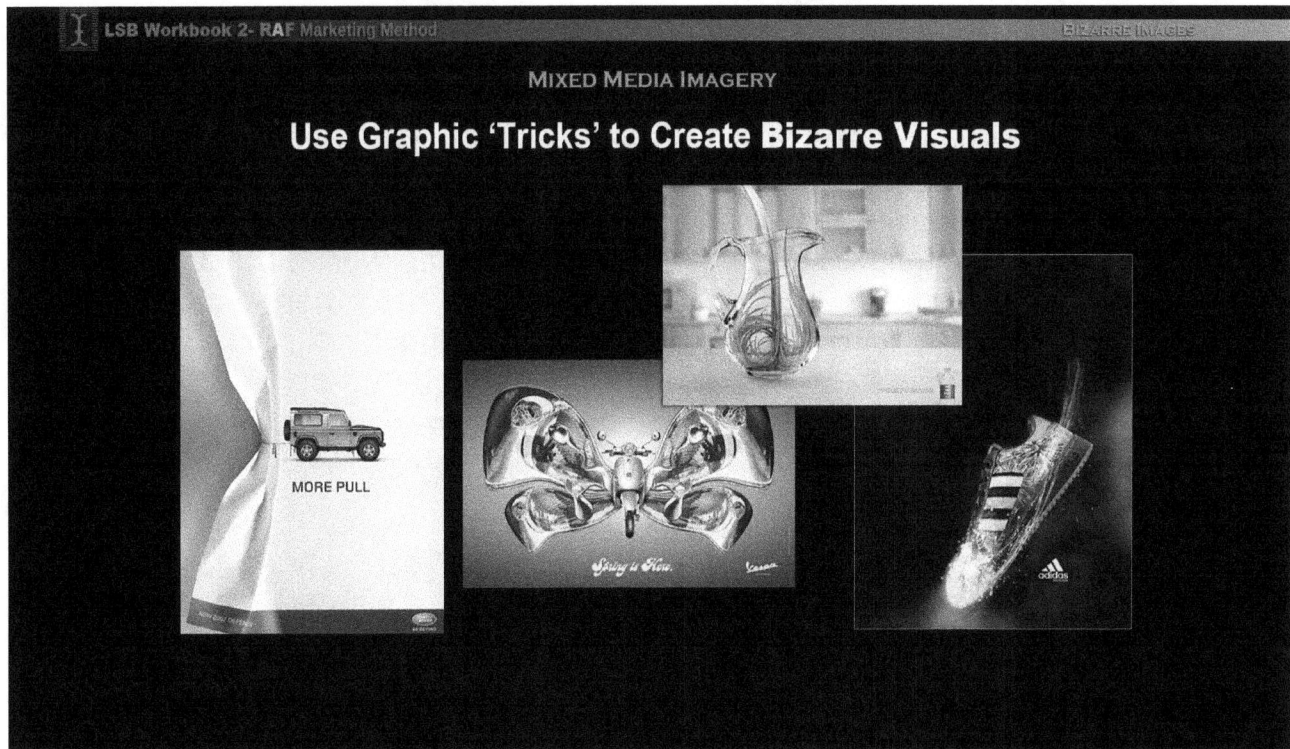

Utilizing layering techniques to create special effects in your imagery will save you time and money. *Land Rover's*, "More Pull," campaign, shows their jeep-like vehicle 'pulling' the left side of the advert's paper, visually crumpling the paper up, as if their car is towing the side of the page. To construct this campaign they shot a photo of a crumpled piece of paper, and a photo of their car, and layered these two images together to create the complete image. *Land Rover* created a simple, quick, cleaver, and cost effective campaign with special effect through layering!

Visual Impact
Regardless of the type of imagery you use—one-point perspective, or bizarre—

visual impact is essential for viewer engagement. And while you now know some effective types of visual images, even an image in one-point perspective will not have impact if there is too much visual content in the picture.

All marketing efforts should be designed to sell a product, service, or brand. It is the graphic designer's job to visually, and instantly communicate the campaign message. Deciphering your messaging should *not* be the job of the viewer! They won't bother trying to figure out what you are trying to tell them. They'll leave your website, or turn the page on your magazine ad if the message isn't instantly clear, *and* applies, even vaguely, to their needs and interests.

Visual content with impact should be HIGH CONTRAST, and have ONE (1) MAIN visually dominant subject.

During the 2016 race for the U.S. Presidency, the *New York Times* launched a PPC (pay-per-click) campaign to promote reading their newspaper. They split the standard display ad space (300 x 250 pixels) into nine, yes, *nine,* rectangles, with pictures of the candidates running for office. Every small picture was rather detailed, not just the face of the candidate, but also showed the background of where each were standing as well. Most of the images were not high contrast, and it was hard to even see the candidates among all the other visual content in the small pictures, especially if viewed on a small cellphone screen. Some of the candidates were so small it was hard to make out who they were.

Only one of the rectangles was filled with just text. A browned, old-time image of a page of newsprint filled the rectangular space. Overlaying the browned newsprint, the *New York Times* Old English typeface identity was set above what looked like a torn piece of white paper with a quote on it, centered in the rectangle.

What was wrong with this *NYT* campaign?
1. There was *way* too much imagery in this small digital display ad.
2. The *best bit*, or UVP of the campaign—the text only box with the headline describing the value of reading the *NYT*—was buried within nine boxes, each of which had too much visual content.
3. The text only box had too much visual information. From the old-time newsprint background, to the *NYT* logo over it, to the torn paper with a very long sentence on it, the designer 'buried the lead,' or the *best bit* about what the *NYT* was selling.
4. The torn paper blended with the light brown newsprint behind it, without enough contrast between the paper and the background to make the copy pop.
5. The torn paper was centered in the box, and therefore did not generate any visual tension.
6. An old-time newspaper page as a background is a turn-off for most of today's readers. We don't want old news. We want high-impact, high-contrast images that are trending today.

The layout of any digital campaign, and the contrast within the image itself, becomes extremely important in our mobile world, looking at everything on small to teeny screens. We must begin the design process for all digital marketing *mobile up*. In other words, all your digital marketing campaigns will be designed for a mobile interface (UI) *first*. Imagine viewing this *New York Times* campaign on your cellphone. I could hardly see what was going on in the ad on my laptop.

Regardless if you are creating digital or print campaigns, we need our marketing efforts to have the most impact possible. Part of the process to achieving impact is using a **high-contrast image with ONE (1) main subject** *per campaign*.

This is LEAN Startup Marketing
You've likely productized your idea, or offering in development, by now, and have eight (8) Productization lists, filled with keywords and phrases to use in your marketing efforts. You [should] have memorable corporate and product identities, on your computer anyway, in a scalable **vector** file, as well as **jpeg** and **png-24** file formats.

We've reviewed design basics and color theory, graphic design and typography, layout and eye-tracking, as well as image and document reproduction. And you now know how to recognize images with impact, so you, or those you hire, can design and produce professional advertising and marketing tools and campaigns that get the greatest response. (You [should] already have a lot of the copy content that you'll need to develop these campaigns from your Productization lists. You'll learn how to *arrange* the keywords and phrases on your lists for the most effective marketing communications in the Copywriting Module of LSM Workbook.)

Beyond your product and corporate identities, LSB Workbook 2: BRANDING takes you step-by-step through the process of creating the marketing campaigns you'll need to produce to brand your startup, and build a sustainable company.

In the following modules, we'll examined pre-launch marketing tools you must develop for your new venture. We'll begin with a review of an array of digital marketing options available today. We'll identify techniques for creating effective UI (user interface) and UX (user experience) design. You'll discover the components required for engagement on your corporate website. You'll learn to create Landing Pages to get people to your website, as well as PPC and video marketing campaigns for launch and beyond that get noticed, and foster interest in your new offering and budding brand. (We'll drill down on producing effective social media marketing (SMM), email and PR campaigns in LSL Workbook 3: LAUNCH.)

Professional imagery will be required with each campaign your publish online, or print. But with little to no budget for photography, videography, or illustration, where do you get the high-quality visual content you need to create and produce effective marketing campaigns?

Now that you understand what gives an image impact, and why, as well as how to reproduce professional quality campaigns across digital and print mediums, it's time to begin setting up your startup's **Visual Libraries**. Let's examine where to get free, to low-cost striking visual (and audio) content for creating your marketing campaigns, next.

-Building Your Visual Library-

As a startup, you can hardly afford to spend a lot of money on professional photography, or videos, or even really cool music, or fonts, for your advertising campaigns. So, how do we come by professional-quality visual and audio content, as well as typefaces that communicate the look and feel you want with hardly any money?

Still Imagery

Looking for a quality photo or illustration with impact for the homepage of your corporate website for free? You can get thousands from *Google*, and many other 'free images' websites. We'll examine how to lift high-resolution jpegs, gifs, and png images, as well as copyright-free images, from *Google* next, but for now, search: "copyright-free images," to find imagery you can legally use in your

marketing campaigns. Here are a few results from my quick search:
- **Pexels**: pexels(dot)com
- **Stock Snap**: stocksnap(dot)io
- **Unsplash**: unsplash(dot)com
- **Startup Stock Photos**: startupstockphotos(dot)com (Right-click on the image to download.)

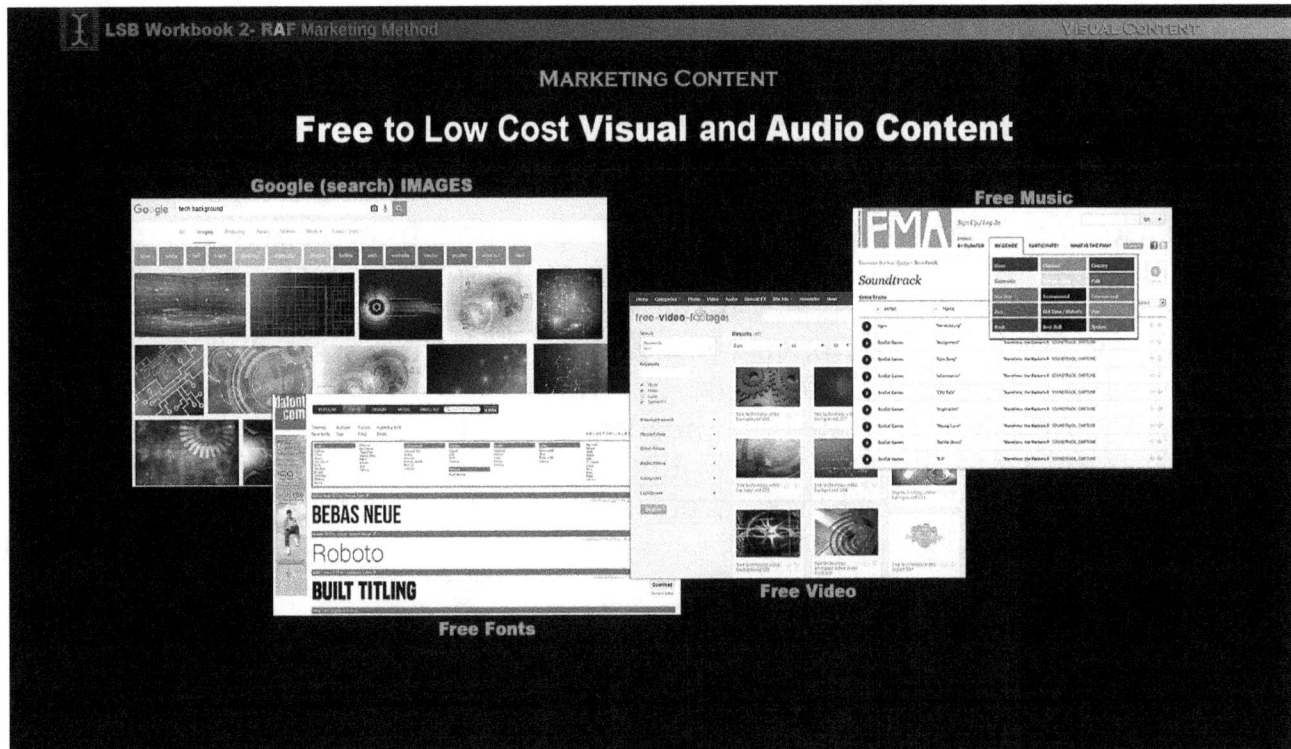

There are tons of these **stock photo** sites with copyright-free images online. Most are free! All you have to do is download the photos to your computer to use wherever, on whatever you want. You don't even have to give the photographer credit on most of them. Additionally, you can layer several images to create unique imagery for any of your marketing campaigns. (We'll go over the legality of layering copyright images to create an original work next.)

Video

Need a quick sequence or scene to include in your website 'Welcome' video, perhaps a powerful handshake between two business women, or a ruckus celebration at an office party?

There are copyright-free, stock videos all over the internet, many of which are completely free! Build video campaigns with short clips, between 0.5 – 15 seconds (max). You can also combine .5 second clips with other short clips, or still images, to create an original video work. Below are a few sites I found when I googled: "free videos for commercial use."

- **PEXEL** (video): videos.pexels(dot)com
- **Vimeo**: vimeo(dot)com/search?price=free
- **Coverr**(dot)co

Be sure to download only **HD** (**high-density**) **MP4 videos**, to ensure quality reproduction across multiple devices.

Once on any one of these platforms, **iterative search** for videos to use in your marketing efforts with keywords and phrases from your Productization lists (LSM Workbook 1). Doing so will assure that the video content you capture and/or create is relate directly [or indirectly] to your offering.

You can *Google*: "free video backgrounds," and find free, copyright-free video content from high-tech, to floating balloons. You can use these backgrounds on your website pages, your landing pages, even your SMM campaigns. Run your headline, add a bit of descriptive text, put in your CTA, and don't forget your company logo over the background. With video content representing your industry, and/or offerings, the right headline, and a valuable CTA (all of which you'll learn to write in the Copywriting Module of LSL Workbook 3), your marketing campaigns will look professional, get response, and motivate conversion.

Rotating GIFs

As previously mentioned, an **animated gif** is a series of still images, presented in a specific order that simulates animation. We often see them as memes, making fun of something in a continuous loop. Also mentioned, sometimes, certain online platforms don't allow for videos. Other platforms, like *WordPress(dot)com*, expect you to pay a premium to upload videos because of they are large data files that take up a lot of server space, and the platform makes you pay for monopolizing their servers.

We know that motion attracts attention. To get motion into our campaigns without video, or paying a premium to upload them, we often use **gif animation**, or **rotating gifs** (same thing).

You commonly see them presenting in an endless loop. They are frequently used as slideshows on the homepage of websites, displaying their range of products and/or services. Unlike video, rotating gifs generally have low resolution, so it helps your digital marketing load quickly onto our devices.

Most smartphones have apps that allow you to create animated gifs to use in your SMM campaigns, and other marketing efforts. Here's a popular site for free animated gifs:
- **Giphy**(dot)com

You can also turn video clips into animated GIFs, as long as the content is short, less than 5 seconds. GIF animation renders poor quality! Complex imagery will not reproduce well, so be careful of poor reproduction quality when using gif animations. And don't forget, many platforms will only show the first image in a rotating gif. Be sure whatever platform you post your gifs, the site will run the entire animation.

Audio
There's free music online. Almost any style, any genre, from Rock, to Pop, to old-time Swing. You can use music clips as background sound to your videos, slideshows, or as a soundtrack for your website or landing page.
- **FMA,** freemusicarchive(dot)org, is a free, copyright-free music site, where you can download the music of your choice, and use it as additional marketing content for your digital campaigns.

Fonts
If you don't like the fonts that you have available, you can always find more fonts for no money at all. Look up "free fonts," online. Beware, that a lot of these free sites won't let you download fonts without 'signing-up' to their site. You do not have to sign-up to get free fonts. There are sites you simply download the font without giving up any information. The best I've found to date:
- **DeFont**(dot)com
- **1001FreeFonts**(dot)com

Capturing and Storing Visual Content
You now know some of the factors that make an image striking, attention-grabbing, and you know *where* to find them. In the next module, we're going to go step-by-step through the process of capturing (lifting) high-resolution, professional quality image from *Google*, and videos from *YouTube* and others, to use in your pre-launch, launch, and beyond, marketing efforts.

Next, we drill down on how to set up your startup's **Visual Libraries**, and then fill them with high-quality, free, to low-cost visual content to use in your marketing efforts—from your websites, and landing pages, to your digital and print campaigns.

◆◆◆◆◆

MODULE 17: IMAGE CAPTURE

LSB Workbook 2: BRANDING, is about designing and producing marketing efforts that brand your startup into a sustainable company. To build brand awareness, you're going to need striking identities, and attention-grabbing campaigns filled with imagery that has impact.

We're almost ready to learn how to capture (lift) images from *Google*, and video content from *YouTube,* for idea generation, *and* for reproduction in your company's marketing efforts. But first, we must examine the legality of lifting and using other people's content to help you effectively market your business, for profit.

Copyright Restrictions

Copyright laws vary per country, and per jurisdiction in the U.S. If you feel you may be violating copyright laws with any content you reuse in your marketing efforts, research the content for possible copyright restrictions, to avoid lawsuits from the original content creator before you publish your campaigns. Follow the basic guidelines below, and you'll likely stay in the 'safe' zone for reusing imagery, and even audio content, legally.

- You go to Hollywood, and then up the coast to San Francisco, and take exquisite pictures (and even video) of *public* tourist attractions for your new peer-to-peer tour guide app. You own the copyrights to those photos, and/or videos, and you can use them as you please, in most cases. (Some national parks require permits to shoot imagery for commercial use.)

- You snap a picture of an accident scene, or take a video of a busy Manhattan street, with people walking while on their cellphones. You own the copyrights to that imagery, which you can use in marketing your addicting new mobile video game, or other mobile offering.

It is LEGAL to photograph or videotape anything and anyone in any *public* space, within reasonable community standards, according to *Wikipedia*. If you choose to create—shoot, or video your own visual content—be sure you are using equipment that supports high-resolution output. Do *not* use your cellphone to generate visual content for most of your marketing efforts, unless you are specifically looking for a grainy, low-quality reproduction.

It is ILLEGAL is reuse photography, video, or audio content created by someone else for your company's marketing efforts, without explicit written permission from the original copyright holder.

We'll examine how to find and lift quality imagery, video, and audio content you *can* legally utilize in your company's pre-launch through launch [and beyond] marketing efforts, next. *First*, you must set up your **Visual Libraries**, to store the great visual and audio content you capture.

Content and Visual Libraries

We reviewed the **Iterative Search** process to search for your offering's competition in LSM Workbook 1. You now use the same Iterative Search methods of using keywords from your Productization lists for finding imagery—pictures, illustrations, video, and audio content that directly or indirectly relates to your offerings, and/or startup. But before finding visual and audio content for your marketing efforts, you have to have someplace to *put* what you'll collect.

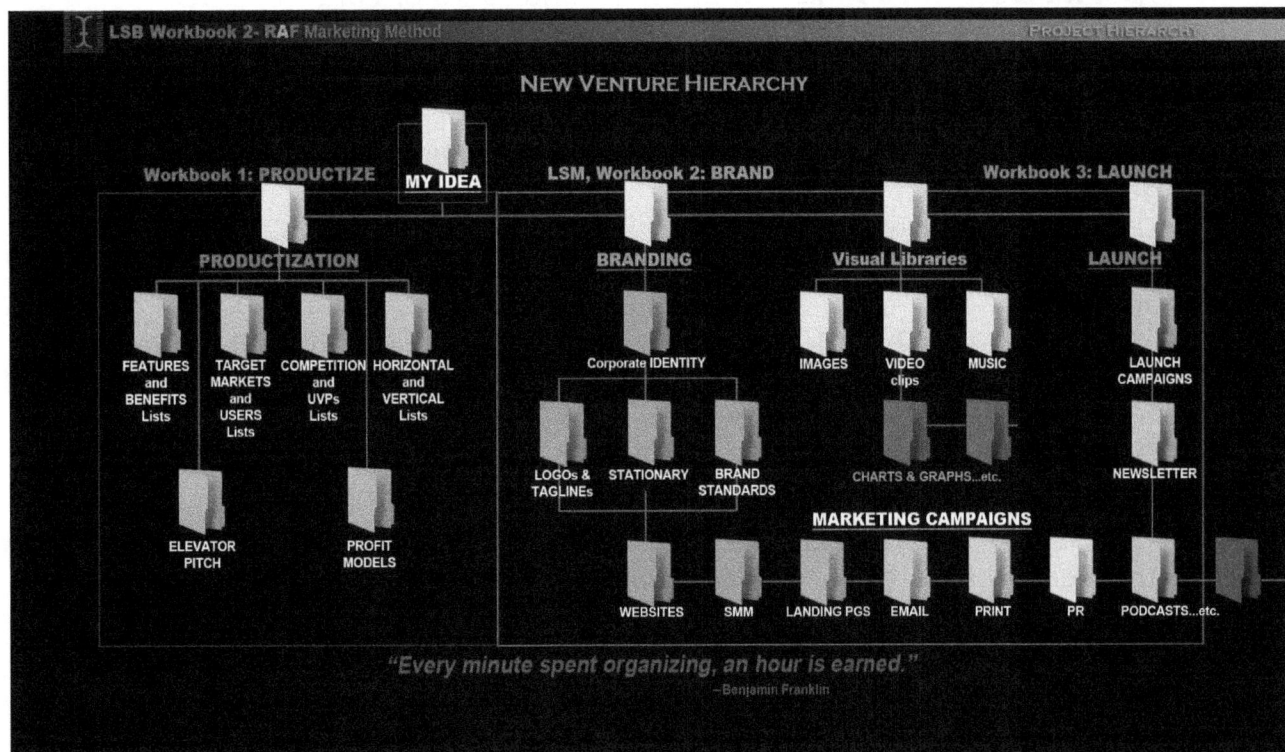

Remember the **Startup Hierarchy** module in LSM Workbook 1? We went step-by-step through the process of setting up your new venture's hierarchy, with *"A place for everything, and everything in its place."* You [should] have begun this organizational process by now, of setting up the required folders to **Get Ready** in the **RAF Marketing Method**—the **Productization** phase in the startup process. These folders should now be filled with documents—your Productization Lists, your Elevator Pitch draft, and the roll-out Profit Model for your startup.

It's now time to **Take Aim** in the **RAF Marketing Method**, and implement your **Branding** hierarchy. You must set up **Identity folders** for your offering and corporate identities, as well as folders for the **marketing campaigns** you'll produce in this Branding Workbook. You also need to set up your company's

Business and **Visual Libraries**, and fill these folders with documentation, and visual and audio content related to your company, and what you plan to sell.

1. Go to your Startup Hierarchy folder, which you established in LSM Workbook 1. Open a new folder inside your GREAT IDEA folder (or rename "Great Idea" with the name of your startup). Title this folder "**BRANDING.**"

2. Inside your BRANDING folder, open four (4) folders to store your identities. Title them as follows:
   - **Corporate Identity**—for your corporate I.D. and Tagline
   - **Offering Identity**—for your offering's I.D. and Tagline
   - **Brand Standards**—list of all colors and fonts of corporate I.D.
   - **Stationery**—business cards; digital and print letterheads

3. Open a new folder inside your GREAT IDEA folder (or rename "Great Idea" with the name of your startup). Title this new folder: "**VISUAL LIBRARIES.**"

4. Inside your VISUAL LIBRARIES folder, open five (5) folders to store your imagery. Title them as follows:
   - **IMAGES**—for photographs, illustrations, even sequential pictures for rotating GIFs—the **still imagery** you collect that relates to your offering/s and company.
   - **VIDEO**—for videos, and video clips you collect that are related to your offering and company.
   - **MUSIC**—You'll store all the sound tracks (MP3) you collect that reflect the tone of your offering and company here.
   - **IDEA Generation/FPO**—(FPO means "for position only," which we'll review in a minute.) You'll store all the copyright-protected images and video content you collect related to your offering and company here.
   - **FONTS**—You'll store all the typefaces you collect here.

5. Inside your Startup Hierarchy folder, open another folder inside your GREAT IDEA folder. Title this *new* folder: "**BUSINESS LIBRARIES.**"

6. Inside your BUSINESS LIBRARIES folder, open several folders to store your company's documentation. Title them as follows:
   - **LEGAL DOCS**—You'll store all your startup's initial legal documentation, like your company's 'non-disclosure agreements' (NDA), and/or software licensing agreements.
   - **HR DOCS**—This folder is for all your hiring documentation, such as resumes, and/or H1B visa applications, if you choose to hire temporary, off-shore employees.

Getting the pattern? Of course, you can name and organize your folders in whatever paradigm works best for you. The point is, you will continually set up more and more folders within your Startup Hierarchy. You'll fill them with files of identities, visual and audio content, as well as business documentation, and also each marketing effort you produce. Every folder in your company's hierarchy should be accessible by the appropriate people working within, or for your company. Access to the right information whenever needed makes the stakeholder's job more efficient, and their marketing campaigns more effective, whether they are sitting next to you in your office space in Palo Alto, or half a world away in India.

Iterative Search for Images

Google has, by far, the best crawlers on the net, and will return the most images per search, so begin with *Google* IMAGES. The *Google Search* homepage defaults to searching the world wide web (the internet). To get to *Google Images*, look in the upper right corner of your device screen (UI), to the blue 'Sign In' button. Next to, or near that button it will say "Images."

Click on "Images."

You will be taken to another *Google* search interface (UI), that looks like the regular *Google Search* UI, only this one says "Images" just under the *Google* logo that resides above their search bar. You'll use this UI to search for images related to your offering and company.

My first novel, REVERB, is about a musician who learns to love someone other than his muse. The main character, James, is a master guitarist.

I begin my iterative search in *Google* Images, with words from my Productization lists, which I created when I productized my novel—got it *ready* (RAF Marketing Method) for branding and marketing. The keywords below came *directly* from REVERB's Productization lists. I used these keywords and phrases to search for images to use in marketing my novel.

REVERB is about the emotional awakening of a rock guitarist.
Keyword searches: *Guitarist. Electric guitars. Rock musicians. Music notes. Music backgrounds. Streaming music. Reverb. Rock concert*...etc.

REVERB, is also a love story. A romance.
Keyword searches: *Romance. Love. Relationships. Lovers. Married. Dating. Single. Sex. Couple kissing. Hugging. Holding hands. Couple on beach*...etc.

Part of REVERB takes place on the Greek island, Corfu.

Keyword searches: *Greek islands. Corfu. Tropical islands. Sand castles. Sunsets over beaches. Beaches*...etc.

In REVERB, the woman James meets has a child. She is a new mom.
Keyword searches: *Parents. Toddles. Moms. Dads. Families. Family. Family vacations. Kids*...etc.

As you can see, I have many keywords and key phrases as image search terms. I'll use them all, and many more, to find professional-quality images to use for my print and digital marketing campaigns. I'll use the same keywords and phrases searching for videos that have a direct or indirect association with my novel. I'll break up these videos into very short clips, combine them, layer them, and then use them in marketing REVERB online, and with print campaigns for my novel as well.

'Usage Rights' Filters

I begin my search for professional-quality, high-resolution images to use in marketing my novel by entering my first search term: "guitarist," into the *Google Images* search bar, and click enter.

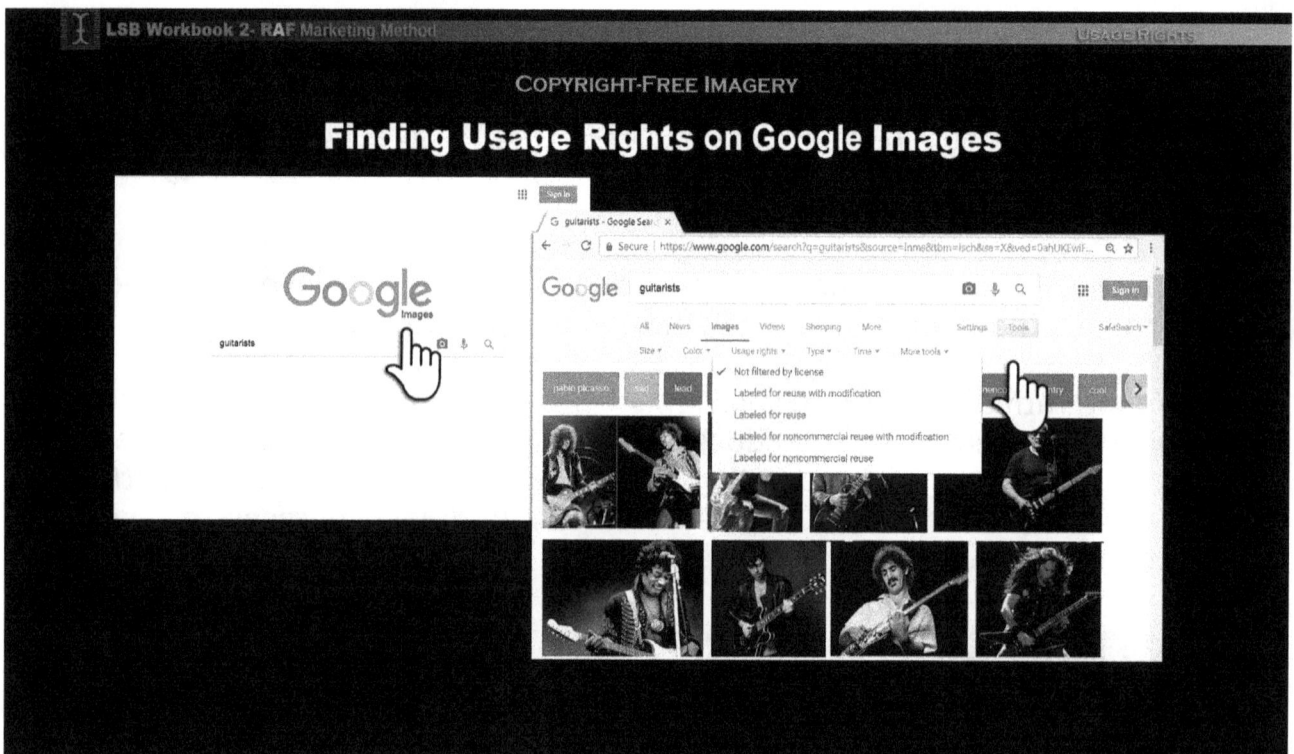

Google serves up many rows of small, 'thumbnail' images of guitarist, hundreds, possibly thousands, in fact, if I scroll down through the many rows of thumbnail images *Google* returns. But can I legally use any of them?

The answer is likely, no, unless I get permission from the copyright holder, which would take longer than I want to spend, *if* I could find them.

Sure, I can use *Pexel*, or another stock photo company to get the copyright-free, high-density (HD) images I need, but I am limited to their selection. I already have enough limitations on my campaigns, like always selling features and benefits of my novel to fulfill the desire of my target audience. And I need to include a great incentive to get people to *act* on my CTA. And I have to consider effective design, and layout, and eye-tracking and...bla bla...so I want to view as much imagery as possible to find pictures with impact that I may want.

To find images on *Google* that I can *legally* use in my digital or print marketing efforts, *without* permission, I click on "Tools," just below the search bar, now at the of screen. A drop-down menu gives me many options, such as "Size; Color; Type." I choose "**Usage rights.**"

Several options appear in a drop-down menu, listing the different types of usage rights *Google* offers in their image returns.

- **Not filtered by license**—returns every image *Google* finds on the internet, regardless of who holds the copyright. This is *Google Images* default position. To limit thumbnail image returns to *legally* usable images, you must choose another classifier.

- **Labeled for reuse with modification**—if you alter the image you lift substantially (typically 70% or more), you can reuse it in your marketing efforts. This works great for generating unique layered visual content using existing images, avoiding the expense of shooting photography.

- **Labeled for reuse**—you can reuse it for anything, to post on your *Facebook* feed, or on your company's marketing efforts (except for hate or inflammatory campaigns).

- **Labeled for noncommercial reuse with modification**—you can use it on your *personal* feeds, for fun, like sharing cat videos, but only if you add something to it, like a mustache on the cat, or turning an image into a meme.

- **Labeled for noncommercial reuse**—you can republish it *as is* on your *personal* feeds, or print party invitations for your kids birthdays, or your wedding anniversary...etc.

Each of these classifiers tells you what images you can legally use for reproduction. Only **"Labeled for reuse," are 100% copyright-free images** you can use (mostly) any way you want. All the other topic classifiers limit the commercial use of the images *Google* returns with each search query.

To demonstrate how to build a IMAGES Library of *Google* images to use in your marketing efforts, I'm going to collect some images with impact for marketing my novel, REVERB. I'll begin my image search using, "Labeled for reuse with modifications," under Usage rights, to adhere to current, common copyright laws.

Searching for "guitarists" under "Labeled for reuse with modifications," *Google* still returns hundreds of thumbnail photos and illustrations of guitarists, but only hundreds. I no longer have thousands of images to choose from, and I can only use an image I lift if I substantially modify it. How substantially? Well, oddly, that is left to a judge to determine if I'm sued by the copyright holder for copyright infringement.

A good rule to stick by is change the original image [at least] 70% or more. I can crop the guitarist's image to show only a close up of his hand strumming the guitar, so there is virtually no way to tell what the rest of the original image looks like. I can strip the guitarist out of the original scene, and put him against a different background, then layer other images over him, like music notes, so my new picture is unrecognizable from its original image.

Search With No Limits

I recommend you do *not* use any limitation in your initial searches. I suggest that you always use *Google's* default, "**Not filtered by license**," in your first round of searches for visual content to use in your marketing efforts. You can always limit your results with the "Usage rights" filter when you're looking for imagery to legally use for reproduction in your campaigns.

Without limitations on search results, *Google* will return a full palette of images on the internet from my search term "guitarists." I receive thousands of thumbnail pictures. Every one of these images is an 'idea generator.' Even if I cannot use the image in my marketing efforts because it's copyright-protected, or not enough pixels for quality reproduction, I can still find, lift, and store images that grabbed my attention. If the picture was powerful enough to get *my* attention, it'll likely draw notice from others as well.

Store all images related to your offering, company, and campaign messaging, that are *not* usable for reproduction, in your "**Idea Generation/FPO**" folder, inside your Visual Libraries. Your Idea Generation/FPO folder is essentially a **swipe file**. You'll peruse this file of images you lift and store to generate ideas for your company's marketing and advertising campaigns.

Beyond idea generation, you can also use these copyright-protected, or low quality images, to direct those you hire to create the specific imagery you want.

FPO, or **For Position Only**, is a term used by graphic designers to indicate an image's position and size within the layout of a web page or print campaign. FPO images are *not* used for reproduction, only for placement, to communicate what the high-resolution, copyright-free image will look like—how big it'll appear, how it is cropped, and where it goes on the layout.

Let's say I hire a photographer to take several copyright-free, high-resolution pictures of guitars to use in marketing my novel, REVERB. I'll use these images on everything from my book cover, to my SMM campaigns, so they need to be HD (high-density) quality photos.

I peruse my Idea Generation/FPO folder, and see several shots of guitars that I like, and would like my photographer to imitate. Not an exact replication of the images, but having this file of pictures, I'm able to communicate what I'm looking for, and direct the photographer to create the imagery I want by supplying him with a visual, FPO reference.

Swiping (lifting and storing) attention-grabbing images related to your offering and company will help you down the line to generate ideas for your marketing efforts, and communicate them effectively to those you hire.

Take every visual—photography or illustration with impact—that directly or indirectly relates to your offerings, company, and industry. Put these images in their appropriate files inside your Visual Libraries, on *your* computer's hard drive. Copyright-free, HD visual content that you can use in your marketing efforts belong in your IMAGES folder. Low resolution, or copyright-protected images that you can *not* use for reproduction belong in your IDEA Generation/FPO folder.

Image Capture

When you're lifting an image for idea generation, you don't necessarily need to be concerned with the pixel density of that image. (Always *try* to lift high pixel density imagery, because you never know how you'll use the image down the line.) However, when you're lifting a picture off *Google Images,* or pulling an image off of a stock photo site for reproduction in a print or digital campaign, be sure the pixel density is high (HD), for *quality* reproduction.

So, I'm looking for images of "guitarists" that I can lift directly off *Google*, to use in an ad campaign for my novel. I limit *Google's* returns to "Labeled for reuse," *and* "Labeled for reuse with modifications," under Usage Rights, to adhere to typical copyright laws, while getting the most thumbnail image returns possible.

Google returns rows and rows of small images of guitarists, or music related imagery I can use directly, or with modifications, in my marketing efforts for REVERB. And while there are a ton of pictures I see that I'd love to use, only a few—the high-density images—will reproduce with clarity, and retain their quality beyond the small thumbnail representations on the web page of *Google's* returns.

4. Rename, and 5. Save image to *your* IMAGE LIBRARY.
1. Click on thumbnail of desired image.
2. Right-click on larger image, and 3. Right-click on "Save image as."

To find the *high-density* images on *Google Images'* crowded page of thumbnail returns, simply let your cursor linger over any one of the small pictures. At the bottom of each, a dark gray banner will pop up. There are numbers on the left, followed by the name of whoever uploaded the image to the internet:

1240 x 960 – RocknRoll.com

The numbers are pixels, width by height, representing the **pixel density** of the picture. The higher these numbers, the higher the pixel density of the original image.

The pixel density numbers that pop up do NOT represent the pixel density of the thumbnail images you see. The pixel density of any of the thumbnail images that *Google* returns is likely less than 250 x 150 pixels. These small images are only *representations* of the original images. Each original, full density image (the pixel measurements you see in the popup gray bar), reside on a separate web page, (that we'll review how to access in a minute).

Follow the five-step process below to lift the images you want from *Google Images*, in the density you need for quality reproduction:

1. Slide your cursor over the thumbnail images of pictures that impact *you*, and note the pixel density of each. Anything less than 1000 x 800px is considered too low density for quality reproduction, unless the image will reproduced rather small. Images *under* 1000px will likely look grainy in print, or in digital reproduction the edges in the imagery will look pixelated, especially if the image is enlarged. Low density imagery can be lifted for your Idea Generation/FPO folder, but generally *not* for professional-quality reproduction.

   If you find a 400 x 350px striking, clear, copyright-free image that you love, and is perfect for the digital campaign you're creating, you must reproduce the image at its *original size*, or *smaller*, and exclusively online, since we only need 72 ppi for quality digital reproduction online, as we reviewed earlier in Image Reproduction.

2. When you see an image that has impact, that is [at least] 1000 x 800 pixels, and that you want to use in a current campaign, or down the line, click on the thumbnail image. Do *not* right-click on the thumbnail image [to save it]. Left click on the thumbnail image, which, in most cases, links to the full density picture you want to capture, and store.

   The *Google Images* web page of thumbnail pictures will 'split' open, to allow a dark gray panel to emerge between the rows of thumbnails. On this panel, to the left, is the original, full density, or *actual size* picture of the thumbnail image you clicked on. In most cases, this picture is the actual pixel density shown in the small pop-up banner under the thumbnail image.

To the right of the image is its title. Under the title is a hyperlink, in smaller text, identifing *who* uploaded the image. Under this link may appear a brief description of the content on the web page the link will take you to. (This description becomes crucial to SEO: search engine optimization. We'll review how to write effective SEO descriptions in the Copywriting Module of LSL Workbook 3.)

The original image you want is being served up from somewhere. Under the brief text description of the picture (if there is one), are two buttons. "*Visit*," meaning go to the site where the image is being served from, and "*Share*," meaning share the image on your social media pages. Do neither. No need. You came for the high-density image, take it, and move on with your search to get more. The point is to collect the most HD imagery related to what you are selling, as quickly as possible, to use legally, and present professionally, in your marketing efforts.

Right-click on the single image [you came for] on the left of the split panel to save the full density picture, with pixel density that matches the numbers you saw on the thin banner under the thumbnail you clicked on to 'split' the page.

Beware, *Google* is getting tighter about allowing users to lift high-quality pictures from their image library. More and more often, you'll click on a thumbnail image to get to the high-density picture you want to capture, and the larger image in the 'split' screen will *not* be the full pixel density it says it is.

3. After right-clicking on the original, full density image, a drop down menu appears with several choices for what you'd like to *do* with the picture. Click "**Save image as**..."

A UI of your desktop appears, essentially asking you where you want to put this image file. Only at this point can you see the file format type. More often than not, the file will be a jpeg, which is great, and worth taking. So are png. So are gif, sometimes, but beware of their poor reproduction quality, especially if enlarged, or used for print. PDFs are essentially 'snapshots' of a document, and also generally reproduce poorly, peculiarly if altered in size. Do *not* save a URL address. It is worthless, as a URL is just a location on the internet, *not* an image you can use it in your campaigns.

4. Re-title the image before saving it. This is very important! You should rename images you take off the internet before saving them to your computer. Give them titles that will remind you what the image is,

without having to open it, as you'll likely collect hundreds to thousands of images as your company grows. Additionally, the metadata (hidden identifiers) on the visual content in your marketing campaigns should have no tags identifying the original image creator, even if it is copyright-free.

5. **Save the original full-density image** (jpeg; png; gif) to your IMAGES folder, inside your Visual Libraries folder, on your computer's hard drive. Low density imagery, store in your Idea Generation/FPO folder. Back up all libraries on to the Cloud, but *always* store them on your company's servers as well!

Striking, high-density jpeg and png images of many guitarists and musical references now resides on *my* computer, in my IMAGES folder. I use these images, and others I have created, in my marketing efforts to sell my novel, REVERB, whether directly, if copyright-free, or by layering many images to create a new, unique image. I can use this visual content whenever I want, on whatever campaign I want, print or online, and likely both down the line. I'll bring most of these images into *Photoshop*, or *Paint*, crop them, and layer them. I'll give them to those I hire to use in my multi-channel advertising campaigns. Remember, images with impact get a *lot* more response than just text marketing efforts. The more quality images you collect, that you have to choose from when creating your campaigns, the better!

Remember, for clear, sharp, professional-quality visual content in your company's multi-channel marketing efforts, it is wise to lift and save images with 1000 x 800 *minimum* pixel density. Save reproducible images with impact in your IMAGES folder. Save all non-reproducible, yet attention-grabbing images in your IDEA Generation/FPO folder.

Lifting and Utilizing Video

Using keywords from your Productization lists, perform the **Iterative Search** process to find video content directly or indirectly related to your offering, company and industry. Research: "free stock video" to find free or low cost, downloadable, MP4, or *Quicktime* (*Apple's* standard video format) videos to use in *your* marketing campaigns.

Here are a few from my quick search (other than the sites mentioned earlier):
- **Videvo**(dot)net
- **Videezy**(dot)com
- **StockFootageForFree**(dot)com

Free stock video from *Pexel*, or *Videvo*, and their like, are also copyright-free, unless otherwise noted. You generally need no attribution to the video creator to use them in your marketing campaigns.

Websites, such as *Vimeo,* not only have video footage you can buy, but they also have a filter in their site search to access just their *free* video library. *YouTube* has the same thing, called *YouTube Stock*. Also search *YouTube* for "free video content."

So, do as I say, *right now*. Go to *YouTube*, and iterative search for free video content related to your offering, company and industry. You'll find a lot! Everything from tech backgrounds to drone flights over popular places are *free* to use in your company's campaigns. Most have download buttons, or links to download buttons to get the video content onto your computer.

The selection is broad, but isn't close to the number of returns you'll get *without* searching: "free," or even "copyright-free" content. To get exactly the video content that you want, search for an image without imposing any limits, such as "free" or "copyright free."

Similar to lifting images from *Google*, it is illegal to use videos in your marketing efforts that someone else created, unless you get their permission to do so. However, layering videos, or adding special effects, or *substantially* changing the video content, you are essentially creating an original artwork. Or, taking ½ to one second out of a full video is virtually untraceable, as long as you are not using a famous person's image in that one second clip. String enough ½ to one second clips together, and perhaps mix them with still images and copy, and you can create a complete marketing video.

Use keywords and phrases from your Productization lists to get the full palette of videos *YouTube* has that are directly or indirectly related to your offering. Go to a video you like, and it's likely there is no download button to capture the video, like with their free content. How do you lift the video to use in your marketing campaigns? Two ways. One, if you have video editing software, there is generally a "record" button. Bring the *YouTube* video to full screen, and record directly off your screen. You will get some quality loss, but if you reduce the video clip, and keep it very short, it likely won't be noticeable. To retain the original quality of the video, your second choice is to use a **video converter**.

Search: "free video converter," online, and you'll find many. Use apps that do *not* require signing up to use their conversion service. There are plenty of free image and video converters online, so, no need to sign up to their platform. It is dangerous to sign up on any platform these days, as the site sells your information and email address to affiliate marketers.

Beware, a lot of these sites have a ton of SPAM on them. Why? As stated, it is illegal to capture video content to use in *your* marketing material. Do not press any download buttons other than the one to download the video you've converted. There will be many download buttons that are SPAM, and can infect your computer with malware.

That being said, video converters use the URL of the web page the video is on, and converts the video content to a downloadable MP4. Video is lossly, which means it loses quality with reproduction. Find the cleanest, clearest videos you can, as most have been uploaded many 'generations' from the original video, and the quality diminishes with each 'generation' drop.

When converting high-density (HD) video content, the quality loss is nominal, and usually undetectable. Conversion is limited to the *original quality of the video uploaded*. If the original video isn't HD, saving it to HD format will *not* improve the quality, so don't bother. Don't limit what you take to HD only. Take standard formats as well, usually 720px, (instead of 1080px of full HD).

MP4 is the default video standard for the internet. If a site or platform accepts video, it will be MP4. *Quicktime* is an *Apple* invention, and came before MP4. You can use a video converter to convert *Quicktime* video to MP4, for platforms that don't accept *Quicktime*.

More often than not, you'll have to download an entire video, but you'll only want to use a ½ to one second sequence of it. If the video is longer than five minutes, and you know you'll only want a very small clip of it, now, or down the line, you can *screen-grab*, aka *record* the particular section of the video you want. Even if you don't have video editing software, *Microsoft Office* has *PowerPoint* (*PPT*), an app that lets you create slide presentations that include video content. It also has recording capabilities that lets you capture video content as it plays on your screen. Just press the "Record Screen" tab.

As mentioned, the issue with screen-grabs is one of quality. First, video gobbles a lot of memory, so *PPT* limits the size of the reproduction to rather small. Additionally, screen-grab apps literally capture your screen resolution as it plays the video. If your monitor resolution is lower than 1920 x 1080 (HD), the screen-grab video quality will suffer.

SAVE each video you lift in your VIDEO folder, inside your Visual Libraries, within your Startup Hierarchy. Always save the clip you capture with a unique name that clearly identifies its content. And be sure to keep the original video you capture *unaltered*. You may want to lift several sequences out of any given video in your library for campaigns down the line.

Once you have a library of video content that relates to your business, you can bring each into a video editing program, and take out just the sequence you want to use in your marketing effort. You can bring many videos into the editing software and layer them, by playing with the opacity of each to create an original work. SAVE any videos you bring through video editing software, or video content that you create in **HD quality, MP4**, for the best possible reproduction of your video marketing efforts.

There are many free video editing software programs available. Search: "free video editing software" for programs that are simple to use. Be sure there are lots of tutorials (from *YouTube,* or the software developers) available, that show you how to use it. Free video editing software I found from my quick search:

- **Lightworks**—lwks(dot)com
- **OpenShot**(dot)org
- **VSDC**—videosoftdev(dot)com

When creating *your* video campaigns, or when directing videographers to produce campaigns for your offering and/or company, be sure to adhere to the standards listed in the Video Marketing section of Module 21: Digital Marketing Campaigns. Use the bullet list of best practices as a checklist to make sure you are designing and producing video marketing that converts your target audience, as well as brands and *sells* your new venture.

Animated GIFs

As mentioned, we use **animated gif** when we want motion in our marketing campaigns, but the platform our campaign is running on does not accept video. Case in point—put up a free website with *Wordpress.com*, and unless you 'upgrade,' to a paid account, they won't let you upload video content directly. The only way to show video on a free *Wordpress.com* site is to use an embedded URL on the page of your site that you want the video to appear, which links to the *YouTube* web page the video is on. However, *WP.com will* accept animated GIFs, so you can still have **headers** on your free website that *auto-play* when someone lands on your site.

You can use an online converter to convert video to GIF animation.

- **OnlineConverter** (video.online-convert(dot)com/convert-to-mp4) has a ton of conversion options, and you don't need to 'join; sign-up,' or give them any information.

Be careful of animated gif quality! It isn't very good, so be sure your animations are sharp, clear, professional, before posting them, or using them in your marketing efforts.

Create LEAN Marketing Campaigns

Armed with powerful, flexible identities, a library of free, copyright-free, visual content, and free software to create images and video with impact, you can now create professional-quality marketing for your new venture. But how do you put it all together in to striking branding and advertising campaigns, that gets attention and motivates *action,* at little to no cost?

There are two easy, free, to low cost, ways, to create, produce, and publish digital and print marketing:

1. **Digital campaigns ONLY**: Online **templates** (minimal, to no coding required) are available to create professional websites, landing pages, newsletters, blogs, and email campaigns. These pre-coded templates are **responsive**—size to your device screens—and translate well across different computer operating systems, and various browsers.

In module 19, we'll review Online Technology, and identify free webhosting sites with digital templates to easily create your online marketing. These webhosts will not only deliver your websites and landing pages to the internet, but they'll help you efficiently build your campaigns as well. All you need is the visual and copy content, to fill in the templates. (We'll closely examine email hosting and marketing, in LSL Workbook 3.)

2. **Print and digital campaigns**: Free, or low cost, desktop publishing (DTP) software is available! To design your company's **print** brochures, direct (snail) mail campaigns, displays, trade show booth, packaging, and/or signage, a desktop publishing program is essential. You'll develop many digital marketing efforts with desktop publishing software as well, when using a template is not practical.

You can get a free trial of *Adobe InDesign*, (which most pro designers use), to create and produce both print and digital marketing efforts. I googled: "free desktop publishing software," and found a couple of free DTP applications that work equally as well:
   - **Scribus**(dot)com
   - **LucidPress**(dot)com

Next, we examine **UI** (user interface), and **UX** (**user experience**) design, and effective digital navigation. We also explore the world of **search engine optimization** (**SEO**), to create marketing efforts that achieve high ranking in *Google* search returns. Online Marketing is next.

STOP! Complete PROJECT #2 before moving on.

◆◆◆

LSB Workbook 2: PROJECT #2
COLLECT CONTENT for VISUAL LIBRARIES

Like to binge-watch series on *Netflix,* or other streaming video service? While you're sitting there vaguely staring at your TV or cellphone, open your laptop (or tablet). Go to *Google IMAGES*, *Pexels*, *YouTube*, and other stock imagery and video sites, and search for visual content for your marketing efforts. Iterative search with keywords and phrases from your Productization lists, (LSM Workbook 1), to assure your are finding visual content directly or indirectly related to your offering, and industry.

Shift your focus from whatever you're binge-watching to the **thumbnail images and videos** *Google, Pexels,* or *YouTube* returns. What captures your attention? Don't bother to stop and think about why. Just *take them.*

1. **Lift all visual content that grabs your attention**, regardless if its **reproduction** quality. Capture and store these images, video, audio, fonts...etc. in their appropriate folders, inside your **Visual Libraries** folder, within your **Startup Hierarchy**, that you set up earlier in this module.

   Add low quality images, and images that are copyright-protected to your **IDEA Generation/FPO** folder. Add high-density (HD), reproduction-quality images and videos in their proper **IMAGE** or **VIDEO folders**. Even if these images are copyright-protected, you can still use them to create original works with **layering**!

2. **Back up to your Visual Libraries to your company's cloud** for easy access by any stakeholder working on a given campaign. Uploading your **Visual Libraries** to your startup's cloud provides relevant stakeholders in your organization with a copy of all your visual content.

3. **You should be continually looking for, capturing, and storing visual content** related to your offerings or industry for your company's pre-launch, launch, and beyond, marketing efforts. Constantly growing your **Visual Libraries** will give you, and those you hire to build your company's marketing efforts, a wide range of visual content to choose from. This will ensure that each campaign has *unique* imagery with impact!

While binge-watch a TV series, or, by carving out a specific time slot each week, you should be filling your **Visual Libraries** with attention-grabbing **visual content** for your marketing campaigns as often as possible, throughout the life cycle of your business. Additionally, if you don't lift imagery *now*, it likely won't be available to lift in the future, as copyright laws are getting more and more restrictive about reuse.

◆◆◆
◆◆◆◆◆

MODULE 18: ONLINE MARKETING

Typical Types of Digital Marketing

In the Marketing 101 module of LSM Workbook 1, we shattered the myth that digital (online) marketing has a different foundation than traditional marketing.

Marketing is selling, in print, online, or on Mars.

To convince people to buy our products and services, or into our messaging, marketing pros seek to understand what motivates our behavior, our *psychology*. We examine what *really* gets people to act, which hasn't changed in any substantive way since we became human.

Effective marketing sells **features & benefits of your offering, to fulfill a desire**, or solve a problem, **for a specific group of people**, regardless if it's a digital or print campaign.

Digital marketing became an additional medium to traditional marketing in the mid-1990s, with the advent of the *NCSA Mosaic* browser, the predecessor to the WYSIWYG (visual) browser, *Netscape*, which brought the World Wide Web to the average computer user. Of course, the internet has expanded since then, especially since the arrival of cloud computing, which gives us access to not only our own information, but everything online as well, on most every electronic device we own.

Digital marketing, or any digital communication, exist on a **web page**. Web pages are the content that fill the World Wide Web. These pages are written in **HTML** (hypertext markup language), and are translated by your browser, such as *Chrome*, or *Explorer*, or *Safari*, or *Android* (mobile), which displays the images from the HTML web page on to your screens. Web pages can either be static, such as a landing page, or dynamic, like your *Twitter* feed. A website is a collection of web pages. A *YouTube* web page has videos on it, as well as text, (and ads).

Effective digital marketing has global reach, and is cost-effective. Websites, landing pages, posts to our timelines, and other social media marketing (SMM) efforts are often little, to no cost, to publish online. Online marketing can be tightly targeted. It can be personalized, actually address specific users, as with email campaigns. Email is considered a critical component of any online marketing strategy, since email is the #1 way we sell online today, second only to in-person networking.

Many digital venues, like your company's *Facebook,* and *LinkedIn* profile pages, are free to put marketing on. Building followers over time, through social media networking, will expand the reach of each campaign, so they are viewed by more people. *Effective* SMM works to convert (try; sign-up), and sell (buy; subscribe).

We'll drill down and detail best practices for several online venues individually. But for now, let's explore a few types of digital marketing that we use today, not only to sell our offerings, but also to build our brand awareness to specific target users, and extend our reach globally.

• **Websites are virtual stores**, each page of the site is like an aisle of products in the supermarket. The 'products' are your company's offerings, each described in detail. Your virtual store has pages on how to use your offerings, where to buy them, sign-up for your services, or maybe even get a trial version to test it out. Your website should show some of your employees, at least the CEO, to your management teams. It shows your company's values, mission, and the volunteer work for your communities. And like a real store, your virtual store— your website—is dynamic, with a consistent stream of valuable *new* content. Websites are mandatory for most any business today. We'll closely examine website development in the following module.

• **Landing pages**, and **Microsites** deliver ONE (1) main message as a stand-alone web page, (generally) distinct from your main website. They are essentially a marketing *campaign*, to motivate people to click through to your site, or give their name and email to receive an incentive offer, such as a free gift or download. **Landing pages** are designed for one *focused* objective—click; sign-up; try; buy. We'll drill down on Landing Page development in Module 21— Digital Campaigns.

- **Pay-Per-Click (PPC) advertising** is everywhere! We see it on the sides and top of almost every site we visit on the web now. PPC ads are in our *Instagram* and *Twitter* feeds—it'll say 'Sponsored,' or 'Promoted,' in small letters, usually under the original poster's (OP) identity. This means the company paid *Facebook* (who owns *Instagram*) to put their ad in your feed, as, from analyzing your *Instagram* board, *Facebook's* algorithms thinks that you'll find some value in the ad content. We'll discuss the fallacy of this reasoning in the PPC advertising module.

- **Video Marketing** is growing, fast! And should be. We live in real time, not still images, and effective video draws people into the unfolding scenes, and increases user engagement. Video marketing is utilized as a Social Media Marketing (SMM) tool. Posting videos is FREE on *YouTube,* or most any other social platform these days. It is an effective *lean* marketing solution! We'll review video development and scripting in the Digital Campaigns module.

- **Social Media Marketing (SMM)** offers us many social platforms to create business pages for our products and company. SMM is also free, when we post on our company feeds. You should create business pages on the popular social platforms, like *Facebook, Twitter, LinkedIn, Instagram, YouTube*...etc. You should also create pages on startup sites, like *Angel.co*. In fact, putting pages up on 'safe' social sites related to your offerings or business will increase your SEO (Search Engine Optimization) ranking. We'll examine search engine ranking, and how to increase your SEO in the last segment of this module.

-UI vs. UX-

Which came first: the chicken, or the egg? Why does it matter? We hear the acronyms **UI** and **UX** bantered about all the time, as if they are separate entities. But one can not exist without the other, just like the chicken and the egg.

UI: User Interface—what you see on the screens of your devices, from your mobile phone to your computer monitor. UIs should be simple to use, easy to learn, clear, and intuitive to navigate within the user interface. We'll review effective navigation next.

UX: User Experience—what you *do* with the UI on your devices. Play a video, or an online game. Click on an ad. Look up information. Post on your timeline. Even fingering your screen to unlock it, or enlarge an image, or swiping it to search beyond the screen's limited view means you—the user—are engaging in an experience with what is on the screen.

The primary function of digital marketing in the social media marketing (SMM) landscape, is to extend each campaign's reach. You can help build awareness of your brand—your particular offerings in association with your corporate identity—to your potential target customer on a global scale with SMM. "Going viral," (generally) means a digital campaign has reached millions of views. Take special note of the word "views." How do views translate into *sales*? Well, truth be told, with SMM, a lot of the time, they don't. Just blindly extending your reach by posting SMM with keywords and hashtag tricks (we'll review later) all over the net, to no particular target audience, is generally a waste of your energy and time.

Remember, **effective marketing sells features & benefits of your offering, that fulfills a desire or solves a problem for a specific group of people**.

Make sure every digital web page, from your landing pages to website pages to your social media platform pages, tout the *best bits* about your offering. Each marketing effort should be creative in their own right, whether direct selling, educational, funny, quirky, witty, bold, brazen, emotional...etc. But addressing what your offering IS, DOES, and for WHO, in some manner or style, is a must, to attract the attention of those [you reach], among all the other online marketing we are bombarded by daily.

Once you have a campaign that immediately demonstrates (communicates) a *unique* benefit of your offering, and/or company, to a particular audience, the best way to get them to stay on any one of your web pages as long as possible is to engage them in taking an action, such as play, watch, click, post, swipe...etc.

There are many ways, and opportunities, to engage viewers to interact with your digital marketing, and create a user experience (UX).

- **Create a great video**, and have it auto-play—start playing automatically—when someone comes on to the web page, to engage them in watching.

- **Rotating Gifs**—create a slideshow of pictures. Put a headline, and a CTA button over each image. Encourage clicks with headlines that match the images. Focus each headline on a solution your offering provides, or an incentive your campaign is offering. A bright colored CTA button to 'Learn More,' or 'Get offer,' should be on each image. CTAs link to the web page/s that pay off the headline on each picture in the rotating gif as they scroll by automatically.

- **Put a customer service CHAT box on your website homepage** to engage customers, and potential customers, to talk with you (or your customer service reps). Within moments of landing on your site, have an automatic chat box pop up that says, "Hi. How can I help you?" This will engage visitors to your website to ask for what they are looking for, instead of aimlessly going through your site, or clicking off the moment they land on your homepage.

- **Offer free trials of your offering.** Let visitors to your landing pages and website try your online game, or platform, or software service, for free, *and* without having to download it to their computer, if possible. Launching a SaaS Freemium model is a quick and easy way for startups to build a user base!

- **Use** [obvious/bright/high contrast] **buttons with common keywords** to encourage clicks: *Play. Try. Get* (promo code; exclusive offer). Getting sign-ups to receive some incentive, like a special offer, helps you garner names and email addresses to use in your email campaigns down the line.

- **Recommendations for YOU.** When we see recommendations targeted at us directly, or the web page we're on shows us others who bought, or looked at similar items, it piques our interest, and increases engagement to click.

- **Augmented Reality (AR)**, superimposes a computer-generated image or text on a user's tablet or mobile screen over the real world, providing a composite view of real life with the virtual images or text added into the scene. Think *Pokeman Go*, which was an early version of this technology. AR is now becoming widely used in marketing, though AR apps are required to view the marketing effort, which limits the viewers to those willing to download the app.

User engagement leads to greater retention (keeping the customers we already have), and conversion (getting new customers). Beyond the above examples, THINK of unique ways to engage your viewers with each campaign you create. Below are some typical online UX that are commonly used to engage viewers in a variety of ways:

- Competitions and Contests
- Polls; Surveys; Vote
- Limited Giveaways
- Games; Puzzles
- IM Chat (Instant Messaging)
- Share/Upload (Snapchat; Instagram)
- Tutorials; How-To videos
- 'Push' and Update Alerts
- Petitions; Cause Support

These are just a few UX marketing tools *known* to extend engagement. But be creative, and think outside of the box of what is known, for new ways to engage your target audiences, and funnel them through the sales process!

Effective navigation of *any* UI is essential to creating responsive digital marketing that *gets response*. Let's explore what it takes to create effective navigation for your website/s, microsites, and digital campaigns, next.

-Digital Navigation-

Marketing 101: The CTA

To get people to do what we want, we must *tell them* what we want them to *do*.

In marketing terms, think of **online navigation** akin to one or more CTAs on any given web page. Remember, a web page is any online digital media, from websites, to landing pages, to a *Facebook* profile page.

Digital navigation essentially shows people what we want them to do, with Direct CTAs of colorful buttons on our ads, to Indirect CTAs like the navigation bar on our websites.

Effective navigation not only tells us where something is on a web page, but also *sells* us on clicking to access another page, hopefully, eventually, to the purchase page or sign-up form. Effective navigation engages us, and funnels us through the conversion steps, eventually, to sales.

There are three main categories of digital navigation:
- **Main Navigation**: Global navigation for all the pages of a website or microsite.
- **Local Navigation**: Interior web pages.
- **Contextual Navigation**: Associative characteristics.

- **Main Navigation** links, aka 'global' or 'primary' navigation generally represents the top-level pages of a website's structure—or the pages just below the homepage. The links in the main navigation are expected to consistently lead to pages within the site.

The main navigation provides an overview to what is on the site. It allows visitors to quickly understand the site content using broad **topic classifiers**— the *headings* you choose for your site navigation.

These topic classifiers of your main navigation are an important marketing tool! Your navigation headings should not just tell visitors about what is on your site, but *sell* them on engaging with it. Instead of using the word "About" as a link in your main navigation, *sell* visitors on clicking to find out more about your company with a *marketing* classifier, using enticing keywords related to your offering or company, *and* an interactive interface to keep them engaged.

The homepage of the website *Discover Los Angeles* predominately displays a slide show (rotating gif), with great photos of popular L.A. locations, from Hollywood to Disneyland. Their main navigation has only three navigation links above the slide show. *What to Do* (instead of 'About'), which has a pull-down menu of *Restaurants, Nightlife, Culture, Activities*...etc., topic headings. *How to Explore* (instead of 'Information'), which has a pull-down menu of everything from *Transportation*, to an interactive map of *Neighborhoods*. *Where to Stay* (instead of 'Lodging'), that has a pull-down menu of *Family* to *Business* to *Historic Hotels*. Their *marketing* headings are effectively communicating what their site IS, and DOES. Their pull-down menus target specific groups of people, like parents and professionals.

The topic classifiers you choose for your main navigation headers are an important SEO (Search Engine Optimization) tool, too! *Google*, and most other search engines, 'spider' or 'crawl' the internet continuously. They are searching for keywords, aka topic classifiers, that define what any given web page has on it. If your main navigation headers match the content on your website, or landing page the navigation appears on, *Google* will rank that web page higher —closer to #1 in their search returns.

The main navigation for your website should [generally] be shown on every page of your site. But, there are times when main navigation should not be shown, or should vary its form—turn into the three bar "menu" icon, instead of showing topic classifiers. Online purchasing (e-commerce) should be seamless, and constrain people from leaving in the middle of the sales process. Cart pages, Checkout pages, Payment pages, should only have navigation links that drive the completion of the sale forward.

- **Local Navigation** links are hierarchically below the main navigation pages. These are generally represented with pull-down menus that appear when we hover-over, or click on a main navigation header. It is also common, especially on homepages, to place main navigation along the top of the web page, and have local navigation as vertical links listed on the left side of the web page.

  Local navigation provides additional context to the main navigation, utilizing more headers, that further identify and define the content on the site. Effective local navigation gives *Google* additional topic classifiers. If these keywords correlate with the content of a web page, it will help increase that particular page's SEO ranking.

Retaining both main and local navigation page for page is unnecessary, and quite frankly, annoying to see. Drop the local navigation on the interior pages of your website. Most of us know by now that if we click on the corporate identity in the upper left corner of most sites, it'll take us to the homepage of that website. Main navigation can become the three bar "menu" icon on interior pages of a website or microsite, either next to the corporate I.D., or on the top right side of any given web page. Use only the navigation necessary to motivate people to *act*, and *engage* in each 'next steps' your CTA links direct.

- **Contextual Navigation** links are often embedded in the bodycopy, or text on a web page. Used frequently in blogging, keywords and key phrases are highlighted as links that take visitors to other pages on that site, or to a landing page of the company's current campaign.

  Other contextual navigation links include:
    - The BACK, NEXT or PREVIOUS links, typically seen at the end of a blog, or video post, to engage viewers to read more, or watch another video.

    - **Direct contextual navigation**, such as link headers like, "Recommendation for YOU."

    - **Indirect contextual navigation** are recommendations using correlations, such as "Those who purchased (or looked at) this, also looked at this." You see these at the bottom of purchase pages. *Amazon* uses them a lot on their product pages.

Contextual navigation ICON links motivate engagement. You typically see them on everything for websites, to blogs and vlogs, to newsletters and landing pages.
    - Video PLAY, STOP, and PAUSE buttons.

- Download and Upload buttons.
- Social media icons, for one-click sharing on social platforms.
- Share; Like; Favorite; Retweet-type icons.

Whether main or local navigation, or contextually embedded links in the copy of your website pages or site blog, *remember*, however navigation appears—as topic classifiers of keywords, or icons, buttons, or menu bars, they are simply *links* to other web pages. This means, by default, that each navigation link is either a Direct or Implied CTA, calling people to take an action, and click. Websites, landing pages, or PPC ads, navigation on *all d*igital marketing must be *specific*, responsive, clear, obvious, intuitive, because to get people to engage with our navigation links, we must give them a reason they should.

-Search Engine Optimization-

SEO Marketing

Search Engine Optimization (**SEO**), or, more precisely, creating SEO content that will get your web pages higher ranking, as in, closer to #1 in search returns, is a massive subject, and one we are not going to delve too deeply into here.

Creating a sustainable business from an idea, or even marketing an existing business through Productization, branding, and launch campaigns, requires a substantial diversity of knowledge. Lean Startup Workbooks are designed to give you a broad breadth of information, a step-by-step *process* to help pave your own path to actualizing a startup, for profit. You will be introduced to many techniques to increase your marketing ROI—the return on your marketing investments. To find out more, on any of the subjects introduced in these workbooks, just use the iterative search method introduced in LSM Workbook 1, and *Google* for answers! Researching anything you want to know empowers you to become your own greatest resource.

The Good, Bad, and Truth About SEO

According to the [trending] statistics, 48% of consumers start mobile research with a search engine, while 33% go directly to the site they want (*Smart Insight*, 2017). While this may or may not be facts, we all use *Google*, a *lot*, to search for what we want to know.

Most all of us don't bother to look at the dozen or more web pages that *Google* returns with each of our search queries. We rarely get beyond the first page of links that *Google thinks* relates to our search terms. We don't have to. We've learned that using a few *specific* keywords or key phrases related to our query will likely guide *Google* to return links that directly answer, or relate to our inquiry on their very first page of returns, and often even in the first few link returns on that first page.

The order of the list of links that *Google* returns—from the first link on the first page, to the last link on the last page—is considered each link's **rank**, or [numerical] list position. The closer to the top of the list on the first page of *Google* returns, the closer to #1 in ranking.

First link return, on first page of [any] search returns= #1 [SEO] RANK.

Remember, whatever the stats, we *all* use *Google*, as well as on-site search engines, like on *Amazon* or *Facebook,* or even on our own company website, to encourage site engagement. Optimizing the words and images on your web pages to get as close to that coveted #1 spot on *Google's* returns when someone searches for an offering similar to yours, is akin to striking marketing gold.

A True SEO Tale
I hired a web developer over a decade ago to produce a website I designed for one of my startup clients. Maybe nine months later, I called her to have her bid on another project. She told he she was no longer doing web development, but devoting all her time, energy, and even some money, into starting her own business.

Envy probably leeched from every pour in my body as I listened to her describe the idea she'd launched only ten months early, and was already *clearing* over $10,000 a month.

Her idea was simple, but unique for its time, 2008, when internet commerce wasn't as popular as it is today. She combined her knowledge of traditional print and digital reproduction, and created a digital printing service. Visitors to her site got to choose from a wide variety of stunning announcement and invitation templates. Weddings to birthdays, to death announcement, these beautiful templates were displayed on her web pages in an array of thumbnail pictures. Click on any one, and the UI allowed you to fill in names, dates, locations, and personal information on the template you chose. They were digitally printed on thick paper to your desired amount, and mailed to the buyer within 48 hours, anywhere in the U.S.

It was a great service that was clearly needed. She told me in the first few months of the roll-out of her website, (and publishing a consistent stream of SMM posts announcing her launch), she was getting 20 to 30 orders a *day*. Even better, her website link was #1 on Google returns with search queries like "invitations" or "announcements." In fact, she was considering purchasing a digital printing press to eliminate the cost of contracting a printer.

Five months later, she called me looking for work. Her fledgling business was struggling. She'd been "thrown off of *Google*" a couple months earlier, a month after she'd told me of her success. They'd "blocked" her website from appearing in their search returns, she'd said. Since then, her phone stopped ringing, and people stopped visiting her site, and her sales dried up to just a trickle of what they were.

What? I'd never heard of being "thrown off of *Google*." They are *the* premiere search engine. It is the function of their service to return web page links of legitimate businesses related to our search queries. Wasn't internet censorship illegal in the U.S.?

Google didn't just bury the list position of her website links. They *removed* all of her website links from their platform. Her company was not among *Google's* search returns when someone searched for anything similar to what she was offering, including search keywords like "invitations" or "announcements." Even if someone looked up her business name directly, her website, and all links to her website were gone from *Google's* returns.

Why?

A few weeks after I initially spoke with her about her successful new startup, she hired an SEO marketing firm. They claimed their firm would use exclusive SEO techniques to increase her reach far beyond her meager SMM on *Facebook* and *Twitter*. This SEO firm promised my web developer that, for a mere $10,000, they could take her from a small business to a global company. And she believed them, and hired them.

One month later, *Google* sent her an email saying they were removing her from their search results for violating their user agreement. Her crimes: '**Over-stuffing, over-optimizing**,' and link-backs to her website were appearing on sites that *Google* considered '**bad neighborhoods**.' The email went on to explain that if she wanted to object to the charges, she could do so by emailing them. However, *Google* would only restore her web links to their search returns if she fixed her SEO violations.

My web developer then invested *another* $10,000 in another marketing firm. This new firm promised to remove all her website links from the 'bad neighborhoods' that the first firm stuck her URLs on, but it was simply not possible to find and remove them all. She sent literally hundreds of emails to *Google's* legal department, and got no response. Two and a half *years* after *Google* removed her links from their search returns, they sent her an email saying they were returning her to their search results. Unfortunately, she had already lost her business.

My web developer screwed up by hiring a self-proclaimed SEO marketing firm she knew nothing about, who claimed they knew all about this newly evolving marketing technique we're all still trying to figure out.

What did that SEO firm do wrong that got my web developer in trouble with *Google*?

- **Overstuffed**—they used the same terms in their SMM posts repeatedly.
  Example: *Are you looking for stunning invitations and announcements quickly, for less? If you're looking for stunning invitations and announcements quickly, for less, look no further. Create your beautiful invitations or announcements with our templates quickly on our website. Order your professional invitations or announcements for less, today.*

DON'T DO IT. *Google* doesn't like it, but even more to the point, it's boring, repetitive, and bad marketing.

- **Over-optimize**—they used too many anchored links (back to her website) on keywords in their post's text. Anchor links, usually indicated by an underline, turn text—words or phrases—into clickable links.
  Example: *Create your <u>stunning invitations</u> and <u>announcements</u> quickly, easily, and <u>for less</u>, today. <u>Personalize</u>, and <u>invite</u> your besties to your next big bash.*

  And/or...the evil SEO firm used misleading keywords or key phrases that had nothing to do with what she was selling, to increase the SEO ranking using trending (though unrelated) keywords.

Example: *This is your invitation to the best Hollywood parties and meet famous celebrates like Bruce Springsteen and Oprah Winfrey.*

DON'T DO IT. *Google* doesn't like it, but more to the point, it's stupid marketing. This type of post may get someone's attention, but they are likely not interested in the invitation and announcement templates my web developer was selling.

Effective marketing means communicating what we have to offer to our target audiences. Over-stuffing, and over-optimizing, are often considered one and the same, just expressed in a variety of different ways by those trying to game search return results.

- **Bad neighborhoods**—are pornography sites, or racist sites, such as the KKK, or 'hate' websites expressing extremist views, according to *Google*. The evil SEO firm my developer hired put her website URL in the 'comment' box, or 'discussion forum' on these types of sites. NOT smart! Google doesn't like it!

When your company URL appears on another website, this is known as a **LINK-BACK**. *Google* considers most *legitimate* companies 'good neighborhoods.' However, for a link-back to increase your SEO, the 'good neighborhood' must have some relationship to what you are selling. A bakery might have a link to my developers invitation site on their site, since they sell wedding and birthday cakes, and these occasions often require invitations. It is unlikely that a site selling chainsaws has the same target audience as those interested in invitations and announcements. Therefore, putting her invitation template website URL on the chainsaw site would not increase her SEO, and possibly flag *Google's* violation detection algorithms *Penguin* and *Panda*, for an infraction.

The Function of Search Engines

Marketing pros know the power of SEO—reaching #1 in *Google* returns in their company's industry, and similar categories. Many try to game the system to get to that #1 ranking.

Google's job, and that of any search engine, is to return the most RELEVENT links to your queries. But evil marketers make performing *Google's* job function particularly difficult by over-optimizing, and putting link-backs on 'bad neighborhood' sites, or sites with no relationship to what is being sold. It may help the ranking of their company, but *Google* returns irrelevant, and often improper links to our queries. (Pornography is notorious for using SEO tricks.)

DON'T PLAY SEO GAMES! Even if you get away with it, **effective marketing sells <u>features and benefits of your offering</u> and/or company, to fulfill a desire of a specific group of people.**

The most effective, and *safe* use of SEO, is working within the perimeters of what *Google* finds relevant:

- Current, up-to-date news, information, entertainment, reviews, ratings, new content from trusted sources...etc.

- FRESH content, on websites, blogs, new campaigns, PR. New SMM content as often as possible. Daily posts, are bare minimum.

- Content, copy *and* images/video/audio, that matches or relates to the offering being sold, or represented.

- 'Natural' or 'organic' link-backs, from *legitimate* sites (people genuinely interested in your offerings and website), as well as online references though articles, interviews, and PR.

- Title tags, categories, topic classifiers, image ALT text, that *accurately* reflect the offering, its contents, and campaign promise.

- Text, sprinkled [lightly] with link-anchored keywords that lead to web pages of *relevant* content to the original link-anchored text.

- Link-backs to your URLs from *trusted* outside sources, such as websites, blogs, vlogs...etc., that *relate* to your offerings.

- Hashtags that *accurately* categorize your published digital content—in all your online marketing efforts, from blogs to your SMM campaigns.
- URLs, and/or subdomains that contain keywords associated with your offering, or particular campaign messaging.

- One main URL (company or product name), and subdomains for landing pages and digital marketing. (Working with domains, and web hosting, is next.)

SEO Best Practices

So, let's put what *Google* (and most search engines) finds relevant into *action*, to increase your digital marketing efforts SEO:

- Use keywords and key phrases *directly associated* with your offering, and company, in your online campaigns. This is *safe*, SEO friendly content.

- Consistently publish safe, **fresh content**, on your website, blogs, newsletters, PPC campaigns, PR, and SMM posts as often as possible.

Daily posts are bare minimum, and keep you up-to-date.

- Use keywords, title tags, categories, topic classifiers, image ALT text, that *accurately reflect* your offering, *and* your campaign promise.

- Search *Twitter* for the popularity of a hashtag. Input hashtagged #keyword into *Twitter's* search, and look under their "Latest" tab at the top of your *Twitter* UI, for currently *trending* hashtags. If the hashtag is *currently* popular, it will have a tweet (posts) in that #keyword's timeline every 1 to 3 minutes, by a wide variety of original posters (OP).

  Google Trends is a keyword and key phrase search tool that identifies what keywords are trending in *Google* searches in real time, for the U.S., and globally (trends.google(dot)com/trends).

- Check *Google Adwords Keyword Planner* for the popularity of a keyword or key phrase. You don't have to buy it to find the keyword rank, according to *Google*, but *Twitter* has more accurate *current* data on hashtag popularity. *Instagram* does too. Input your hashtagged #keyword into their search bar, and a popup window of the same, or similar hashtags, will appear right below the search bar. It'll show how many *Instagram* users have used this hashtag, but unlike *Twitter*, does not show this in real time.

- **Link-anchor** your blog, or website text, with only a *few* keywords directly related to your offering, and/or company. The links should take viewers to your website's internal pages, or an external landing page *directly related to your offering*, company, and campaign promise.

- Garner **link-backs** from *trusted* outside sources. Contact companies related (*not* competing) to yours. Ask them if they would like *you* to put a link-back of *their* site on yours, then ask them to post *your* link on their site.

  A recent client of mine produced custom-made chef knives. In the process of developing his website, I contacted many popular chefs, and sent them one of his knives to try out. A few got back to me with positive feedback, and I asked them for a testimonial, and promised a link-back to their website on my client's site. Two offered to put a link to my client's site on their site in return.

- Don't use more than three to five hashtags *related to your offering* on all your company's SMM posts.

- Use **subdomains** added on to your corporate URLs for your landing pages, blogs, vlogs, and interior website pages.

Utilizing the bullet points above will increase your SEO ranking, and allow *Google* to deliver on their promise of returning the most *relevant* link returns to our queries. This makes *Google* happy, and they will reward your online marketing efforts with higher ranking of your web pages in your company's industry segment, and/or your offering's category.

How It All Works

Most of us think we know how the internet works. Maybe you do, maybe you don't. But wherever you are on the learning curve of digital media, it is mandatory you understand some of the basic workings of the world wide web to create effective digital marketing. We drill deep into the virtual world of online technology, next.

◆◆◆◆◆

MODULE 19: ONLINE TECHNOLOGY

Traditional Marketing vs. Digital Marketing

Traditional and digital marketing have the exact same purpose—*to get people to do what we direct them to do*. The only difference between traditional marketing, and online marketing, now known as digital marketing, lies in how their respective technologies reproduce their content, or publish media.

Traditional print campaigns, whether it be a direct mail (snail mail) campaign, a brochure, or an ad in a printed magazine, use the offset or digital CMYK, 4/C (four color) printing process discussed earlier in the Design Fundamental's module. Even trade-show booths have backdrops and podiums that require printing to emblazon them with imagery and text.

Print campaigns are *one shot and done*. Once the marketing material is printed, it is permanently on the paper or substrate (like plastic for packaging, or metal for signage).

This is *not* the case with our digital marketing efforts. Design and publish a website, and you'd better be changing the content consistently, or your site won't get the traction—views, engagements, higher SEO—you want it to. Landing pages and PPC ads are A/B [Split] tested all the time. A/B testing means we run online campaigns that look identical, but change ONE element, such as the headline, to see which headline gets greater response.

The online platform is an exciting new frontier for marketing opportunities! It offers many forms of creative expression, from still pictures, to moving text, to video. It not only grants every one of us global reach for little to no cash, digital marketing can, and *should* be flexible, fluid, and responsive to our online behavior—change in response to the reception, and engagement, each marketing campaign receives.

Digital media requires advanced technology behind the marketing campaign served up (reproduced) to your mobile or tablet screen. While it isn't necessary for you to understand intricate details about online technology, it is required you get the basics to effectively market your offering and company online.

Let's begin with some basics about online technology. Some you many know, and some you may not. We'll start with the foundation of online tech—an overview of how it all works, to empower you to create digital marketing that will give your offering, and startup, an online presence.

Is It an OS or Browser

We'll begin with how your computer functions, and how your access to the internet happens, by reviewing the difference between an **Operating System** and a **Browser**.

Your **operating system** (**OS**) controls your computer and everything attached to your computer. Your OS controls the operations your computer performs, as well as your printers, speakers, disks, keyboard, mouse, monitors, external mics...etc. Your OS will likely be installed on your computer, or mobile phone when you purchase it. All *Apple* devices, from their *iPhones* to their tablets, run on *Apple's* OS, known as iOS. If you have a *Samsung* cellphone, you'll likely have an *Android* OS, by *Google*, performing the operations of your phone.

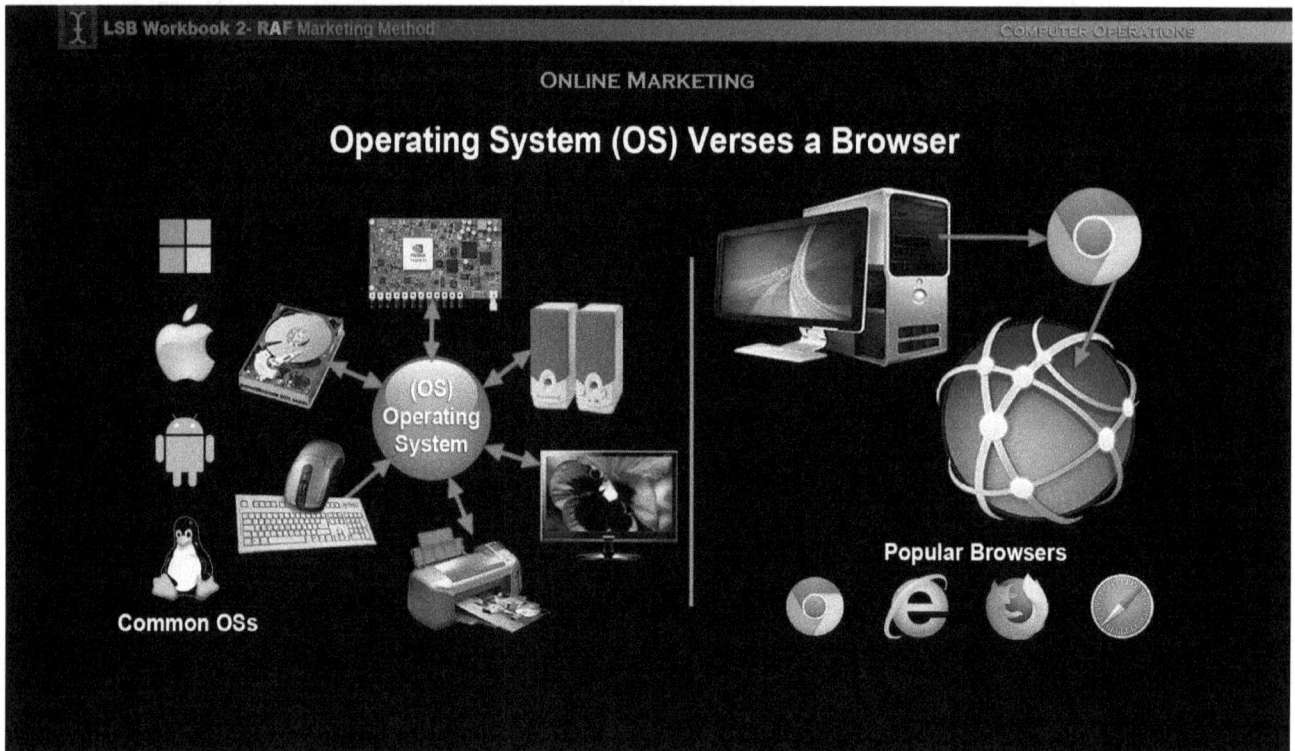

A **browser** is *not* an operational part of your computer, tablet or mobile. You don't need a browser for your digital device to function. You *do* need a browser to access the internet. Your phone, or laptop's **user interface** (**UI**), is just a window in which to access your browser—a **SaaS** (software as a service) application. Open the browser software, and the app provides a *portal* to the internet.

Your computer, or phone, or tablet's operating system, talks to the browser, which then talks to the world wide web (www). *Chrome,* by *Google*, is one of the most widely used commercial browsers. Software developers usually prefer browsers with built in development tools, such as *Firefox*. While it is likely your new computer or mobile comes with a previously installed browser, unlike your computer's OS, you don't have to stick with the browser the manufacturer put on your device. Is *Chrome* too slow for you, or you find its UI too hard to navigate? Easily (download) switch to *MS Explorer*, or *Safari* (for *Apple* only).

Most computers have only one operating system. However, you can put several browsers on your computer, and use them simultaneously. You may want the convenience of a browser with a simple UI, like *Chrome*, but need the development tools that *Firefox* offers. Additionally, you may have several email accounts and want to view them concurrently. Since most browsers will only let you log into one email account at a time, having multiple browsers lets you see multiple emails at the same time.

-Webhosting-

A **webhost** is an online service, that provides **servers** to *store* your digital marketing efforts, and a network connection to *display* your campaigns online. Your website, your landing pages, videos, e-newsletters, email, and online advertising campaigns, are all delivered to our device screens via a webhost.

All digital content needs to reside on a server, so it can be *served up* to our devices when 'called.' It can be *AWS (Amazon Web Services)* servers, at an *Amazon* warehouse, or servers located at your company, but all digital content must reside on *some* digital storage unit, *somewhere*—aka, a server.

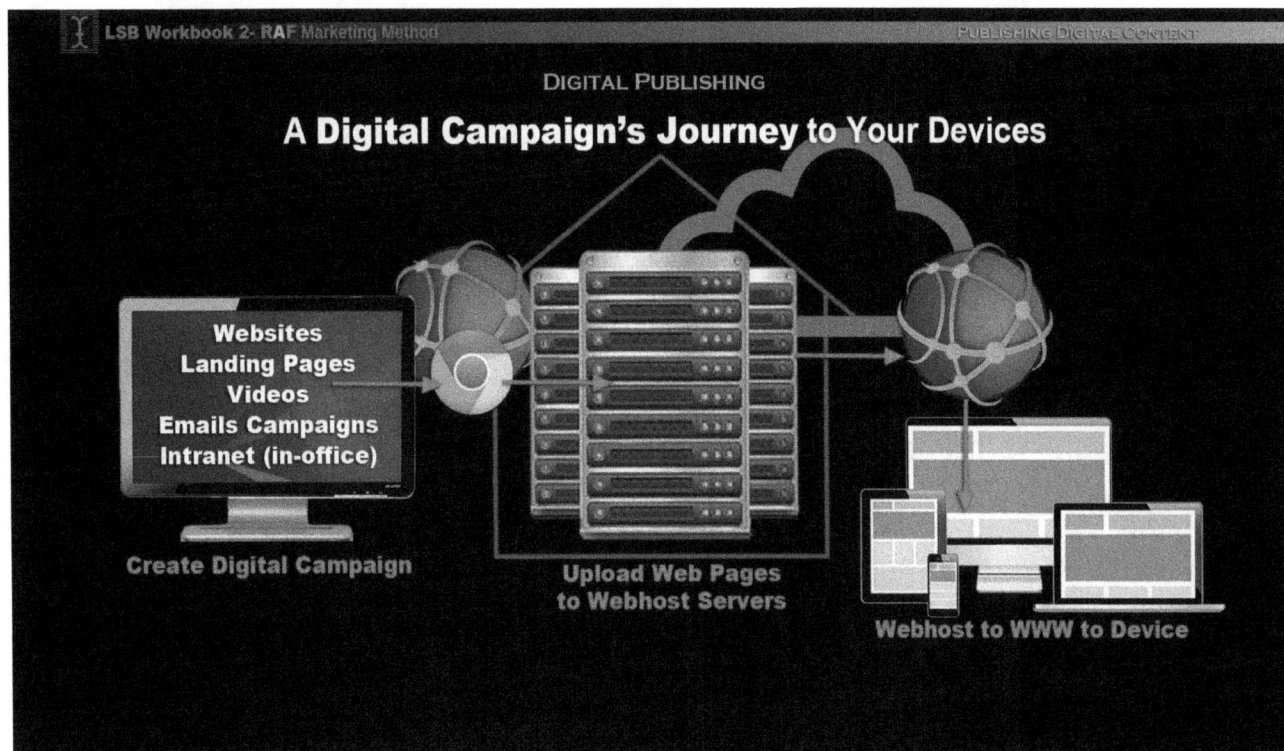

Every web page on the internet has its own unique URL, aka web page address. This address is 'called,' or *requested,* from the server the URL is located on. Any online 'link' is a URL address. Every time a web page is called—when we press on a link, *any* link—we are requesting access to that particular web page's URL.

The more digital marketing you create, and the more traffic your web pages get, the more servers you'll need to store and serve up your digital marketing efforts. Sure, you can build your own network of servers for your new venture, but this is a very expensive proposition, since the more you grow, the more servers your business will require. Startups, to major corporations, like *Netflix, Comcast, Samsung,* and many others, use webhosting services to mitigate the expense of continually adding servers, and to avoid the hassle of troubleshooting them.

Webhosting services house banks and banks of servers on which they 'rent' virtual space. When you build and house your website on a webhost, they will manage a lot of your site security, for secure communications and e-commerce, with software that prevents hacking. Most webhosts will provide templates for building websites, landing pages, blogs, newsletters, PPC ads, and other marketing campaigns. They'll manage the technical maintenance of your site—keep it functioning on the internet as you designed it to. Webhosts often collect statistical data on user behavior—track the behavior of visitors to your site—how long they stayed on a web page, what pages they viewed, if they purchased, or how far they got in the purchase process before leaving your site. You can use this data (if you have a lot of it), to more effectively identify and market to your target audiences.

Like most online service providers, webhosts cost money, sometimes a lot of it, depending on what services you purchase from them. Another advantage to using a webhost, is that you self-host your site, meaning *you* have control over the content you want to put up, any number of web pages—websites to landing pages to ad campaigns, with as many images, videos, and links as you desire. *You* determine your pricing, not some **VAR** (**value added reseller**), like *Google Play*, or *iTunes,* where your *one page* of content resides on *their* servers.

Webhosts provide instant scalability. As your business grows, you can purchase more servers as needed. You'll need more virtual space to house your expanding collection of online branding and marketing campaigns. To keep your website up and running, you'll need additional bandwidth to accommodate the increase in your online traffic—the visitors to your site. The more server space you buy, the more expensive your webhosting will be.

To clarify further, your corporate URL is like the address of your [online] store. Webhosting, on the other hand, is akin to the location of your store, including the space in your store where you put the shelves of goods for sale. Inside your store is also where you network—establish a connection with your target audience.

URL Registrars vs DNS vs Webhosts
When you buy a domain name (URL) for your website, you are purchasing it from

a **Registrar** (whether you know it or not, as URLs often come as part of a package deal from webhost providers).

A domain name should only be purchased through an accredited domain name registrar. Many webhosts, such as *GoDaddy*, are also accredited domain registrars. A registrar may or may not offer hosting services, though most do now. These certified registrars manage local and global directories of billions of existing URLs. They 'reserve' your website address—your URL—and each unique domain name you purchase. URLs must renew annually through the registrar, to remain in their indexed directories.

Two separate web pages can NOT have the same exact URL. Accredited domain registrars prevent the duplication of domain names.

When you purchase a URL from a webhost registrar, like *GoDaddy*, they 'hold' your URL, whether you choose to use them as your webhost or not, unless you go through the complex and time consuming process of switching registrars. Having your URL 'mapped' from *GoDaddy* to another webhost is easier than switching, but usually cost money annually to maintain the 'mapping.' Avoid the hassle and expense of having to switch registrars down the line by carefully researching which webhost will work best for your company's needs, at launch, and in the foreseeable future.

URL and DNS are often associated as the same thing, but they are not. The internet is a mathematical system, so all URLs must be translated into numbers to be displayed over the internet. We now know a URL is any specific web page address. As reviewed in Module 15—Identity Development, the 2ⁿᵈ level domain (2LD) of any URL is the company name, or some rendition of a name, so we can easily identify who the digital marketing is from.

DNS, aka **domain name system**—lets us use actual names, or words in our URLs, then translates those letters into a sting of numbers, like 73.189.192.13, called an IP (Internet protocol) address. Think of it as calling "Mom," instead of 888-123-4567. These numbers tell the web browser where to go to get to the site, which is stored on your webhost's servers.

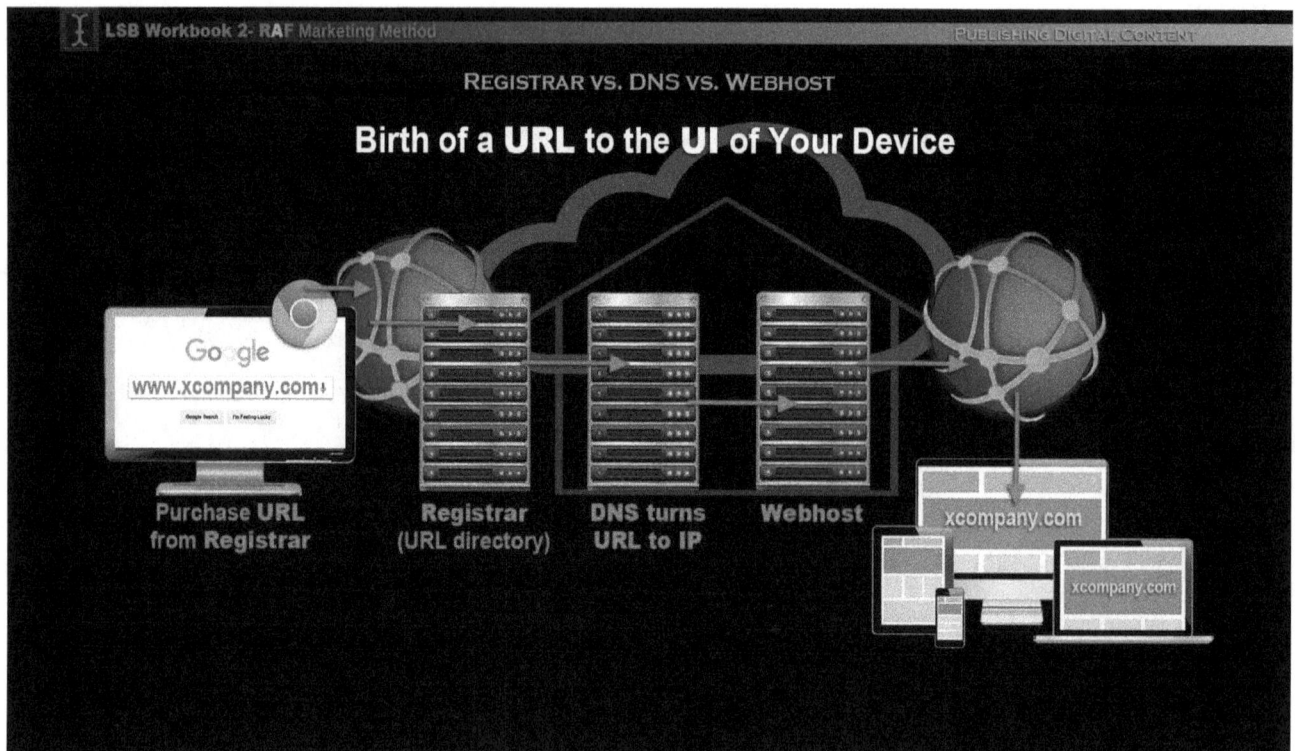

Domain Name vs. Subdomains vs. Subpages

Remember, every web page on the internet has a unique address, i.e. domain name, aka URL. But a web page can mean many things. A video plays on a web page, whether it be on a *YouTube* page, or an *Instagram* feed. Social media platform feeds, like your *Facebook* profile, are dynamic web pages, in which content is consistently delivered to *your* specific 'page/timeline.'

To build your company brand, your corporate URL should be fairly consistent across all digital media. How do you achieve this when you need a *unique* URL for every digital campaign you produce?

Subdomains and **Subpages**.

Remember, your company name is your 2LD (following the 3LD, www; https; ftp, etc.). Your top level domain (TLD), or the .com; .net; .org...etc., extensions, complete your corporate URL.

A corporate identity URL: https://companyname.com. (The 's' in https, means it has internet *security* protocol, which we'll review next).

We use our corporate URL for a lot of our digital marketing campaigns. We do this to build brand awareness. People look to the URL to identify who the web page belongs to, or email campaign is coming from. So does *Google's* search crawlers! Keywords added to your corporate URL that relate directly, or indirectly (though not *too* obscure) to what your landing page, or website page is offering, will increase your SEO ranking.

To build our brand, we consistently use our corporate URL for our digital marketing campaigns. Since each web page we publish must have its own unique URL, or web page address, we *add on* identifiers to our company URL.

This is where **subdomains** and **subpages** come in. A web page with a subdomain in the URL looks like this: https://**blog**.companyname.com. This URL puts visitors directly on the company's blog page.

To get to a specific blog post, a subpage is utilized. A URL with a subdomain *and* a subpage will look like this: https://**blog**.companyname.com/**latestnews**

Subdomains and subpages usually resides on the same servers the corporate website does, even though they may or may not be part of the company website itself. They may be landing pages, or PPC ads, or e-newsletters in your company's digital marketing arsenal.

A subdomain and subpages added to a URL for a landing page that is *not* a page on your company website could look like this:
https://**landing**.companyname.com/**lean-startup-marketing/course-sale**

Most webhosts offer unlimited subdomains and subpages, but registrars charge annually to maintain your primary domain name (URL). Instead of buying separate URLs for every digital marketing effort, use subdomains and subpages for each online campaign. It'll save you money, as well as help increase your company's SEO ranking, since your company name is repeated in your URL again and again with each digital campaign.

Get satisfied customers, good reviews, and/or link-backs from legitimate sources, and your corporate URL will become a trusted source, not only to *Google's* search algorithms, but to potential target users as well.

Webhosts vs CMS
You need both a URL, and webhosting for each web page you produce. You do not need to *pay* a webhost to put up your website, nor do you need to *buy* URLs, aka domain names, for your offerings and company.

Each LEAN Startup Workbook, in the RAF Marketing Method series, teaches you how to start a startup for little, to no money. But webhosts cost money! Buying banks and banks of servers for your company costs money too. Lots of it! Before making these types of monetary investments up front, it may be smarter to begin your digital branding and marketing efforts with a **Content Management System** (**CMS**) from *Wordpress* or *Wix*, for free.

A CMS is an online platform that helps you not only build websites, landing pages, and such, it also allows non-developers, and code-phobic marketing pros to easily design, upload, and manage their digital content.

CMS platforms generally fall into two categories. Each has their own unique features, benefits, and drawbacks.

• *WordPress; Drupal* are rather complex, customizable, open-source platforms for web publishing. *WordPress.org* is by far the most widely used CMS out there, but must be managed through a webhost. Almost 30% of all digital media globally is built on *WordPress.org* (WP). *Disney Corp.*, *CNN*, the *New Yorker* magazine all run on *WP.org*. These Fortune 500 corps are their own webhosts, or employ *Amazon Web Services (AWS),* or other webhost, for a monthly fee, to publish their content online.

While *WP.org* is a difficult CMS to master, it is fairly straightforward to learn the simpler version of the program: *WordPress.COM*. *WP*.<u>com</u> is free, and you don't need a webhost, as they act as their own webhost. You can even get free website templates, *and* URLs, and publish your digital marketing online through *WP*.<u>com</u>, at little to no cost. Before choosing either the *WP*.org*, or WP*.com platform, search: "*Wordpress*.COM vs. *Wordpress*.ORG," to find which will work best for your startup's needs.

• *Wix; Weebly; Squarespace*—are **WYSIWYG (what you see is what you get**), *visual,* drag-and-drop platforms that make it easy to design and publish a website, for free, with no coding, or technical experience required. While they have many web page templates to choose from, even e-commerce templates that make it easy to set up an online store, these platforms often have limited flexibility. You are restricted to just what the template provides, unlike *WordPress*, where you can input "plug-ins," which are prepackaged modules of code, as well as hand coding, to add functionality, such as games, news feeds and/or analytics, to your website.

A warning about getting a free corporate identity URL from *WordPress* or *Wix,* instead of buying one for your business...

It's true, you can set up a professional looking, and functioning website, even an e-commerce site, for free with *WP*, or *Wix*, or most any of the website builders out there. While running your website through these platforms is fine, obviously, with *Wordpress* running so much of the internet, you want your company URL to be a unique identifier for your company alone.

When you get a free URL from *WP*.com, it'll look like this: https://companyname.wordpress.com. Your URL's 2LD is *not* your startup's name, but becomes the *subdomain* to *WP*.

Free *Wix* URLs look like this:
https://username.wixsite.com/companyname
Again, your company name becomes a subpage to *Wix*, with their free URLs.

To appeal to viewers, as well as search engines, your URL must look/read like a professional business or organization. These CMS platforms are not giving you a URL for nothing because they are altruistic. YOU are their product. Every time you publish a digital marketing campaign, you are also selling *them*, in your company's URL. Getting a free URL, avoiding monthly fees, might seem like a good idea, but your URL will be branding these hosting platforms more than your own digital address. Instead of branding *your* business, you are branding *WordPress*, or *Wix*, with *their* name in *your* corporate URL. Not smart marketing!

The only text that should follow your company name is your TLD, or top level domain, of .com; .net; .org...etc.

You can purchase your own unique corporate domain name (URL) through most website builder platforms, without having to purchase their webhosting. It costs anywhere between $10 to $20 to purchase *just* a URL (that is publicly available) from a registrar. Webhosts that are not a registrar, generally offer a conduit to a registrar, and will sell you a unique URL indirectly. To 'hold' the URL year after year, generally costs around $15 to $30 annually, as of this writing. In other words, buying and holding a URL is not much more than a few *Starbuck's* lattes. It is wise when starting a startup to pass on a couple lattes a year to help brand your new venture with its own unique corporate domain name (URL).

Digital Marketing Best Practices

Implement the following lean launch solutions, as well as the others introduced throughout the Lean Startup series, for *real world* lean startup marketing:

1. **Purchase** [at least] **your corporate URL from a registrar** (not a free URL from a webhost), **with a .com TLD**. Use SUBDOMAINS and SUBPAGES for your digital marketing efforts beyond your corporate website.

2. **Purchase two or more URLs** with .com, and/or .org, or other TLD, that all 'point,' or 'map,' to your corporate website.

3. **Use a free hosting site**, like *Wordpress.*COM or *Wix* to build your first website (with or without e-commerce), at little to no cost. Use the imagery you've collected, or created, and stored in your Visual Libraries, to produce an engaging and visually striking website. (While several website pages with

pictures and videos are fine, free webhosting offers limited bandwidth, and can NOT accommodate a website laden with a lot of visual content.) Even if you do not use this website as your final corporate site at launch, you can use it to direct those you hire to show them the content you'd like to include, and where the content should reside on each web page of your site.

4. **You'll have to buy webhosting**, or banks of servers, if you are building a social media platform like *Facebook*, or a dynamic news feed like *Buzzfeed*, to handle the videos, visual, and interactive content uploaded to these types of sites. Check *AWS*, as *Amazon Web Services* offers templates for these types of hosting platforms.

5. **Build your digital marketing content on a CMS platform**. Whether building a website, or landing pages, or newsletters, using a CMS allows you, and other stakeholders in your organization, to update or change any of, or even part of, whatever digital content that you grant them access to.

Operating in Digital Clouds

Cloud computing connects a network of remote servers hosted on the internet, to store, manage, and process data, (unlike your personal computer, which connects *to* the 'cloud,' but isn't a server *on* the cloud). Cloud computing lets us access the same digital content—from databases, to applications—on most any digital device, whether a tablet, mobile phone, or laptop. The digital content, like the streaming movies on *Netflix,* resides in the cloud, and can be accessed from your personal device, or your friend's device, or a computer at your local library, or a public computer in a hotel lobby in another country.

Websites to landing pages, your webhosting must link to an online cloud to access your published digital content from the internet.

There are three basic levels to cloud computing:
- **SaaS**
- **PaaS**
- **LaaS**

• **Saas**: **Software as a Service** is the one which most of us are familiar with. Technically, it is software that is generally licensed on a subscription basis, and is accessible, and fully functional, through the cloud. The software *is* the service, and performs its functions within the cloud, not on your computer. Most of us use software services daily. Every time you use *Google Docs*, writing or sharing documents through their platform, you are utilizing *Google's* desktop publishing software service.

Some other well known **SaaS** product types:

- **CRM—customer relationship management** software, from email services like *Outlook; Gmail; Zoho*, to full service CRMs like *Salesforce*.
- Collaboration [and communication] tools like *Slack, Zoom* or *Skype*.
- Online games—MMO[G] or MMORPG (massive multiplayer online [role playing] game).
- Creative software tools—*Adobe Creative Suite; Camtasia Video Editing*
- EdTech—online course and education programs.
- P2P—peer-to-peer services, like the ride-sharing service *Lift*, or house sharing, like *AirBnB*.

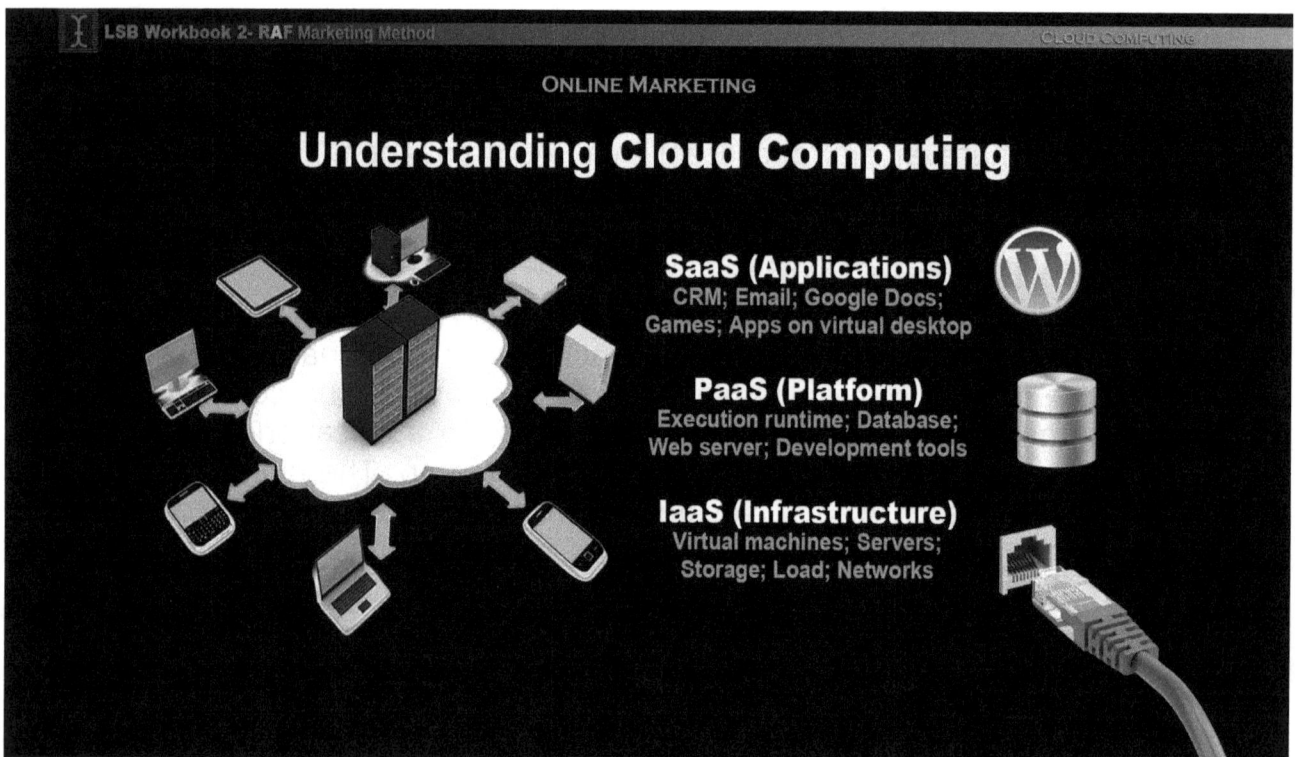

- **Paas: Platform as a Service** is a cloud service that provides a platform that allows users to develop, run and manage their applications from anywhere. PaaS vendors offer a development environment to software developers. They typically provide the servers, storage, networks, operating systems, database, security and other services needed to develop and maintain software applications. *Amazon Web Services (AWS)– Elastic Beanstalk* is a PaaS service. So are offerings from *RedHat*, and even *Salesforce*.

- **IaaS: Infrastructure as a Service** provides you access to your own computers, networks and storage systems, and give you the flexibility to easily scale up (or down) your operations. IaaS vendors, like *AWS*, or *Cisco Systems*, allow you to configure, and reconfigure your company's infrastructure as needed. Add servers to handle more online traffic, or virtual machine to increase your developers compute power.

Why is any of this technical stuff important? You better know how to set up your digital marketing (websites, to online campaigns), and even inner-office communications, to effectively develop and market your new venture in our current digital cloud landscape.

A basic understanding of how the internet works, enables you to, at least, design and produce marketing within the perimeters of the digital landscape. This little bit of technical information presented here, also gives you the knowledge to ask a few of the right questions when hiring IT vendors for your startup.

-E-Commerce Basics-

Once you have your product and company names, your identities, your logos, taglines, and several similar URLs that all point to your company website/s, we move on to how you *sell* your offerings online.

Transport Layer Security, aka **TLS**—as of this writing, is the current successor to **Secure Socket Layer (SSL)**. TLS is a security protocol for data encryption and authentication between applications and servers. To conduct business securely through the internet, whether sending email, or managing financial transactions, we need TLS on our websites, and any other platforms where secure communication is necessary. This software service *tries* to make sure the credit card that pays for our offering rightfully belongs to the same individual who actually made the purchase.

TLS gets online purchase transactions right most of the time, but many of us have had charges on our credit card for purchases we did not make. More often than not, in these cases, our credit card number is stolen, and used until the card is terminated. The computer has no idea if the credit card being used for an online purchase belongs to the person using it, unless it is reported stolen, or purchases are flagged as identity theft.

SSL, and now, TLS, was developed to mitigate the staggering loss of almost $200 *billion* in credit card fraud (2017 estimate) annually. The CC companies pass on this loss to the card holders. And we all pay for this fraud with exorbitant interest rates on our credit card balances.

How SSL/TLS Works

Below is a brief description of how internet security works. Why do you need to know this? To set up an e-commerce site, you need to have security. Even if you are not selling stuff on your site, your computer's security software, such as *Norton Utility*, wants to know that you are visiting a secure web page. You must make sure that everything you build for online access has security protocols.

1. The browser on your computer or mobile phone requests an SSL or TLS from the server (the place/space where your digital content resides).

   These servers, that 'serve up' your web pages to our device screens, can be *Amazon's* servers, aka *AWS,* or other webhosting services, like *HostWinds*. We then access these pages on our device screens through our web browsers.

2. The server responds to the browser's request with an SSL/TLS Certificate, and then encrypts all future transmissions between the server and browser. This certification allows the server and the browser to perform financial transactions securely.

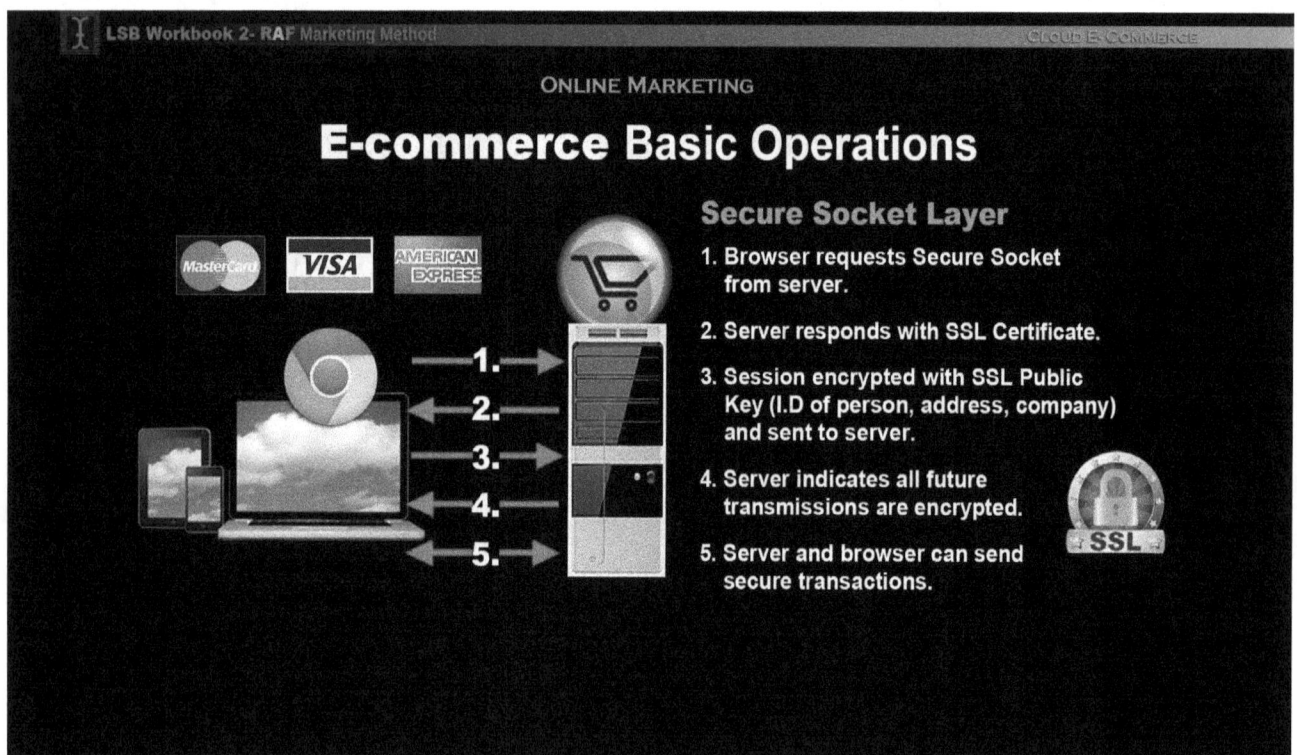

If you want to create digital marketing campaigns, and/or sell your offerings online, you need to know how to securely deliver your digital content to the web. You also must know where your virtual marketing efforts will reside online, and how your campaigns are 'served up' to our devices, so viewers of your marketing efforts know they can safely engage with your web pages.

Working with VARs
Right about now, you're likely thinking, '*WAIT! I still don't get how to set up a secure socket layer to sell my offerings on my website that I don't have yet!*

No worries! Most webhosts have templates for websites, landing pages, newsletter...etc., with built in security, so you don't need to code it in. Just be sure when hiring someone to build your site, and other digital marketing efforts, from scratch, that they know how to put in TLS protocols.

It is highly recommended that you have a website, even if you have no intention of starting a company. If you are an artist—a writer, musician, designer...etc.—you still need to brand your offerings to your name, or *a name*, to market whatever it is you want to sell. You'll need an identity, and a great tagline describing your offerings, however, you may not need to build a website to sell your stuff.

VARs—Value Added Resellers, add a valuable service, or sometimes even a product to an existing offering, giving the original offering *added value*.

Sales Platform VARs, like *Amazon, Etsy, Ebay, iStore, Google Play,*
sell your creations on their high traffic platforms for a percentage of each sale.

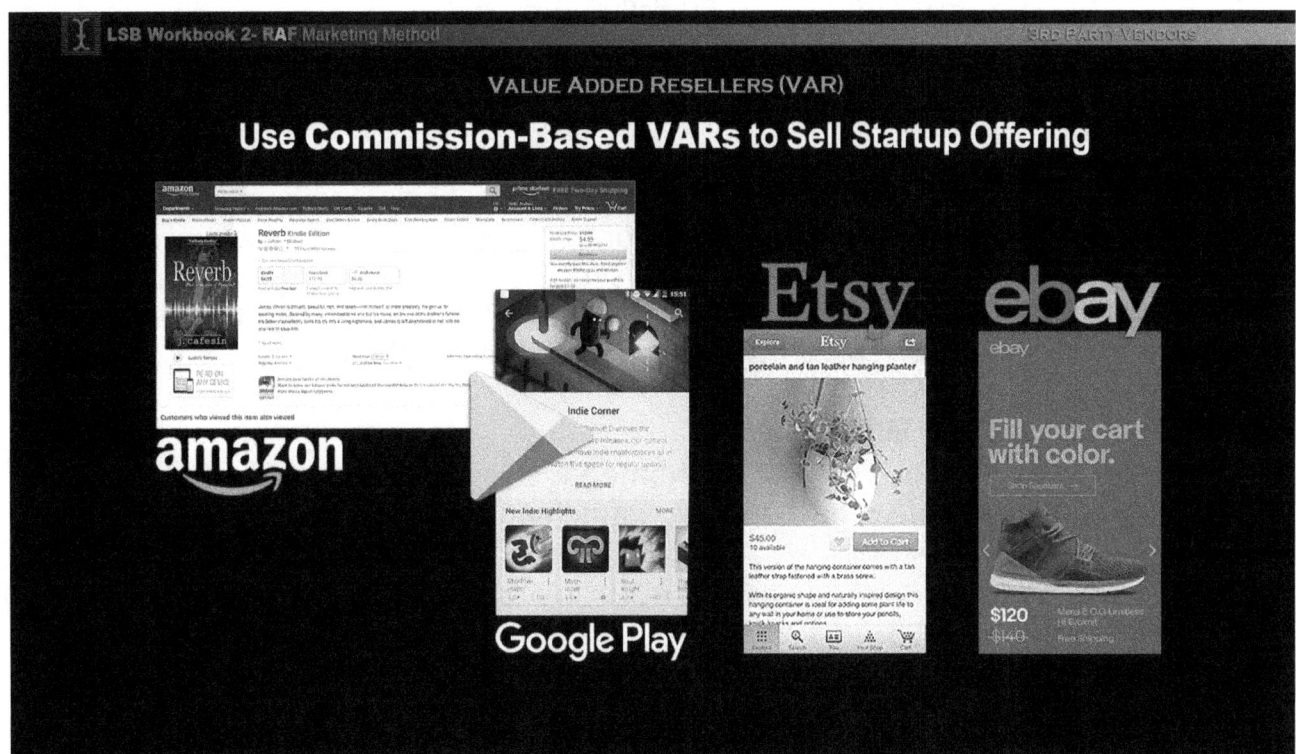

So, let's say you wrote a book, or a video game, and you'd like to sell it online. You don't have any desire to start a company. You simply want to sell your book or game. You may, down the line, write another book, or code another game, and become a gaming company, but right now, you just want to sell what you've created.

Amazon.com will publish your book, or your video game for download, on their website. These VARs give you an SSL/TLS sales page in which to sell your offering directly to consumers. The web page provides a place for a picture and/or video of your offering (or related imagery), a space for text about the features (including specifications) and benefits of your offering, and a CTA, usually a "Buy Now" button. All financial transactions happen on *Amazon.com's* servers, which are set up with trusted security protocols.

Your sales page on the *Amazon* platform IS your website. For providing you a web page on their site, they charge a commission on each sale of your book or game. The commission rate is determined per platform, so *Google Play* likely has a different pay structure than *Etsy*. Carefully research VARs, to find a sales platform that works for your needs, and sales goals. You can also sell your offerings on multiple platforms!

When selling a book or a video game, there are advantages and disadvantages to going with a VAR instead of setting up your own website:
Advantages:
- No website setup or maintenance.
- No SSL/TLS setup needed to do e-commerce.
- High traffic platforms have global reach.

Disadvantages:
- High commission rates severely cut into your profits.
- You are at the mercy of the VARs changing policies and commission rates.
- The VAR platform will push sales of your offering at a discount, and you get only the sale price profit, minus their commission. (You agree to let most of them 'incentive price' your offering when you signed up with them.)

Why Websites Are Wise
Your website is your storefront. Your homepage is the exterior facade for what you have to offer, even if you are initially launching only one product or service.

As mentioned, it is wise to have a separate website for your products, and even a page on your site about *you*, the creator, regardless if you are selling through a VAR. You don't need to set-up any e-commerce on your website if you are using a VAR to sell your product or service. Your CTAs on the web pages of your site will direct viewers to your VAR's sales page. With your own website to build your brand awareness, your sales page on their platform is just a *sales tool*.

Your website is online for people who want to know more about your offering/s, and about *you*—as an author, artist, or game developer. A website will help you build your brand, and establish a URL link, so people who don't know about your product or service *yet,* may find it in a search for similar offerings.

It is *smart marketing* to publish and maintain a dynamic website—changing text and images often (to increase SEO)—for as long as you are selling your offering online, *regardless* of the *sales* platform you choose to use.

Take <u>A</u>im and Brand Your Venture with a Website
At this junction in the RAF, Lean Startup Marketing process, you should now have:

- Eight (8) Productization lists—1A – 4B (LSM Workbook 1).
- Product *and* corporate names and identities, as well as logos and taglines for both.
- Brand standards guide for your corporate I.D.
- One or more corporate URLs.
- Webhosting (or personal servers continually connected to the web).
- A CMS to build your website, and digital marketing campaigns.

You've learned about design, and working with color, as well as print (4/C process), and digital reproduction (RGB), to successfully publish your marketing campaigns both off, and online.

Before we can market our new venture with ad campaigns and landing pages, we begin the branding process by opening our storefront—building a website for our new company. A website makes people aware we have arrived (SEO)—as search engines pick up our URLs and serve them up in search returns. It also gives our business credibility, as well as a *place* to send those who see our campaigns, and want to learn more about our offerings, and/or business.

Next, we examine what makes an *effective* website, beyond the obvious of creating a responsive user interface (UI), and navigation that is simple, and intuitive, as we've previously discussed. A website is, or should be, an ongoing, dynamic digital campaign.

◆◆◆◆◆

MODULE 20: THE CORPORATE WEBSITE

The **RAF Marketing Method** is a lean process to turning an idea into an offering of value, and marketing a startup (or any business) for profit. You are a third of the way into the process of building and launching a sustainable startup once you've gotten your offering **R**EADY—initiated Productization lists, elevator pitches, and profit models (LSM Workbook 1).

You are half way into the process of effectively actualizing a sustainable business, when you've taken **A**IM, by branding your offerings and company with names, logos, taglines, brand standards, multiple URLs, and webhosting, to serve up your digital content to the internet.

It is essential the above marketing material is well underway *before* developing your website. To create a digital storefront—a website that excites, and communicates all your company has—you first must have a thorough understanding of what you are selling, which [hopefully] you achieved through performing the Productization process.

All effective branding—from identities, to websites, to billboards—require an intimate understanding of what we are selling, to create campaigns that build brand awareness. A startup is branded by the *reception of the products or services they sell*. The company name is meaningless, until it is branded as valuable by the benefits the offerings provide to one, or many groups of people.

Launching a new company in days of old, the startup would take out ad campaigns in magazines and newspapers. They'd create press releases to notify the press they'd launched. (We'll review creating the press release in LSL Workbook 3.) They'd likely have had a brick and mortar store, or shop, and perhaps sent out a direct mail (snail mail) print campaign to homes of people in the area of their business.

Today, we put up a website to display our products and services, as well as news and information about our company. We invite visitors to our website to hear our story, pique their interest in our offerings, and provide them with a way to contact us with any inquiries. After establishing a corporate identity, the next step in the branding process is to create and publish our primary corporate website.

Website Anatomy

What, exactly, are typical website components? That depends on the industry, company, and their offerings. Website components—or the web pages that make up your website—are *industry specific*. The website user interface (UI) of a local pizza place will look a lot different than the UI of a news feed, like *Buzzfeed*, or the *Huffington Post*.

Taking this into consideration, we're going to drill down on *how* to create an effective website to market your offerings and company. Let's begin with some basic website components that apply to many types of businesses, whether you're selling a product, service, or even a political or social cause/message.

There are [at least] six (6) basic web pages in a standard business website.
- **Home Page**
- **About Company**
- **Products/Services/Message**
- **E-commerce** (or Get; Try; Subscribe)
- **On-site Blog**
- **Contact Info**

We'll discuss each of these web pages in depth, in a minute, but this module is about enabling you to create a website (or direct those you hire to create an effective site for you), so lets start at the beginning of this process.

Website Templates

So, you have to put together a website, but are freaked out about coding one? No worries! Website templates are available FREE from many webhosts. Since websites come in a variety of types, so do the templates, so you'll have many to choose from. Simply google: "free website templates," to find what is available. Be sure whatever template you choose that it is **responsive**—the content per web page will adjust to whatever device screen it is viewed on.

We've discussed the disadvantages of using the URL that you can get for free from webhosts—that *their* name appears in *your* corporate URL. But, you can purchase a URL with your company name only, directly from a registrar, or through the webhost providing the free templates. URLs generally cost $18 - $20 annually, and you can still use the free templates. Here are a few webhosts that offer free templates that I found in my quick search:

- Wordpress.**com**
- Wix
- Free-CSS (Wix)
- Weebly
- SquareSpace

Digital Sitemaps

A SITEMAP is a directory of the web pages on a website, or microsite. When conceiving what your site should look like, and the components necessary to create a complete storefront for your offerings and company, do NOT begin creating your site on your computer. Even if you are using online templates, do NOT design and layout your website using the template.

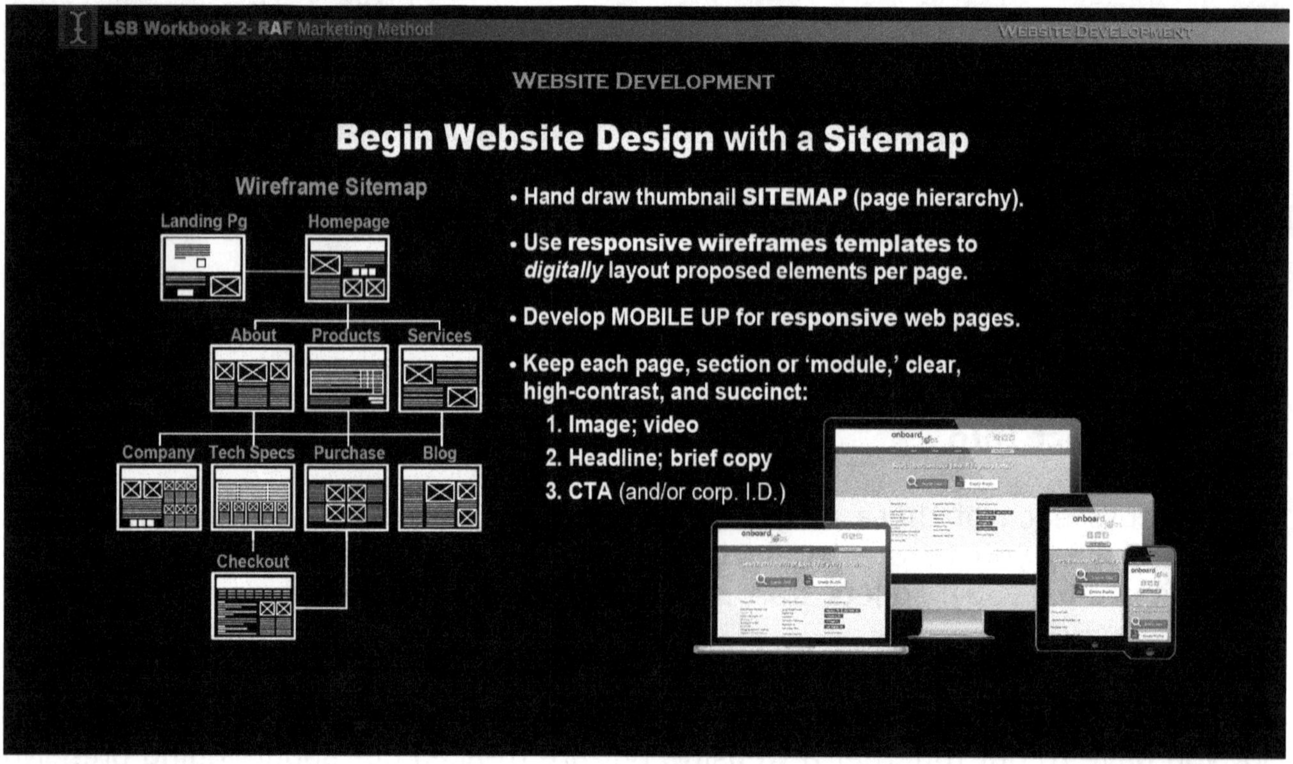

Begin your site development process with HAND-DRAWN THUMBNAILS. These are small sketches, used to explore many ideas quickly. Do NOT use online **wireframes**—templates for creating thumbnail drawings—to build your site either. **Hand drawing**, even if you do not draw well, will help you figure out which pages are needed to communicate how great your offering, and company, are, and in what order your information should be presented. Your thumbnail sitemap should not only show small sketches of the content for each web page, but also illustrate the page hierarchy of your website, effectively defining your site navigation.

Using this thumbnail design technique gives you the ability to *play* with the development of your website, until it has continuity, like reading a captivating story, with content that leads the viewer naturally from one page to the next.

Create your website sitemap using the following criteria:
1. **Develop and design your website mobile up**, for a responsive website. Your website will be viewed on cellphones *and* large computer monitors. Regardless of the UI display, your website must still communicate the *best bits* about your offering, and company, page for page. In other words, each page of your site must show the UVPs of your offering *first*, above the 'fold' line of any given device.

   Your website navigation should be intuitive, obvious, even on a small, mobile screen. You should **include a CTA on every single page of your website**, even if it's only, "Read Our Newest Blog," or, "Meet Our Staff," referral links to other pages on your site.

   To assure all this comes together in a professional, responsive website, be sure to order the importance of each element you put on each web page.

2. **Use digital wireframes if you are coding your website**, or **put your site content into your chosen template page for page**. Utilize digital wireframes to convert your hand-drawn thumbnails to code, to begin the development/design process online. These grid-based wireframes help you *place*, or *layout* each web page, as well as each element—images, headlines, copy, videos, and CTAs *per page* of your site. You should already have a good idea what these elements for each page are, from your final thumbnail sitemap. Make sure to work with a wireframe that's responsive—will scale to fit the UI of any device—to assure all your website content appears to your specifications.

3. **Keep each web page clear, succinct, and specific** to the benefits that the features of your offering provide a specific target audience.

   Common elements per page:
   • **Logo** Identity is usually in upper left corner of the fixed header on any given website page, and generally links to your website homepage.

- **Image/s**, and/or video.
- **Headline**, and subhead, or tagline/slogan where applicable.
- Brief **copy blocks** with still images, or video for complex descriptions.
- **CTA** should be the last thing on the web page, or module, even if only your corporate I.D., to get viewers to *remember your company,'* with your implied CTA, aka branding campaigns.)

4. **Your website is** a **dynamic** part of your ongoing marketing efforts. Don't forget to build your website with a CMS platform like *Wordpress*, even if you are coding it in HTML/CSS/Java...etc. It must be updated continually to get any SEO traction. Make updating simple, and error free. Be sure each page of your site is not only succinct and specific, but flexible enough to add and update pages and elements, from imagery to copy content, with ease. Remember, search engines, like *Google*, are looking for new, up-to-date content. Changing your site pages and elements on the page often will assure you stay closer to #1 in search engine returns.

The Homepage

Your corporate website **HOMEPAGE is your digital storefront**. It is the first thing a visitor to your site sees, assuming they weren't clicking on a link in a promotion that takes them to a specific page in your site. Your company's website homepage should instantly communicate what your business IS, and what your core products DO, overall. (You already have all this information in your Productization lists, that you began in LSM Workbook 1.)

Similar to your corporate identity, websites utilize '**umbrella branding**.' Umbrella branding is NOT tightly targeted to a specific audience, but should speak to the full range of your target markets. Your company may offer several types of products or services, or will, down the line, but the homepage of your website should represent an overview of what your company is marketing/selling. And it should do so above the 'fold line' of any given UI—the bottom of the screen on your mobile, or monitor.

GoPro sells FPP (first person perspective) cameras. They also sell drones, video editing applications, camera bags, and related accessories. *GoPro's* corporate homepage must show their wide range of products and services instantly. This does *not* mean they stick every offering the company sells on their homepage. They show visitors to their site an extreme sports video—someone skiing off a cliff, or flying in a 'base' suit—that starts playing as soon as you arrive on their homepage. The video clips are quick, 5 seconds before moving on to another, and each clip is so arresting, and remains so breathtaking as it plays, it keeps us on the page, and more likely to read other page elements, and ultimately click on their CTA.

Most all sustainable companies sell more than one product, or even service. Hair salons often sell beauty products. Social media platforms like *Facebook*, or news platforms like the *Huffington Post,* sell advertising space (affiliate marketing), but both are also selling the latest news, updates, networking opportunities, and more. Remember, your corporate website employs 'umbrella branding' to represent *all* your company offers. You must demonstrate the value of your products, services, and company, to a broad cross-section of your target markets, to invite the widest possible audience into your 'store.'

Website URL links are delivered globally in search returns. We never know who may find us. We want to attract the attention of as many as possible, even those we've not considered in our first targeting efforts during Productization. If the homepage of our corporate website instantly communicates what our company has, and does, overall, anyone interested in what we are selling will likely be attracted to our site. For our corporate website development, we don't need to focus this particular marketing effort on a specific target user, but let our corporate site identify its own.

Corporate Homepage Best Practices
- **Websites are industry specific.** Format your company's homepage per industry standards. Don't reinvent the wheel. Follow trending layout, and navigation practices, such as putting your logo in the upper left corner of any web page, and have it always link to your homepage. A generation of working online, and we've been trained to expect certain behavior from specific

elements in specific locations on a web page.

- Homepage should demonstrate your offering/s value to a broad cross-section of target markets.

- Keep your homepage's main messaging *visual*, and clearly *show*, even with a powerful headline of visual words (which we'll review in the Copywriting Module of LSL Workbook 3), the *best things*, or UVPs (unique value propositions) about your offering/s, and company. Use images with impact, and video clips that command attention from your Visual Libraries. Create slide shows of your offering, or related to your products and services, to instantly communicate who your company is, and what you produce.

- **All web pages must be responsive.** Keep your primary CTA above the 'fold' line. Vertical or horizontal scrolling (swiping finger directly on the device screen) must be enabled to access web page sections *below* the 'fold' line.

- One click CTAs should engage automatic scrolling to the desired information, or link to interior web pages that pay off the CTA.

- Homepage should be updated continually to increase your website SEO. Each page of your site should be succinct and specific, but must be *flexible* enough to add and update pages, and site elements, easily, which is why we develop websites, and other digital marketing, on CMS (content management system) platforms.

Website About Pages

Corporate **ABOUT pages** should share our company's journey with the viewer, but also *sell* them on our company, the people running it, users testimonials of our offerings, positive press...etc. About page 'mission statements' are the purest form of content marketing, in that they are written in a storytelling way, as are the biographies of the C-level executives (CEO; CFO; CTO). About pages should welcome the visitor in a personal manner (not a bullet list of benefits, like when selling an offering directly). About pages are basically *implied CTAs,* that help brand the company with a specific perception, and a personal touch.

Marketing is selling. All web pages on any website are online to sell something to the site visitor. About pages are online to indirectly sell visitors on embracing our company's story, and our mission.

Who, and what, are we selling on our about pages?

- Sell website visitors on the competency of our company, management, and staff. Our about pages sell the *perception* that our offerings are of the highest quality (even consulting services), because the people involved in creating them are of the highest caliber.

- Sell potential hires on joining our company with our engaging story, and mission forward. About pages sell our executive staff with the highest credentials. They sell our fantastic work environment, with endless free food, drinks, and foosball.

- Brand our company as socially responsible with our mission, and values statements. About pages often include philanthropic causes, charitable contributions, and volunteering events. They may also include industry news, favorable press, company events. Remember, you want your website to be changing its contents often. Posting news and events, even office shenanigans, on your about pages are great for SEO.

The about pages on your corporate website should include [at least] three sections, modules, or web pages:

- **Company story**—how your offering came into being, and how your company began around this original idea for the products or services your business produces.

- **Mission/Philosophy statement**—what is the core purpose for your organization? Why does your business exist?

- **Executive staff**—the C-level executives, and accomplished staff, with a picture and a brief bio for each [important] member of your team.

Website Product Pages

As we've discussed, website design is predicated on what we are selling. A real estate website, like *Zillow,* shows housing for sale and rent. Their website homepage, like most real estate sites, wisely have a fill-in field to show you the type of housing you want, in the location you're looking for. Once you've filled the form in, and press enter, the site takes you to their main **PRODUCT** page, their SaaS (software-as-a-service) UI, which shows the available housing with your criteria, and a map of where each address is located. If you scroll down, you'll find an array of information about area school ratings, transportation, crime stats...etc.

A product can mean many things. If you are selling a software service (SaaS), like *Zillow*, or even a social platform like *LinkedIn*, your sites product page/s will likely look a *lot* different than if you're selling a consumer product like vitamins, or baked goods. *Zillow's* product pages (the available housing in the area of your choice) are paying off the homepage CTA—the fill-in field of the location of the housing you are seeking.

You've already defined what your offering IS, what it DOES, and for WHO in LSM Workbook 1. You have the features and benefits, as well as the target markets and users of your offering in your Productization lists. By now, you should also have your offering's differentiators, or best UVP lists, as well. Utilize these lists to determine the best design to represent your offering's unique strengths, with the most obvious, intuitive navigation possible.

Product Page Best Practices

• Use imagery of the product or service, *in use*, where applicable. With food, or beverages, show people eating, or drinking it. Fashion should show someone, even a model, wearing it.

  With SaaS, show the functions your software performs, as in real estate sites showing pictures and prices of housing. For software companies, that sell PaaS and LaaS infrastructure hardware and software, use related imagery, showing connectivity, networking, technology oriented referential images.

  For consulting services, focus on using imagery in the industry that you consult in. Make your marketing efforts personal, and use images of presenting at meetings, shaking hands with a team of colleagues, or smiles all around the boardroom table...etc.

• Limit text/copy to:
  ✔ **HEADLINE**= Product name.

✔ **SUBHEAD**= Best UVP of the offering.
✔ **Bodycopy** (if at all)= *brief* descriptor, and/or bullet points list of features, benefits, and/or solution of your offering. Sometimes, additional information is required, such as technical specifications. Be sure to put these below the 'fold' line, and *after* the CTA, or use a clickable link to access them on another web page in your site (*not* listed in your navigation menu).
✔ **CTAs**= differs per site offering, and per page of site. Every marketing effort must have a direct or implied CTA (or it ain't marketing). So be sure to include an incentive to buy; try; sign-up; learn more; get gift; contact; or simply *remember* your company (branding), on *every* page, module, section, of every marketing campaign you produce.

• Create videos to describe complex products, services, or software. Do *not* put long text descriptions of complex SaaS applications, or any other product or service on your product pages. Only *brief* descriptors of each offering, with "read more," if absolutely necessary, like with technical specification. To show the full capacity of complex offerings, use video.

• **Make the homepage an interactive product page with SaaS offerings.** SaaS offerings often deliver their product on the homepage, and therefore require no product page. The software *is* the service, i.e. *software-as-a-service* (SaaS). Music, and movie streaming, use a SaaS product model. *TripAdvisor,* a search service to find travel packages, offers its service on their homepage. The homepage acts as a CTA tp engage with their service. If you use their fill-in field, and input your search criteria, the app takes you to their product/service page, which lists all of the travel packages *TripAdvisor* gathered, via your specifications, from the internet.

E-Commerce web pages

Onsite **shopping cart**, and **purchase pages**, should concertize the sale with simple, obvious, check-out navigation, so the visitor follows through with the purchase. Shopping cart pages, and purchase pages, should also *sell more* than just the offering being purchased. E-commerce pages on your corporate website should be developed with garnering additional sales in mind.

I considered purchasing a laptop from *Best Buy*, a national chain of technology devices, from cellphones, to entertainment systems. I picked one I liked on their website, and went to the shopping cart page to purchase it. Essentially, this page is a marketing play, as my order is always confirmed on the check-out/purchase page where I input my credit card.

The shopping cart page is on a website to *sell more!* Free shipping; product warranties; special offers; recommendations; these are all meant to attract impulse buyers, to get them to buy more, and raise their overall purchase price.

All check-out/purchase pages on your website must have SSL/TLS security, to make sure all financial transactions are safe. Your webhost should offer SSL/TLS. *Wordpress*, *GoDaddy*, *Wix, Weebly,* all have one-click enabled TLS.

E-commerce Pages Best Practices

• Offer an immediate incentive to encourage follow-through to purchase, such as special savings, or free shipping.

• Increase total sale price with warranties, add-on features, benefits, or components. Car rental companies now offer GPS mapping, baby seats, satellite music service...etc., for additional fees. Software companies may include more functionality, as in premium services.

• Attract impulse buyers with special offers, or 'gifts,' related to their potential purchase. Show the offer prominently, and place it close to the "confirm order" button.

• Add targeted recommendations (with great ratings, if applicable), of similar, or related offerings to the one in their shopping cart.

• Add support messaging, such as lowest price matching offers, or money-back guarantees, to reduce customer risk of purchasing.

- Provide customer support (live chat), near checkout to minimize cart abandonment, and help concertize follow-through of the sale.

- Utilize pop-up windows for recommendations, or special offers, to push these incentives, so customers don't miss them on a crowded purchase page.

Many times we are selling our products or services through a VAR (value-added reseller), as we reviewed earlier. A cart, or purchase page, is not strictly required for your website when selling through the VAR model. CTAs on the product page should link directly to your sales page on the VAR platform. When utilizing a VAR for SSL/TLS sales transactions, your website product page essentially becomes your shopping cart and purchase pages.

Website Blogs

ONSITE BLOGS, as opposed to *commercial* blogs like *Mashable*, increase site engagement by providing visitors entertaining, informative articles, podcasts, even videos, directly on our company website. Onsite blogs also increase our website SEO, by continually publishing new, dynamic, and [engaging] content. Remember, *new* content is highly relevant to search engines, and they'll rank our site higher, closer to the top of their search returns, if we consistently update our onsite blog with content that is related to what our company offers.

We utilize onsite blog in a variety of way. As mentioned, it increases SEO ranking if you update the content often. It is also a way to attract people to your website.

Much like newspaper articles, putting up an interesting post on your blog attracts readers. You can, and should, social media market (SMM) a line or two about each new blog post, on your corporate profile pages on *Facebook*, *Twitter* and *Instagram*..etc, with a link to the full blog post on your website. An onsite blog is also a way to collect email addresses. Every blog post should have an opt-in form at the end of the post for viewers to subscribe to your website blog. A pop-up fill-in form for subscribing to your blog can be utilized after 20 – 30 seconds of the viewer reading. Collecting emails is an important marketing tool to be used for email campaigning down the line.

Anchored links—keywords and phrases that are highlighted as links—within your blog content, get readers to other web pages within your website. Using a few per blog post will help increase your SEO ranking, and also get readers of your blog to explore other pages of your website. Be sure that the anchored keyword link is directly associated with whatever page the link sends your readers to.

Onsite blogs are not limited to words. Today, we can create an onsite **vlog**—a video blog—where each post is a video article! These posts can be slide shows, to full videos, but, again, should relate directly or indirectly to your offerings, company, and industry. Be sure to put captions on every vlog post! Video should always communicate with, and without sound. It doesn't hurt to mix it up a bit, and one week post a blog article, the next week post a video story! You can also create a weekly **podcast**—an online radio show—of blog articles and videos you publish on your website blog.

Onsite blogs or vlogs are a great marketing tools. New blog posts should be added weekly, monthly, on the outside, and touted through your social media marketing channels with each new post.

Onsite Blog Best Practices

- **Content is king!** Write new content directly or indirectly associated with your offering, and/or company as often as possible. Daily, weekly, or, *at least*, monthly.

- Optimize each blog posts for SEO using keywords and phrases directly or indirectly related to your offering in your articles, podcasts, audio, and video scripts and captions. Make sure all content, even re-posted content from others, has copy directly inline with your products, services, and/or industry.

- Link anchor keywords and phrases within your copy content to other pages on your website, or to your landing page campaigns, where applicable. The goal is to keep people engaged with your site, or other marketing efforts.

- Include images, or videos, in your blog posts to increase engagement.

- Break up long blog text by sprinkling significant sentences throughout the post as subheads.

- Create podcasts of each blog or vlog post, and release it simultaneously, or a few days after you post your onsite blog. Creating an ongoing podcast will not only increase your SEO, but also build your brand awareness.

• SMM (social media market) each new blog or vlog posts. Include comments, and social proof of interest, such as Likes, or Shares, of your blog posts in your SMM campaigns. Don't limit your SMM blog campaigns to just new posts. You can SMM old blog posts as well, especially if they suddenly relate to currently trending news.

Re-posting Content

Creating and populating an **onsite blog** with posts is time consuming. Writing articles related to our business, especially if we suck at writing engaging and coherent material, is hard! If writing your company blog yourself seems more than you can handle, consider re-posting other bloggers, vloggers, and previously published content.

While this is not the best blogging approach, as it does not optimize your search rank, it is often an easy way to populate your company blog in the beginning. Additionally, re-posting content from others can garner link-backs, from *'safe neighborhoods,'* which is the #1 way to increase your search ranking. The more link-backs from valid websites, the higher your SEO ranking.

When you re-post content belonging to others, you are required to get their permission. In doing so, you'll let them know that you'll be linking to their site, i.e. providing a link-back of *their* URL on *your* blog post. This is also your opportunity to share with them industry information you've discovered, or a similar blog on your site to the original poster's (OP) content that you are re-posting. Ask the OP to put a link to *your* blog's web page, which relates to theirs, as, in fact, you show some of their content on your site in re-posting them.

There are some basic rules for reprinting and re-posting other blogger's content, but copyright laws are changing all the time. They are becoming more restrictive, so be sure to check with the OP before re-posting any of their original content.

- Reprinting, or re-posting entire articles, blogs or vlogs (video blog) requires the approval of (and credit to) the original poster (OP). It is also *not* recommended. *Google* requires 'fresh,' unique content related directly, or indirectly to what you are offering (but there better be *some* connection, or *Google's* algorithms are going to label you malicious), to increase your search rank.

- Re-posting the headline, image, and a summary description, with a link to the original blog post requires giving the original publisher (OP) written credit. This generally does not call for the OP's approval, as with re-posting full blogs, as long as *your* summary of their content is unique, and you give them credit, as well as provide a link to the original post or video.

- Always accurately credit sources, and link the credited source to the original content you are re-posting.

- *Google* does not consider duplicate content on your site grounds for blocking you from their search returns, unless it appears you are intending to deceive and manipulate their search engine. Be careful to re-post material directly related to your industry and business to avoid alerting *Penguin* and/or *Panda*, *Google's* primary malicious-intent detecting algorithms.

Types of Onsite Blogs

Now that you know why website blogs are important, and why you should have one on your corporate website, what, exactly, do you write about, especially daily, or even weekly?

Listed below are some typical blog/vlog types. But you are *not* limited to this list. Be creative! Think of an ongoing blog like a TV, or internet series, and create a weekly blog that not only engages your target audience with entertaining and informative posts, but also attracts new markets you've yet to identity.

- **Informative**—all about your industry, your company, products, services, employees, events, *favorable* press, charitable activities and programs...etc. Company news can be as simple as videos showing your 'lively' work environment, your Friday beer bashes, or foosball competitions. If your startup is selling a consumer good, a food product perhaps, you can show the process of making your great baked goods, even cake decorating. If you're selling a service, like a SaaS product, focus blog content more on industry trends.

- **Recommendations**—pairing of fashion, such as jewelry with seasonal clothing; foods with beverages, including recipes; furniture, or interior design with housing or rental sites; incentive purchases, like reduced prices or discounted items.

Recommendation is becoming more and more popular. Machine learning software utilizes 'collaborative' algorithms to analyze massive data stores of information on each of us. They track what you, and everyone you know, and everyone they know, does on the internet. These algorithms also track what you do offline, from your credit card data, to the locations you visit through the GPS in your phone, and car, and then analyze all this data to establish patterns in our behavior.

These algorithms are designed to 'correlate' our behavior, with people we know, and people similar to us in their behavior patterns, i.e. they visit the same or similar websites, at the same rate of frequency we do. They have purchased similar products as we have, both on and offline, frequent the same locations as often as we do, drive the same way we do (there are accelerometers in our cars now, that record how fast we drive, how often and how hard we brake...etc.), and post similar words and feelings on our social feeds, and text messages.

Verizon, Apple, Amazon, Netflix, and every popular social network—most *any* corporation these days—serves up recommendations, and/or advertising that relates directly or indirectly to your behavior, or the behavior of familiar, and/or similar people to you. Recommendation blogs are more likely to attract the attention of your target audience, as your target users, or their associations, have, at some point, looked into, or purchased something similar to what your company offers. (We'll drill down on recommendation engines, and collaborative filters—the pros and cons, like influencing presidential elections with 'fake' marketing—in LSL Workbook 3: Launch.)

- **How-To Blogs** and Vlogs—such as demonstrating how to use make-up, or to fix a washing machine, or learn HTML/CSS programming, how-to blogs and vlogs are a trending blogging category. How-to blogs and vlogs are excellent marketing tools to engage viewers.

  Sephora's, (beauty products) *YouTube* channel has over a million subscribers. Their videos show how to put on make-up for the "Smoky Eye," look, to "Holiday Party" make-up videos.

  Salesforce, and their affiliates have created thousands of video tutorials that show how to used their **CRM** (customer relationship management) products, analytics, and social networking software.

  It doesn't matter what you are selling, it is likely you can show your target markets how to use your product or service. How-to blogs and vlogs are also great customer relations tools, to offer solutions to recurring problems your customers encounter.

- **Bizarre**—Get creative! Think outside the normal blog types, and create something truly unique. An environmentally-friendly construction company has a "Built It From Trash," blog, with stories and pictures of fantastic buildings and furniture they made, or built by others, from garbage. Another example is *Blendtec*, a line of food blenders. Their unique version of a vlog, "*Will It Blend,*" has become its own internet series. CEO, Tom Dickson, blends bizarre requests from an online poll, such as blending phosphorous light sticks with *Coke*.

- **User-Generated Blogs** and Forums—**user forums** must be heavily marketed to attract users, and moderated for quality control, and therefore are better suited for commercial blogs, like *Reddit*, or *Buzzfeed*.

  Creating a user-upload sharing platform related to your offering, is an excellent onsite blog/vlog alternative to developing and moderating a user forum. Not only can you upload pictures or favorable comments from customers, but visitors to your blog can too! You can also SMM great content uploaded by users. Tell all your followers about the great new upload just added to your website blog, even tout the **original poster** (**OP**) by name with the @ symbol—

@OPname—as they are more likely to retweet, share, or repost your SMM about their upload to your blog.

Does your offering have anything to do with travel, occasions, or *experiences*, like vacations, weddings, sailing, or live cooking classes? Instead of a traditional blog, put up a guestbook, for your customers to upload their pictures and videos of their experience with your offerings. Or, encourage potential customers to upload their images and thoughts related to your offerings, company, and industry.

As with user forums, onsite user-generated blogs require an administrator. The admin reaches out to customers and encourages them to post their experience with the company's offering on the blog web page. The admin must market the blog on social media, as well as create UX campaigns that encourages site engagement, such as contests for best uploads, with a valuable incentive for the winners. It is the admin's job to make sure everything uploaded to the blog is 'clean,' and doesn't offend anyone. And don't forget, they must SMM great uploaded content, and give credit to the OP.

While you don't need to produce your own content for your company's user-generated blog, be aware that it still requires a LOT of work to market and solicit user engagement.

Onsite Blogging for Engagement
A weekly blog post related to your offerings, company, or industry, on your

website increases your SEO ranking. It gives you *content* to SMM, and becomes an integral part of your ongoing marketing efforts. Knowledgeable posts brand your business as an authority in your industry. Visitors to your blogs/vlogs increase your website engagement, which therefore increase your retention rates (keeping the customers you have), and conversion rates (buy; try; subscribe).

Website Contact Pages

While the elements of a **CONTACT** page may seem obvious, there are components that make these pages more (or less) effective at generating response. We *want* people to reach out to us, show interest, ask us questions about our offerings and company!

• First, give website visitors a *reason* why they should contact your company. Have one-click buttons for Product information; Request a demo; Customer service forms. You'll get the greatest response by targeting viewer's desires and issues directly. *Targeted* reasons means: *"We're here to help you solve your specific X-problem."*

• The CTA on a contact page is to motivate visitors to contact your company. *"Let us help you find exactly what you want."* *"Tell us your story, and why you're reaching out today."* Be sure to include a comment box for visitors to express themselves on your contact page!

• Always use a fill-in form on your contact page. Do not publish any personal or employee email addresses. Use only corporate email addresses, such as info@yourcompany.com. A contact form will reduce phishing spam emails, and limit most responses to those interested in communicating with your company directly. Best of all, a contact form gathers email addresses to use for email marketing campaigns down the line.

• If you can afford it, put live chat on your contact page, and/or every web page of your site, to motivate potential customers into paying clients.

• Include your company address, or city location if the only address you have for your company is your home's garage, or dining room table. Do NOT put your personal home address on any marketing material, ever. You may include your phone number, but a toll-free number is always more professional, and therefore recommended. You may choose not to include a phone number, which is fine, however, you must provide a corporate email address with your company name: contact@yourcompany.com.

Do NOT use a free email service, like *Outlook* or *Gmail*. Having a corporate email with a free service looks unprofessional: yourcompany@gmail.com. There are free email services, like *Zoho*, that will use your 2LD name without adding their name to your corporate URL. Your webhost should also provides free corporate email addresses for any given URL.

- Include links to your company's active social media profile pages, such as *Twitter, Facebook, LinkedIn,* to give visitors a way to engage with your business on social platforms.

- After the visitor has filled in, and sent the contact form, redirect them to a thank-you page that explains when and why you'll be contacting them in the future. Include a CTA to keep them engaged with the site, such as, *"Check out our latest blog entry."*

Branding Beyond Websites

The branding process began with giving your productized offering, and startup, names, and a 'voice' with taglines, then creating 'faces,' with product and corporate identities. In this module, we've examined the second phase of the startup branding process—creating and publishing your website, effectively developing and producing your storefront, which house your valuable offerings.

Send viewers of your marketing campaigns to your website for more information, or for special offers, to more effectively funnel them through the conversion process. Having your corporate website URL on most all of your marketing material makes your company look professional, established, even though you may be just starting up. It gives visitors who are legitimately interested in what you have to offer, a place to find out more about your company.

Your startup should have a complete corporate website before beginning the third phase of the branding process—creating digital and print advertising and marketing campaigns. Beyond creating and continually updating your website, you must produce marketing material throughout the life cycle of your business for it to thrive. Next, we explore some typical digital marketing vehicles, such as landing pages, microsites, video advertising, and **PPC (pay-per-click)** campaigns. We'll drill down on *process*—precisely how to create these marketing campaigns, for your new venture.

STOP! Do PROJECT #3 before moving on.

◆◆◆

LSB Workbook 2: PROJECT #3
Your Corporate WEBSITE

1. **HAND-DRAW THUMBNAILS** of your projected hierarchy, aka, a **SITEMAP of your corporate website**. Produce **thumbnails** for *each page* showing the placement of images, headlines, text, CTAs, and logos. Adhere to **layout** and **eye-tracking** best practices! *Remember*, website design is dictated by the *function* (as with many SaaS products), or *content* of your offering/s. **Thumbnail sitemaps** should include [at least] the five (5) website pages listed below, where applicable:
   - **Homepage** (May be the *interactive* UI of your SaaS product, as in the ride-sharing app, *Lift*; or a media platform, like *The Huffington Post.*)
   - **About page**
   - **Products or Services page/s** (plus **e-commerce cart and checkout pages** if selling directly on your company website.)
   - **Contact page**
   - **Blog**

2. **Website Design & Production**
   Use *Wix.com*, or *Wordpress.com,* to **create your startup's website online** (or any other software you choose that allows you to put up a free site using **templates**, if you don't want to build your site with code). Sure, you can hire someone to design a site for you. But walking the process of producing your **website**, by following the steps in this **Branding Workbook**, will give you insight to direct those your hire to efficiently create a responsive, flexible **corporate website** that professionally and effectively promotes and sells your company's offerings and **brand**.
   - **Produce [at least] five (5) pages of your corporate website online:**
     1. Homepage
     2. About page
     3. Products or Services page/s
     5. Contact page
     5. Blog

   Use **visual content** from your **Content Libraries**, and pull reproduction-quality images and video related to your offering and company. Write a **headline**, **subhead** (and **bodycopy** if applicable), and a **CTA** for *every page* of your website utilizing keywords and phrases from your Productization lists.

   Wordpress.com has many free templates to build your site. *"How to Create a Business Website"* is a video tutorial that will teach you, step-by-step, how to populate one of their business template with *your* words and imagery: https://yoursiteon.wordpress(dot)com.

   Wix, Weebly, and others, also offer free tutorials on working with many of their templates as well.

BEFORE PUBLISHING ONLINE, have someone, preferably *many* people, **proofread** your website, *page for page!* (If you are unclear how to create **copy** that coverts from the **keywords** and **phrases** in your **Productization lists**, you may want to wait to publish your website online until after reading the Copywriting Module of LSL Workbook 3.)

◆◆◆

PPC, CPC, CPM...etc.
Beyond our website, another digital marketing tool we utilize to get the word out about our great new offering is PPC (pay per click) advertising. When we buy virtual ad 'space' on a platform like *Facebook, LinkedIn,* or other affiliate sites, the web page our ad appears on is SMM (social media marketing) our campaign for an agreed upon *'price per click,'* or *'view.'*

Imagery will get our PPC campaigns noticed, but using video instead of pictures often engages viewers beyond just a glance. Additionally, beyond PPC advertising, and video marketing campaigns, creating landing pages, microsites, SMM campaigns that you post on your profile pages on social media platforms, are all part of the ongoing marketing you will need to consistently produce.

Marketing on the digital landscape is essential to any business today, to build brand awareness, and become a sustainable company. You must begin, and grow an online presence, to reach your target markets where they likely hang out, and then sell them on your offering/s.

Digital marketing is often free, or inexpensive to produce and publish, especially with extensive Visual Libraries and Productization lists that relate directly and indirectly to your offering/s and company. Additionally, the internet has enormous reach. Today, most nations on the planet are connected to the web.

On the downside, because it's free, or cheap to blast digital campaigns on almost every web page, every *YouTube* channel...etc, *everyone* is marketing online. Effective digital marketing campaigns, that actually convert or sell the viewers, takes creative thinking, and time to create.

Like any marketing you create for your business, digital campaigns have their own set of parameters—formats, established protocols, best practices—to adhere to when creating for the digital landscape we use today. We examine these standards, as well as the good, bad, and utility of digital marketing campaigns, next.

◆◆◆◆◆

MODULE 21: DIGITAL CAMPAIGNS

As previously discussed in Module 18: Online Marketing, there are many types of digital marketing campaigns. Don't worry about choosing which one to employ. You'll eventually use all of them, and hopefully many other creative marketing efforts as well, throughout the life cycle of your business.

Digital marketing is trending as a cost effective way to brand, and even sell your offerings, but by no means is it the *only* way to market your new venture. Live, in-person networking is still the most effective marketing method to date.

Successful digital campaigns, like all **effective marketing, sells features and benefits of your offering, to fulfill a desire of a specific group of people**. But even assuming you do this exactly—put your offering's fantastic UVPs in the headline, add an enticing CTA incentive to the campaign, and launch it online directly to your target customer—there are so many campaigns online now, it's hard to get noticed at all. Response rates to our digital marketing efforts are notoriously low. The ROI is particularly poor, especially since creating a digital campaign takes the same amount of time to produce and publish as traditional marketing vehicles, like print, or PR campaigns.

Since digital marketing is trending, and startups must use traditional *and* trending marketing methods, it is necessary we examine some online advertising tools. Regardless of the low ROI, striking digital campaigns will help you *brand* and promote your business, at little to no monetary cost, for pre-launch, launch, and beyond.

-Paid (and Free) Digital Advertising-

As previously mentioned, digital campaigns have notoriously low conversion rates. They may indeed get higher **CTR—Click Through Rates** (Clicks ÷ Impressions= CTR), but have very low actual *conversion*—people buying, trying, signing up, or subscribing, from a digital ad campaign. It's no wonder. We are bombarded by advertising with almost every web page we visit today.

To complicate matters, the ROI on our digital campaigns will likely remain low with hackers trying to game the digital landscape. *Click farms* execute a form of click fraud. Large groups of low-paid workers, generally operating out of developing countries, are paid to click on the CTA of digital ads, because the *click-farm master* or *farm owner* makes money with every click, i.e. **PPC: pay-per-click** advertising.

Evil companies hire *farm masters* to deplete the advertising budget of their competition. They put ads on the same targeted websites as their competitors. They pay a low **cost-per-click** (**CPC**) rate, to jack up the page ranking of the site, forcing legitimate advertisers to pay a higher CPC rate to have their marketing on that targeted website. Additionally, when *click-farm* workers click on an ad, the money lost by the advertiser through the fake clicks is gained by the *farm master*, rather than by the affiliate network the advertiser paid for the space.

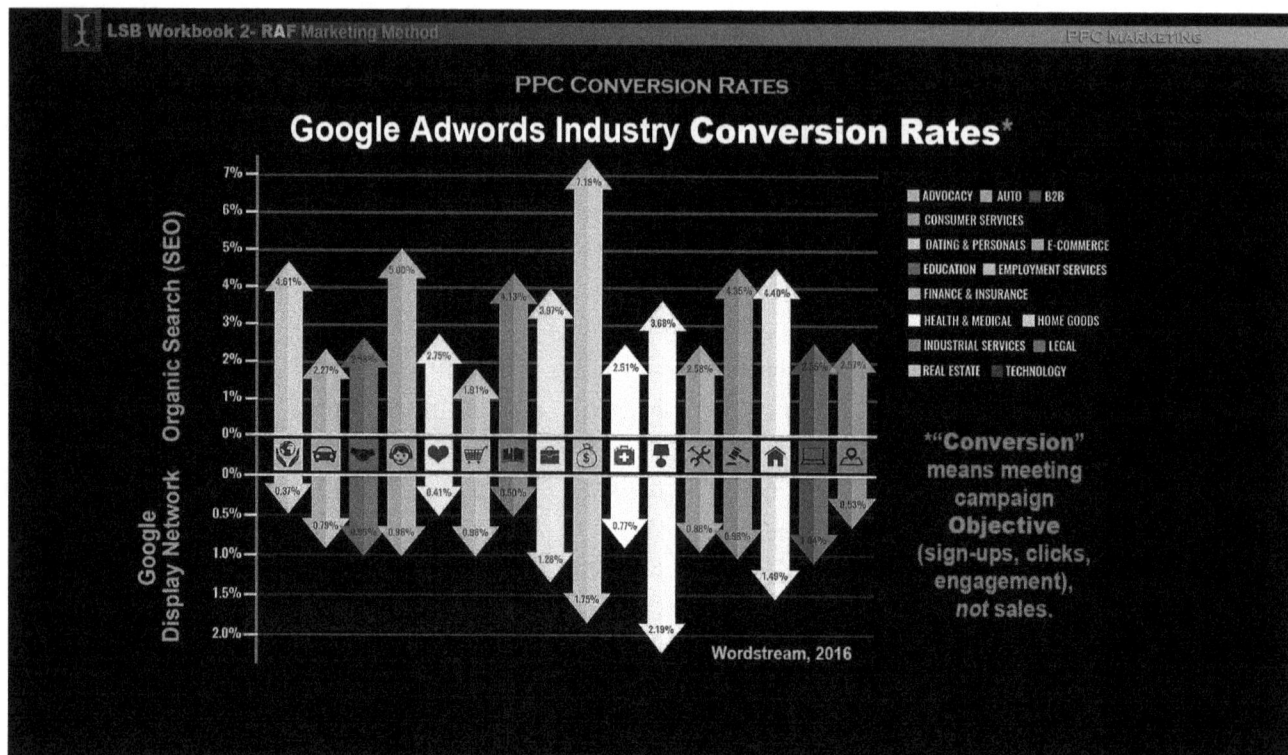

The overarching message here is *beware* of investing a lot of money upfront for paid digital marketing campaigns. You don't need *Facebook* advertising to launch or market your company. You can publish your click-display advertising on every social media site out there for free. Put up profile pages for your company on targeted social platforms, and you have a 'space' to put your click-display ads—on your timelines and feeds—without the cost of PPC. You can even target your ads to specific user types when you post your click ads on group forums aligned with your offering and industry.

Are you selling 'enterprise software,' maybe a business application, or CRM (customer relationship management) system? There's a ton of groups for that on *LinkedIn*, *Meetup*, and other social platforms, where you can publish your ad campaigns, assuming you create ads that invite engagement rather than viewed as spam. (We'll drill down on setting up effective profile pages, how to get targeted followers to your pages, and when and what to post on your timelines/feeds in LSL Workbook 3: Launch.)

Drowning in Acronyms

Every industry has its own colloquialisms. Learning any job function, you'll likely have to learn the *language* of that industry as well. Throughout all three Lean Startup Workbooks, I've put words and phrased in **bold type** again and again, to plant these words and expressions in your mind, and get you familiar with the *language* of traditional and digital marketing.

Marketing, and technology industries are particularly egregious when it comes to using acronyms. There are many acronyms to describe different types of PPC ad campaigns. Here are a few that are commonly used:

- **CPC: Cost Per Click**, aka **PPC: Pay Per Click**: Price advertisers pay every time somebody clicks on their online ads.

- **CPM: Cost Per Thousands Impressions**: Cost of 1,000 'views' of an ad on a website. (This is bullshit. Don't pay for it! Research shows that this model has little to *no* ROI.)

- **CPA: Cost Per Acquisition**: Price advertiser pays for each conversion—engagement (Likes/Shares), clicks, fill-in forms, downloads...etc.

- **RON: Run of Network**: Ad campaign is put on a ton of websites (that likely have nothing to do with your offering). Advertiser does *not* get to choose targeting.*

- **ROC: Run Of Channel**: Online campaigns run on multiple channels, such as websites, blogs and vlogs, of a specific publisher. Advertiser does *not* get to choose targeting.*

- **ROS: Run Of Site**: Ad campaign runs on every page of a given website. Advertiser does *not* get to choose targeting.*

- **RTB: Real-Time Bidding**: Real-time auction selling (and buying) online ad impressions during the time a web page takes to load.

*Effective marketing sells features and benefits of your offering that fulfill a desire of a <u>specific target audience</u>. The ROI with these PPC ad campaigns is absurdly low, because they are not really targeted at all. *Facebook* and *Google* will offer some targeting with certain campaign types, but these are very broad markets, and are likely not targeting your mark. Generally, PPC campaigns with no targeting are large retailers trying to get rid of overstocked items no one wanted, and they are trying to *find* their markets.

PPC= Affiliate Marketing

PPC Advertising is a form of affiliate marketing, as examined in Profit Models in LSM Workbook 1. For PPC campaigns to get any traction at all, yet alone, *conversion*, *you* should be picking your target markets—the affiliate websites, blogs, videos and other online networks your ads will appear. You should know who the potential target customers for your offering are by now, from the Productization lists of target markets and users you produced in LSM Workbook 1.

If you choose to run paid PPC ad campaigns, there are many types of Cost-Per-Click (CPC)-type advertising vehicles. Each has their own strengths and weaknesses, however, most require the same components to motivate response.

- **Search Marketing**—*Google Adwords; Bing Ads; YouTube; Google Display Network (GDN)*

Search CPC campaigns are text ads that appear on the top of search return results. These ads have keywords known to solicit response, that are (generally) purchased with a bidding system, through an affiliate marketer.

They have the word "Ad" in a box next to the link, which is how we know they are not 'organic,' but paid search returns.

Do Search Marketing text ads work? Oddly, they do, if your ad has keywords and messaging that apply directly to the search term. You won't get the response with Search Marketing you'll likely get with live networking, or even print campaigns, but this digital marketing venue is meant to attract potential target markets already interested in what you have, as they were searching for something similar, when the search engine returned your text ad, on top of its other link returns.

Search Marketing ad components: Headline with keywords; Subhead copy with keywords; CTA that links to a website, or a landing page campaign.

- **Shopping Ads**—*Google; Bing; Yahoo; Amazon*
Small product display ads, generally consumer products, that come up on the right side of the list of search returns, or appear under the SHOP or SHOPPING tab of the search interface.

Shopping ad components: Product image; keyword headline; price, ratings, incentives (if applicable); CTA *link* (not button) to website or landing page.

- **Native Display Ads on Social and Affiliate Networks**—*Facebook, LinkedIn; Twitter; YouTube; Google Display Network (GDN); Amazon...etc.*
Text only, to full display advertisements, with images and CTA buttons. *Google,* and other affiliate networks partner with high-traffic websites, videos, and blogs, that (ostensibly) have content related to your offerings, to display your ads on these targeted sites. You may target many of your display campaigns through these affiliate networks.

Run of Site (ROS) ads show only one advertiser on any given web page on a website. Banner ads, skyscraper ads (on the side of the page), in-feed display ads, even the text ads are all only one advertiser on the website. The advantage to this is obvious, as you are the only advertiser, you've got no competition for viewer's attention.

Native Display ad components: Image and/or video; Headline with keywords; Subhead with keywords; CTA with button that links to a website, or a landing page campaign.

- **Responsive ads**—digital ads that automatically adjust their size, appearance, and format to fit the space the ad appears. While affiliate networks sell the perception that these ads 'transform,' to better blend with the web page content on which your ad appears, that's bullshit. The ad simply adjusts to the space it has to fit. If you've designed a display ad, but the affiliate website or blog your ad is shown on only has space for a text ad, then the affiliate network will eliminate the image, and your ad will *only* show your text and CTA, which is turned to a text link, as it will not display even button images.

Responsive ad components: Image and/or video; Headline with keywords; Subhead with keywords; CTA with button, as well as just a link that takes visitors to a website, or a landing page campaign.

- **Remarketing Ads**—*Adroll; Google Adwords Retargeting*
  Text to display ads, that are targeted to potential customers based on their previous online behavior. If a visitor to your site leaves before doing anything but looking, you can get your PPC ad placed on other sites they visit to reignite their initial interest in your company. The ROI with remarketing ads is growing rather substantially. Someone who visited your site, or a site *like* yours, will be more interested in what you are selling. The problem has been accurately tracking, correlating, and assessing behavior. Until now.

  Today, with billions of users online daily, marketers are tracking user behavior more precisely than ever. And we're correlating all this data to find out what you, your family, your friends, and friends of friends are doing to tightly target market to *you*. It's likely you'll buy, read, watch, *do*, what the people in your life, and people similar to you, do. (We'll examine recommendation and correlation engines in LSL Workbook 3.)

<u>Remarketing ad components</u>: Image and/or video; Headline with keywords; Subhead with keywords; CTA with button that links to a website, or a landing page campaign.

Types of PPC Advertising

One or more display ad types may be employed per any given ad campaign. Listed below are some display ad formats for websites, blogs, and other online media platforms. We'll review video ad formats in Video Marketing, next.)

- **Standard**—Typical square, skyscraper, or banner ads, usually on the right side, and/or top of a web page.

- **In-Feed**—ads that appear inside the content of a blog article or website page with similar content or context.

- **Expandable**—ads go from standard to larger sizes, or may even display a video, directly when landing on the web page, or after a moment's delay.

- **Interstitial**—a full page ad (or pop-up) that appears before the expected web page content.

- **Sticky ads**—banner ads, and typical display ads, that 'stick' to a fixed position on the screen regardless of where the viewer scrolls to on the web page.

- **Pop-up**—ads that pop-up the moment you get to a site, or moments to minutes after you are on the site, like when reading a blog post and a pop-up appears.

- **Pop-under**—ads appear behind the main browser window, generally in the bottom left corner of your screen.

- **Reveal**—ads that block part or all of the content of the intended site, and you have to watch part of a video or interact with the ad, even to remove it, to advance to the web page.

- **Exit-intent**—ads that pop-up when the mouse movement predicts the visitor is leaving the web page.

- **Slide-in**—ads that slide in from the top, side or bottom of a web page directly upon landing, or moments after landing on the web page.

- **Mouse-over**—ads that pop-up when visitor mouses over specific words or images on a web page.

- **Background**—ads that replace the background image on a website.

- **Footerbar**—customizable banner ads at the bottom of a web page.

PPC/CPC Advertising Best Practices

PPC In-Feed Display advertisements are designed to fit in social media feeds, aka 'timelines,' of the platform they appear. *LinkedIn's* PPC display ad format is a different size than *Facebook's* platform offers. In-feed Native ads (paid platform PPC ads) adjust to the social media feed format the ad appears on. The word "Promoted," or "Sponsored," in small type usually appears somewhere on the ad to show it a paid ad.

This is *Lean* Startup Marketing, with the emphasis on LEAN. PPC advertising cost money, often with little ROI for anyone but the platform serving up the ads. Be smart with your marketing budget! Sure, you can pay *Facebook* to promote your ad, but you can begin by promoting your company, and its offerings yourself, for free! Attract potential customers with your PPC ads by posting them on your social media profile feeds. We will extensively examine social media marketing (SMM)—building a following of potential and existing customers for your offerings and brand, in LSL Workbook 3.

Paying to publish your PPC ads through an affiliate network, or posting 'click' display ads on your company's profile feeds (that you'll learn to create, and populate with the *right* followers), requires adhering to proven techniques to garner the greatest conversion with your online click advertising efforts.

- First, identify the OBJECTIVE of your ad campaign. Use only ONE objective per campaign. Any more than ONE will confuse the viewer as to *what* specific action you want them to take. *Remember your brand* (with an awareness campaign). *Get more clicks on your PPC ad. Get newsletter sign-ups* (from your landing page campaign). *Sell your consulting services. Get trial downloads of your software.* These are all common **objectives** in traditional and digital marketing efforts. DO NOT use more than ONE objective *per campaign* to motivate a specific action by the viewer.

- Next, identify the type of PPC ads needed—*Display; Text only; In-feed; Pre/Mid/Post-roll video,* or the full array for the greatest impact with each campaign.

- Identify the best platforms to reach your projected target audience—*Facebook; Instagram; Google Display Network...etc.*

- Text to Display ads should deliver only ONE clear, *valuable* message, and have a clear CTA that pays off the headline, for best ROI (and fewer bad clicks).

- Make the ad's headline the campaign offer, or USP (unique selling proposition) for greatest conversion. A temporary price cut incentive campaign for a lighting store may headline: "20% Off All Desk Lamps, Oct 12 – 14," effectively making the headline and campaign offer one and the same.

- Display ads should include a clickable image or video to increase engagement.

- SHOW (don't SELL) your offering. *Show* your product or service being used, enjoyed, and/or appreciated (where applicable).

- Corporate identity must be somewhere on the ad. Logo or full I.D. should be a clickable link to the same web page the CTA of the campaign takes viewers.

- Use 'social proof'—reviews, ratings, testimonials, number of users, and/or high-profile users—to support your campaign messaging.

- Offer a guarantee to win trust and reduce the viewer's risk in clicking on the CTA. The perception we are not making a *permanent* commitment, or giving away, or access to, our personal information, helps us jump the internal hurdles that prevent us from taking an action, like clicking on a link.

- A/B test headlines, CTAs, colors, images, and incentive offers for optimal conversion per campaign. (We'll examine the A/B testing process in LSL Workbook 3.)

- Track the results of each campaign. Paying *Google* or *Facebook* for your PPC ad campaigns, or posting your click advertising on your *Twitter* feed, most any platform or affiliate network will offer you analytic results. But *beware*, you generally need thousands of data points, known as 'events' in data science, and know how to correlate them, for meaningful results that will help you guide your future campaigns for greater response.

Use the bullet points listed above to ensure you are creating digital ad campaigns that maximize conversion with each click campaign you publish.

Whether purchasing keywords for your search marketing campaign, or posting your own display ads on your company's social feeds, digital advertising is a dynamic marketing tool, in constant flux. Research the latest trends in digital marketing, new formats and interactive techniques that may effectively promote your business. Put your company's online campaigns *on the cusp* of a trending platform to realize the greatest ROI with your digital marketing efforts.

Motion Attracts Attention

In any digital display, or print advertising campaign, your most powerful attractor will be the visual component in your marketing efforts. Great imagery is essential to commanding attention, especially with all the other visual marketing we are bombarded with daily. We've examine what makes an image arresting, and [wisely] you've began a lean Visual Library of attention-grabbing imagery to use in your marketing efforts, as reviewed in Module 17 of this Branding workbook.

In many cases, the ad format restricts the type of imagery we can use in our ad campaigns. As discussed, *GDN* (*Google Display Network*) will adjust your ad size, *and* components—take out video, pictures, even link buttons—to accommodate whatever space is available on the web pages it sticks your PPC ads on.

Most digital formats now support still images like photos and illustrations, so we want to use them whenever possible. Include them in your PPC campaigns, with strong headlines that immediately *demonstrate value* to your target audience. These headlines will have to motivate clicking on the CTA with or without your imagery. Remember, *Google*, or any other affiliate network, strips out your visual components where applicable to accommodate their affiliate platforms, or search engine's text only requirement.

While powerful imagery is good for getting attention, moving imagery, like animation, or video is even better! Video Marketing is next.

STOP! Do PROJECT #4 before moving on.

◆◆◆

LSB Workbook 2: PROJECT #4
PPC/SMM Pre-Launch Advertising Campaign

To actually reach anyone today, you must *begin* your startup's marketing process with an intimate knowledge of your offering *and* its target markets (LSM Workbook 1: Get Ready and Productize Your Offering). A billion people may 'view' your **PPC ad** on their social feeds, but it's likely they never actually *saw* it while they were fast swiping their mobile screen looking for whatever it is they came on that web page for. You need digital marketing that grabs attention, *and* gets viewers of your campaigns to *act* on your CTAs.

Even if you do not use the **PPC/SMM campaigns** you create in this project, you'll gain insight to more effectively and efficiently direct those you hire to create campaigns that *brand*, and *convert* your target audiences to buy, try or subscribe. Additionally, you will be able to provide visual representations of what you'd like those you hire to produce for your startup marketing efforts—in other words, *show* them exactly what you want.

1. Define an OBJECTIVE for your initial **pre-launch** PPC/SMM Branding campaign. You've got nothing to sell yet, as you've not launched your startup, or any of its offerings. Remember, this is your first pre-launch campaign.

Think: *'Coming Soon,'* campaign, but it can be anything you want. Do a branding campaign to build awareness of your upcoming offering, with a packaging or screen shot *reveal* of your latest video game. See how many *downloads* you can garner for a trial of a *portion* of your offering to come (that is quality-tested, stable, and functions as promised). Get *subscribers* to your company's blog, or newsletter, or push alerts. Create a *'Learn More'* campaign that links viewers to your corporate website. These are all typical pre-launch campaign types. For the best conversion rates, be sure to link your ad's CTA to a landing page or website that fulfills the **objective** of each marketing effort.

2. **HAND-DRAW THUMBNAIL** sketches of your initial pre-launch PPC/SMM Branding campaign in the general proportions your ads will likely appear on the digital landscape. If you are designing ads for your company's *Facebook* timeline, great! Now, *be sure* the ad fits the space you must fill. Too small, or cut off content looks unprofessional. Always design within the [general] *space* your campaigns will appear.

Adhere to **layout** and **eye-tracking** best practices! Use the **imagery** from your **Visual Libraries** for **idea generation**. Using **keywords** and **phrases**, google to find additional imagery that reflect your offering (from your Productization lists) to create professional-quality PPC/SMM ads that get clicks. (You want *engagement* with your marketing efforts—viewers taking the *action* your CTAs direct, or imply—as in simply *remembering* your brand.)

3. **Produce PPC/SMM Campaign**
   • **Create and digitally produce** [at least] **seven PPC/SMM full Display ads** for your company's pre-launch, digital Branding campaign. Each ad should have a *unique* **image**, **headline**, and **direct CTA** that *rigorously* adheres to the campaign's OBJECTIVE.

If you are going to buy PPC ad space from an affiliate network, like *Google Adwords*, you likely don't need to hire a graphic designer to produce your digital campaign. Reputable affiliate publishers provide templates of the elements needed for them to 'fit' your ads into the space available on most of their affiliate sites. The typical elements, or components of most **Native ad campaigns** are: **Image**; **Headline**; **Subhead** (descriptive copy with a strict character limit); **CTA** (usually **direct CTA**: buy; try; see more; subscribe). These are also the typical ad components of most any **SMM 'click' advertising**.

If you are self-publishing, i.e. social media marketing (SMM), your initial pre-launch Branding **'click' campaign**, identify the *space*—size and format requirements—of each online publisher's platform *before* beginning the digital production process. If you plan to post your SMM 'click' ads on specific *LinkedIn* groups, be sure your ads fit the group's feed! Design the ads in a standard **desktop publishing program**, like *Microsoft Word* or *InDesign*. Use (or supply to those you hire), **reproduction-quality images** from your **Visual Libraries** in your PPC and SMM 'click' campaigns.

When your pre-launch Branding 'click' campaign is of professional-quality, post each of the seven SMM ads, *one at a time*, over the course of a few days to weeks, *before* the official launch your startup. Be sure each ad in your campaign appears multiple times on websites and platforms where your projected target audiences are likely to see it.

Headlines should reflect the USP (unique selling position) of this *specific* pre-launch Branding campaign. Use clear, *specific* direct CTAs that lead viewers to click. Remember, on some web pages and search platforms your 'click' ads may appear as 'text only' ads, *without* images, or even CTA *buttons*. Effective copy becomes critical with PPC/SMM campaigns. We'll carefully examine Copywriting best practices for social media marketing (SMM) in the Copywriting Module of LSL Workbook 3.

◆◆◆

-Video Marketing-

While working with still imagery in our ad campaigns increases engagement over text ads, working with **VIDEO** is even more effective at garnering attention. According to stats from *YouTube* (2017), they have over a billion users, who watch over three billion hours of *YouTube* monthly. According to data from *Facebook*, more than 50% of people who visit their site in the U.S. watch at least one video a day.

Video advertising is growing, fast! And it should. Real life happens in *real time*. Pictures speak louder than words, and scenes unfolding in real time get attention and increase engagement, making it more likely we'll click on the CTA.

Facebook predicts the number of video posts per person will continue to increase substantially, meaning you're competing with a lot of other videos on *Facebook*, and everywhere else you can post videos. So, how do you create videos that grab attention, and keeps viewers watching, then motivates them to click on your CTAs?

Video Marketing Best Practices

It is very important that your videos are *instantly* visually and verbally striking. We achieve this in a variety of ways we'll review next, but, first, let's review some video marketing best practices to create video campaigns that builds brand awareness, and sells your productized offerings.

- First, be entertaining. If your video is *not* entertaining, it won't get attention. Entertainment can mean many things. Flashes of colors, lightning striking, a car crashing, kissing, pets or kids doing cute things—high impact visuals that command our attention.

- Deliver ONE clear, valuable message to a specific target audience throughout the video.

- Limit video length from 5 to 60 seconds, depending on the type of video— promotional; how-to; branding—and the **objective** (buy; try; subscribe) of the campaign.

- Limit the number of words in your script to (generally) between 120 – 150 words *per minute*, to keep voice over, or dialog natural. Script no more than 3 words *a second*.

- Speak directly to your target audience. *Personalize* your message by scripting, "You; Your," and talking directly to your targets. Address *their issues*, in their tone of voice and use of language, and show your offering's solution.

- Show/Sell your message with *and* without sound. Video marketing should be much more visual than verbal, since a lot of people watch videos without sound. When using sound, beyond **voice overs** (**VO**), use sound to enhance the user experience (UX), such as soda hitting ice, or music in the background of the VO.

- Show the product, or service being used, and repeat its name several times throughout the video.

  State, and *show* the location of a brick and mortar business. Pictures of your storefront are great for getting local recognition when you target your marketing efforts at the community of your business location.

  Selling a consumer item, you can show how the offering is used, or is consumed. However, selling SaaS, showing complex, or even simple software services becomes a bit more challenging. When creating videos for SaaS offerings, focus your content on the *solutions your software service provides*, i.e. the software will make your business more profitable. It'll save you time and money. It'll add fun to your day, or life...etc.

- Storyboard and script video *before* beginning production. We'll review effective video scripting techniques in LSL Workbook 3.

- **A/B [Split] test** your video campaigns. Create a variety of videos *with the same campaign message* by altering ONE element or component in the video campaign, such as the VO, the background music, the CTA message or button color. Show each video to a *limited* target audience. Track which video in that campaign got the best response, and reuse this video to your full target audience. (We'll drill down on A/B testing in LSL Workbook 3.)

Categories of Video Marketing Campaigns

There is so much video online now, we really need to capture people's attention in the first 24 frames of the video, or first *second* of viewing, and a talking head just isn't going to do this, unless the words, or the person's face, is striking.

All video marketing *should*:
   1. **Captivate/Entertain**
   2. **Inform.**
   3. **Engage viewer to ACT.**

When developing a video campaign, first determine what category of campaign will deliver your message effectively, and will instantly engage your target audience. Let's begin by examining the three basic types of video campaigns to consider when implementing any video marketing effort.

- **Video COMMERCIALS**: 10 to 30 seconds of video that (typically) follow yesterday's paradigm of television commercials, shown before, in the middle, and after a TV show. Video commercials are typically used for branding, but can also be used for direct incentive selling, such as a sale or special offer.

- **Video ADVERTISING**: 5 to 25 second video 'clips,' that show and sell the campaign message—the best UVP (Unique Value Proposition), and incentive CTA, to motivate an action by the viewer. Video advertising should sell a specific offering with an incentive for *immediate* action. Include ONE direct CTA (see more; try; buy; subscribe) at the end of the video, or throughout, as a clickable link in a corner of your video as it plays. If you are creating a branding video, your CTA is implied, i.e. *remember my company*, and the video does not require a clickable link. We'll examine where to post your video ad campaigns, next.

- **PROMOTIONAL videos**: 15 to 60+ second videos that appear on your company website, and business *YouTube* channel. These are generally to showcase your offerings, and how to utilize them, sprinkled throughout your website to engage and inform visitors.

Complex offerings should be shown with videos, *not* text. Video is visual, and most people are visual learners.

Autodesk produces complicated CAD (computer-aided design) drawing systems. Their software is complex, so *Autodesk* wisely designed their website with product demo videos, showing how their software products works, and what each complex program they offer can do.

- **INFORMERCIALS**—long-form video, typically 30 or 60 *minutes*. Known as *Direct Response Television* (DRTV) commercials, these long-form videos ask viewers to respond directly to the company by calling an 800 number, or visiting a website. They generally run at 2:00 – 6:00 a.m., because air time is less expensive at these early morning hours, when most of us are sleeping. *"Get Rich with Real Estate,"* infomercials are typical DRTVs.

Video Marketing Content

Video marketing uses an array of storytelling techniques, regardless of the category you choose to employ, to sell any given offering, or brand a company. 'How-to' videos are generally promotional videos, that show viewers how to best utilize your product or service.

No need to stress on which video content style is best. You'll likely apply them all, many times over, throughout the life cycle of marketing your business.

- **Talking Head**—We see these constantly because they are cheap to produce, but how many of us sit through them? The actor better be trending famous (not some old has-been), or the spokesperson looks amazingly stunning, or bizarre, or the first sentence out of their mouth is strikingly captivating to garner our attention these days.

- **Slice of Life**—The car manufacturer *Suburu*, shows a child putting his soccer equipment in the car, while the VO talks about the stages of growing up. The VO isn't strictly necessary. The video shows the boy grow to a man, while interacting with the *Suburu* in their driveway. Last scene, the grown teen is driving off to college in the family car. The message is clear: *Suburu produces safe vehicles you can trust to last over time.*

  A **slice of life story** is an effective marketing approach for branding, but they often take time to communicate the message effectively. And, they better open with something pretty dramatic, heart-felt, attention-grabbing, or you're not going to keep anyone watching.

- **Mixed-Media**—combining animation with live action is interesting, but it's expensive, and generally not worth the cost of producing this type of video campaign for a startup launch. If you are a graphic designer, or particularly adept at creating CGI (digital FX), go for it, but be careful of spending too much time creating 'art,' when you should focus your time on producing marketing.

- **Artsy**, or **Off-World**—like mixed-media, artsy videos are expensive to produce, and generally do not give the greatest ROI for the cost involved in putting these types of videos together. If you decide to create a new world to showcase your offerings, be sure it is a high-contrast world, with imagery that pops. (Often, off-world illustration is soft or slightly blurry.)

- **Kinetic Type**—animated text that shows the video script's *words*, literally, displays them in moving type. Kinetic type is an excellent design choice that grabs attention quickly, and gets your messaging read (and heard if sound is on). It is inexpensive to produce, eliminating the cost of actors, sight locations, complex filming and extensive editing.

- **Jingles**—music is great for branding, with a catchy jingle. People will often sing a memorable tune. Regardless of the language, *good* jingles stick, resonate with us. (♫"I am stuck on Band-aid®, cuz Band-aid's stuck on me."♫)

Bad jingles may stick, but annoy the hell out of us. We may not *like* a jingle, such as the "♫ 1-800-Cars for Kids ♫" tune, but, in marketing terms, *remembering* it makes it a *good* jingle. Most of us find bad jingles annoying, and we'll turn off the sound, or click off the video to avoid listening to them. When creating jingles, have several people closest to your target audiences listen to it, to make sure it isn't annoying (unless that's what you're going for).

All advertising, video, or any other form of marketing, should play on people's emotions. The moment you trigger someone to become emotionally invested in any given campaign, you've greatly increased the likelihood they'll respond to your CTA, or recall your company's brand.

Branding, Advertising, or How-to videos, better demonstrate the UVP of the offering, or company's value, within those first 24 frames of video, or most of us are clicking "SKIP," when given the opportunity to do so.

Startup Lean

Full length, video commercials are generally expensive to produce. To present your company professionally, you'll likely need to hire a professional video production team, like *Suburu* does for their video commercials. This is LEAN Startup Marketing. I'm not suggesting you produce commercial videos out of the gate, or at this stage in your startup development.

I recommend developing more advertising 'clips' for early stage startups.

It is mandatory your company produce and consistently publish a wide array of Social Media Marketing (SMM) video campaigns to build your company's brand awareness, and even sell your offerings. Below are some typical types of SSM video campaigns trending today.

- **Company branding**—PR and *positive* press; company news, such as new clients, acquisitions, or growth figures; philanthropy, events and parties. Employee activities in the office, or for a cause, i.e. *'Run for leukemia'* or *'Habitat for Humanity.'*

  Now live is all the rage, so shoot a lot of live video clips of events, or even your company's work environment, and post them on *Facebook, LinkedIn, SnapChat, Instagram*, and every other place your target audience hangs out online.

- **Product marketing**—product upgrades, and new product releases; testimonial videos from satisfied customers of your offerings; incentive advertising campaigns—buy; try; play; download; subscribe. Product marketing is all about the unique value (UVP) of the products and services your company offers.

- **Tutorials**—How-To, or Tutorial videos are hugely popular. They are fantastic for lead generation, to get viewers to fill out a form with their name and email, before they can watch, or continue watching, or after viewing, to subscribe to your company's video channel.

  Educated/Demonstrate videos are probably the most popular video type today. Definitely trending, they are an excellent way to not only educate viewers, but to show how your offering, even your company's brand, can satisfy a desire, or solve their problem.

- **Startup launch** videos, generally take 10 – 60+ seconds to promote your new company and offerings. These are branding videos. The only CTA (if any) is a fill-in form for more information, or click for more.

- **Customer Service**—another effective approach for retention of your customers and target audience is to create videos that address frequently asked questions, or provides solutions to customer issues as they arise, or a monthly video series.

- **Bizarre Series**—weekly competitions, games or polls; on the street interviews; wild, or weird, like the previously mentioned, *"Will It Blend,"* for *BlendTec* blenders. A clothing line could create video clips of *'fashion on the rest of us,'* with regular people on the street wearing high fashion clothing. THINK outside the box, and come up with a weekly series that solves a problem or fulfills a desire (even if just entertainment), of your specific target audiences.

Effective video series are generally used for branding. They are usually short clips, 1 to 5 *minutes* in length, and are directly or indirectly related to your offerings and company. For effective content marketing, the correlation between your series theme and your company's offerings should be clear.

- **Interactive**—this is new, upcoming, but here, a bit. Beyond a clickable CTA, you can allow viewers to interact with your video, like a video game, only it's video marketing! **Virtual Reality** (**VR**), aka **Augmented Reality** (**AR**) add images, clickable links, characters, such as the *Pokemon Go* game, and even full video content to our existing reality, in real time, through our mobile phones and tablets. Research "Interactive Video Marketing," for the latest on these amazing new marketing tools.

Video Marketing Formatting

So, you created some captivating videos for your website, landing pages, and for SMM on your social platforms. But how, and *where* do you post your video marketing campaigns to effectively reach your target audiences?

Much like PPC advertising, video marketing can be published through affiliate networks using the same PPC, CPC, keyword-type payment models. In other words, you pay *Google*, or *Facebook* to run your campaigns—you pay per click, or view, or whatever affiliate program you purchase.

The truth about social networking is you *can* do it yourself (DIY), for free. You, and other stakeholders in your new venture, can post your video marketing on your company's social media profile feeds. You can also post your video campaigns to online groups related to what your business does, and on sites directly or indirectly related to your offerings, company, and industry.

Through the Productization process in LSM Workbook 1, by now you should know *who*—what target markets and users—will find value, or a benefit in the features of your company's offerings. Sure, you can pay *Google*, or *YouTube* to target your video marketing to *their* idea of your potential target markets, but they get paid per click, regardless if *you* make any sales, or even meet your conversion goals.

Build thousands of the *right* followers on your company's social media profiles, and you can post your PPC advertising, and video marketing on your company's social media feeds. Your video campaigns will likely get equal to, or greater response, than leaving your targeting to the affiliate network's discretion.

If you choose to publish your video marketing campaigns through an affiliate network, below are some common, and trending types of video marketing formats that can be purchased from *YouTube*, *Vimeo*, and other popular blogs, vlogs, and frequently visited websites.

In-Stream video campaigns:
- **Pre-Roll**—5 to 24 second video that plays *before* the main video the viewer originally came to see. It is smart marketing to keep pre-roll videos to 5 seconds to deliver your full message, and a clickable CTA!

- **Mid-Roll**—aka **In-Feed**, the video ad *interrupts* the main content on others videos, vlogs, or even blogs. The video pops up, opens and plays within the text of a blog post.

- **Post-Roll**—video ad plays *after* the main video, usually with a direct CTA (buy; try; subscribe; call).

Video Display campaigns:
- **In-Banner**—video ads placed in the banner or sidebar of any given web page or platform, hopefully directly related to the content on the web page where the video is shown. These are generally small display ads, 300 x 250 pixels in size, but are full video display advertisements.

- **Sticky Video Slider** (trending)—video ad slides onto the web page, then fixes itself in the lower left or right corner, or right sidebar, and automatically plays. Sticky means the video display ad stays on the screen and continues to play, even as the viewer scrolls down the web page.

- **Interstitial**—[generally] display video ads that pop-up, and interrupts the intended content, forcing viewers to sit through the video ad before they can continue to visit their desired web page.

On top of posting your video marketing on video platforms, such as *YouTube* or *Vimeo*, you can also post video display advertising across global affiliate networks. Be sure to research which affiliate publishers work best for your needs and budget. But don't forget, you can post your video marketing campaigns on your company's social media profile pages for free! We'll examine how you can garner targeted followers for your new venture's social media pages way beyond any affiliate publisher in the Social Media Marketing module of LSL Workbook 3.

Posting Your Video Marketing

Assuming you don't yet have an extensive base of targeted followers, and want to gain some by paying affiliate networks to post your video marketing efforts, utilize the list below as a *starting point* in your research. New affiliate publishers are coming online all the time. New PPC/CPC programs from trending affiliates are continually being created to more effectively market our campaigns. *Do your research*, and find the best network of affiliate publishers for your marketing needs and budget!

- **Google Adwords for Video**—(part of *GDN)* keyword matches your content to millions of sites, blog, vlogs, and web pages with similar keywords in their content. This is a typical PPC model, and functions the same with video campaigns as with still imagery.

- **YouTube**—Pre-Roll, Mid-Roll, Post-Roll, and In-Banner Display video ad placement that [ostensibly] matches your video content, including video script through captions, to similar content of the web pages on which *YouTube* places your video ad.

- **Bing/Revcontent/Adsterra**—these affiliate publishers all have less 'reach' than GDN, but are cheaper per click/view...etc.

- **Social Platform Marketing**—*Facebook; LinkedIn; Twitter; Instagram* and other social media platforms use the PPC model, and can target by demographics, interests, location, online connections and behavior patterns. Can *you* target better? Most likely, if you've gone through the Productization process introduced in LSM Workbook 1, and productize your offering. And many of these platforms will let you target (to a limited degree) your own audiences.

- **Retargeting**, i.e. Remarketing—*Adroll, Google, Facebook,* and other affiliate publishers, show your video ad to visitors who have previously watched another of your videos, or viewed similar videos to the content in yours. Your video marketing efforts will also appear on websites, blogs, vlogs and other web pages that previous visitors to your website or landing pages have viewed.

- **SMM**—*you* can post your video marketing efforts on your company's social media profile pages, without having to pay for viewers of your videos, or clicks on your CTAs! *You* can also publish your video campaigns on your SMM feeds, on online group feeds associated with your offerings or industry, in webinars or even live presentation, *for free!*

Video marketing is a powerful tool for getting attention, and creating interactive marketing campaigns that get response, but *only* if:
1. Your video is instantly visually and audibly striking.
2. You create an engaging story, that promotes your campaign objective—buy; try; subscribe—with a clickable CTA.
3. You show your product or service in use—or a representation of the best features and benefits of your offering, that fulfills a desire, or solves a problem for a specific group of people.

Follow the basic marketing guidelines introduced in this module to produce video marketing that gets response. Websites, to landing pages, to PPC text, and video campaigns, your company's digital marketing efforts must stand out among all the other online advertising that most of us try to block out while surfing the net.

Your digital marketing must look professional, and demand the viewer's attention, and hopefully manipulate an *action*—convert them to do as your CTA directs.

-Landing Pages-

LANDING PAGES are excellent lean marketing tools to introduce our arrival in a specific industry to a specific online audience, and as a *part* of our ongoing marketing efforts, at little to no cost. Technically, any web page you 'land on' is essentially a *landing page*, however, the term has become synonymous with a specific type of marketing tool. **Landing pages are any single web page**, usually a stand-alone web page that's distinct from your main, or even secondary website. Landing pages typically promote and support a *single campaign objective*. Think of them like an advertising campaign, but instead of published in print magazines, the ads are published on the internet.

Since every web page on the net requires a unique URL, we generally use **subdomains** and **subpage** URLs for our landing pages. To build awareness of our corporate brand requires web addresses that retain the company name as their 2LD, and add subdomains for blog posts, landing pages, and other digital marketing efforts.

Your campaign landing page URLs should look something like this:
https://squeeze.companyname/sign-up-for-savings.

As a single web page, landing pages should have ONE single focused objective, such as get more customers with a sale on your offering, OR (NOT *and*) get sign-ups for your company newsletter. While our corporate website shows all we have, and are, as an organization, landing pages focus on communicating ONE message. *What* message, depends on the campaign.

Imagine you send an email to a friend inquiring about getting together for dinner. In the body of your email, you ask your friend a series of questions, like, when are you available, *and*, what kind of food do you want, *and*, where do you want to eat? It is very unlikely your friend will answer *all* of your questions. It's quite likely your friend with only answer the *very last question* on your email, and not the other two proceeding the last.

Humans have 'goldfish' memories—we forget things we don't consider important. Most marketing efforts don't attract our attention because we perceive that what is being sold has no value to us. Therefore, it is important we keep our advertising campaigns to ONE main message for the viewer to take away, as we already know that people generally won't remember more than one.

Two Typical Types of Landing Pages
There are two commonly used types of landing page campaigns:
  • **Lead Generation**, aka **Squeeze pages**
  • **Click-Through**

Landing pages have other functions as well, such as polls, contest, or games that visitors can play. Remember, a landing page is simply a web page—a digital page/address on the internet. You can create anything on a landing page that you can on any other web page.

Lead Generation Landing Pages
Lead Generation landing pages are used to collect names and email addresses, for email marketing to prospective customers down the line. The CTA on a Lead Gen landing page is the **fill-in form**.

Some basic Lead Gen landing page types:

- Blog, Vlog, Newsletter sign-ups
- 'Gift' incentive campaigns
- Savings incentives (coupons; discount codes)
- Invitations (webinars, podcasts requiring event registration)
- Trial consultation services
- Contests; Giveaway entry
- Limited time trial offers
- Notifications (news; press; beta launches or upgrades)

The fill-in form should only ask for the information you need, such as NAME, and EMAIL, as asking for too much information is a turn-off, and many will click off your landing page with too many fields to fill in.

Click-through Landing Pages

Click-through landing pages are designed to persuade the viewer to click the link to another web page to increase the likelihood of conversion upon arrival. The CTA is the click button, which typically takes visitors to a sign-up form or shopping cart. Conversion rates are generally higher with click-through landing pages, as the viewer was motivated to click for more details.

Some basic click-through landing page best practices:
- Be *very specific* on the what the viewer will get for clicking on your CTA. Click-through landing pages generally have Direct CTAs, beginning with a *verb*, in front of what visitor will get when clicking.

- Make sure to pay-off the CTAs offer in one click. If you're offering a course, one click takes you directly to the course. If you're offering a blog post, one click lands visitors directly on the post. As the viewer reads your post, use a pop-up fill-in form a few seconds into their visit, but don't demand it up-front with click-through. The goal of a click-through landing page is to get the viewer to click on the CTA.

- Use colorful, and/or high-contract [to the background] CTA buttons to garner attention and get response. Be sure your CTAs are easily seen on every marketing effort, and they link to where you want to send your visitors.

- Click-through landing pages can be dual-purposed as homepages on your website, that click-through to interior web pages, or shopping cart or checkout pages of your site.

GoPro's new website uses this design technique to keep their website homepage *fresh*—changing all the time—to increase their SEO, *and* to concertize the messaging of their marketing efforts by publishing it not only as a digital marketing campaign, but as the homepage of their website as well. Each module on their website homepage is a click-through landing page campaign. Each 'landing page/homepage' CTA clicks through to the product page of the particular offering being promoted.

Landing Pages Best Practices

Whether using a lead generation, or click-through landing page, use the bullet points below as a checklist to make sure your landing pages stay on task, and on target for the greatest response.

- Focus on ONE primary message or offer, with direct CTA (Get; Create; Learn more; Sign-up; Trial offer). Be sure to tout the *best UVP* of your offering *and* any given campaign promise or incentive.

- Design simple, bold, succinct! Get to the point *fast*, with a visual that communicates *something* about what you are selling, and a headline (and subhead/tagline if applicable) that reveals or entices.

- Use high-contrast images, videos or rotating gifs to communicate, entice, and motivate engagement—visitor *watches* video or slide show—for better conversion rates. (You should already have a lot of quality, reproducible visual content in your Visual Libraries.)

- Utilize layout and eye-tracking best practices to be sure your UVPs are the first thing seen or headlining the landing page. Be sure the last bit on your web page is the CTA, to motivate an action from the viewer.

- The headline of your landing page must match the messaging of the ad or web page viewers clicked to get there.

- Make your CTA obvious, high-contrast to the background image, and position it above the 'fold' line (the bottom of the device screen).

- Use CTAs known to motivate conversion: Free offer, or limited trial. Discounts. Incentives. Free 'gifts.'

- Be sure to put your corporate I.D. *somewhere* on the landing page, and make it clickable to your website, or another landing page, for a game, contest, or fill-in form.

- Add 'social proof'—known corporate customers, ratings and testimonials somewhere on the landing page to build trust and confidence in your company.

- A/B test different headlines, CTA text or button colors, before rolling out a full SMM and/or email campaign to generate traffic to the landing page.

Microsites

Microsites are landing pages that mirror a website. They look similar to a website, as they have navigation links that lead to other web pages on the microsite, just like a website, and their logo, generally in the left corner, links back to the homepage of the microsite.

Unlike a website, that should have *all* your company is, and offers, microsites, like landing pages, generally have only ONE primary message. Every web page in a microsite has the *same messaging*, just presented in a distinct way. The navigation may have several links, but each web page they take the viewer to in the microsite is selling the same message.

Example:
1. Microsite homepage headline: *"Build Better Websites with WIX."*
2. Microsite navigation links: *"Websites Made Easy," "Code-Free Website Templates,"* are both clickable navigation links. And each link concertizes the headline message on the microsite homepage—you can build better (i.e. easier, faster, more professional looking...etc.) websites with *Wix*.
3. Microsite navigation links take viewers to interior web pages that pays-off the homepage messaging—that using *Wix* will make building your website better.

We typically use microsites over landing pages to market more complex products or services. Many software tools take more explanation than a single landing page to understand the benefits the features of the offering provides. Like websites with many pages, a microsite is more complex than a landing page. It's a lot more time consuming to design and write copy for several pages, instead of a single landing page.

The objective of a microsite is for conversion to happen directly on the microsite—either buy, try, upgrade, or subscribe. A click-through landing page sends you to another web page to convert you. When you click on the CTA on a microsite, it should take you to interior web pages within that microsite, and eventually funnel you to conversion/sales.

We direct viewers to our landing page and microsite campaigns using **SMM** (**social media market**). We post on our timelines, our profile feeds, groups and forums a campaign with a CTA that lands viewers on the landing page or microsite supporting the SMM campaign messaging. For any given campaign, we identify which social media platforms will likely reach our target audience, then focus our SMM efforts on those platforms for the greatest response.

We use email to get people to our landing pages and microsites as well. Utilizing landing pages, we can deliver videos, online games, even AR experiences that would never function through email. Instead of emailing these user experiences (UX), we entice recipients to click on a CTA that links to our landing page or microsite campaigns.

STOP! Do PROJECT #5 before moving on.

◆◆◆

LSB Workbook 2: PROJECT #5
LANDING PAGE CAMPAIGN

LANDING PAGES are often accessed by viewers who saw your PPC/SMM ad online, and clicked on your CTA. These viewers are potential customers, as something in your PPC/SMM campaign motivated them to click through to your landing page.

1. **Create a UX LANDING PAGE campaign**. Engage viewers with a short video, an easy game, poll or contest with prizes for future redemption (when you launch your company). Follow the bullet points from the *Landing Pages Best Practices* list above. Use it as a checklist to be sure you are on task, in the proper order, to achieve the greatest response.

   The campaign **OBJECTIVE** is to get people to *fill out the form*—SQUEEZE page, or *click on the CTA*—CLICK-THROUGH page. (We'll review the process of defining your campaign OBJECTIVE for each marketing effort your company generates in the CCopywriting Module of LSL Workbook 3.)

2. **Create a PPC/SMM ad series** to get people to your **landing page**

campaign. The CTA on the SMM is to your landing page campaign. Be sure the headline of your SMM campaign is the same, or similar to the headline on the landing page the viewer is sent to when clicking on your SMM campaign's CTA.

Design your landing page campaign, with ONE clear, specific message. Your CTA should be the pay off of this message. Remember, give people something they want from your company (even before you launch). A 'free' gift; an 'industry trends' newsletter; a vlog on your offering or startup's journey; reward points for discounts on your offering to come, will often motivate people to fill in the form, or click through to where your landing page sends them.

Begin, by hand-drawing thumbnail sketches of your pre-launch PPC/SMM, and landing page campaign, in the general proportions your ads and landing page will likely appear on the digital landscape. Use the imagery you've collected in your Visual Libraries for idea generation, but also for quality reproduction in this campaign. Use the words—keywords and phrases—from your Productization lists to write the copy. As with all marketing efforts, focus your content on how your landing page campaign message or offer will fulfill a desire or solve a problem of your projected target audience.

Digitally produce your landing page campaign with templates from *Wordpress*, *Wix, Weebly*, or other web development (CMS) platform. If you are not satisfied that what you've produce meets the professional criteria you want, give what you've created to whomever you hire, as a visual reference to communicate what you want them to digitally produce for your landing page campaign. *Walk the process* of creating this integrated **PPC/SMM/landing page campaign**, and you'll gain insight into developing strategic marketing efforts for your business, for pre-launch, launch, and beyond.

◆◆◆

◆◆◆◆◆

Lean Startup Branding
WORKBOOK 2: Branding WRAP-UP

Putting it All Together

We are more than two thirds of the way to fully actualizing and marketing an idea, or product in development, into an offering of value, for profit. We have initialized the R and A, in the RAF Marketing Method.

Let's travel back to the very beginning of this course, **LSM Workbook 1: Productization**, where we examined the practice of marketing...

Real-world **marketing is selling**. That's it. Not very complicated. And, to make it even simpler, you are always selling the same thing:

Effective marketing sells <u>features and benefits</u> of your offering and company, that <u>fulfills a desire</u> of a <u>specific group of people</u>.

You've begun the first step in the startup journey of creating a sustainable company, once you've gotten "**Ready**," and actualized your idea (or even fully developed offering) into a marketable product or service, or even nonprofit, through the Productization process.

You've initialized the second step in the startup process, when you "Take **Aim**" at your offering's potential target audience with the branding and marketing tools and campaigns introduced here, in **LSB Workbook 2**.

As you now know, the branding and advertising process of marketing your offering and company, should begin long before your product development is complete. Your company should be creating and producing your marketing material simultaneously with the development of your offering. If you have a fully developed offering you're hoping to market more effectively, and have yet to '**Get Ready**' and '**Take Aim**, well, better late than never! *Do it now*, to build a solid foundation for a sustainable business, and for greater response to your future marketing efforts.

You will need the following marketing tools and campaigns to productize an IDEA into an product or service of *value*, then effectively brand and sell your offering and company—pre-launch, launch, and beyond—to create a sustainable startup, and grow a thriving business over time.

Pre-Launch Tools and Campaigns
- 8 Productization lists
- Elevator Pitch (Drafts)
- Profit Models

- **Corporate Name and Identity**
- **Product Names and Identities**
- **Product and Corporate Standards Guide** (or video)
- Purchased **URLs**
- A **webhost**—from *Wordpress* or *Wix*, to *Amazon Web Service (AWS)* for self-hosted digital media.
- **Digital Marketing** Campaigns: "Logo reveals" and "Coming soon" campaigns. UX games, contests, savings incentives, pre-order, sign-up [newsletter/blog] interactive campaigns.
- **Print Marketing** Campaigns: [for Brick and Mortar only] "Coming soon," *plus* coupon or incentive, direct mail (snail-mail) campaign. (30% off of a local restaurant or store opening.)

Launch Campaigns
- **Website**/s
- **Landing pages**
- **PPC advertising campaign** (that double as SMM campaigns)
- **SMM** (Social Media Marketing) **Profile Pages** (on Facebook; LinkedIn...etc.)
- **Email** (and direct [print] mail) campaigns
- **Fully integrated, interactive, multi-channel marketing campaigns** including digital, print, PR, SMM, display (where applicable—trade show booths, in-store Brick and Mortar).
- Both digital and print marketing efforts should focus on touting the **features and benefits of your offering** (or campaign messaging), that **fulfills a desire** or solves a problem of **a specific group of people**. All marketing efforts must have an Implied or Direct CTA, that tells the viewer what *action* to take, even if it's simply remembering your brand (as with implied CTAs).

Beyond Launch Tools and Campaign
- **All of the above marketing efforts**, plus:
- **Data collection** and applied **analytics**
- **Website updates**
- **Product and company updates**
- **Live Meetups, Talks/Presentations**
- Online **Webinars, How-To videos** (utilizing your offerings)
- **Positive press,** and your corporate **philanthropy**
- BE CREATIVE, and deliver unique advertising experiences, and interactive marketing campaigns, focused on the *benefits* your offering's *features* provide for *specific groups of people* for the greatest response to your marketing efforts for the life-cycle of your business.

The Power of Knowledge
By now, at the completion of LSB Workbook 2, Step 2 in the RAF Marketing Method—Take Aim, and Brand your new venture—should be well underway.

Armed with **product** and **corporate identities**, and striking imagery in your **Visual Libraries**, you should now have the components to create, or direct those you hire to produce marketing efforts for your offering and company that generate response.

If you are wise—a smart entrepreneur—you'll have begun your startup journey by setting up a foundation for creating a sustainable business. You've already completed LSM Workbook 1, and have engaged in the Productizaiton process. You've produced all eight Productization Lists, as well as Profit Models, and Elevator Pitches for your new venture. If you have *not* productized your offering yet, whether it is still just an idea, or a fully developed product, give your startup a solid foundation that will help your company thrive, and complete the Productization process NOW.

At this second phase in starting up your business, you should at least have a **sitemap** for your **website**, showing what imagery should go where, page for page. You've drawn the placement of headlines and text, and have an idea of what you'd like it to say on each page of your site. Many of the words for your marketing copy are in your **Productization lists**, where you've identified the features, benefits, target markets and users of your offering. Whether producing your company's website yourself, or hiring someone to create a site for you, you still need a sitemap to direct a web developer to produce the site you want.

To create and produce a spectacular site that shows everything your new venture will offer at launch, all you need to know now is *how* to utilize the keywords and phrases on your Productization lists to write marketing copy that will effectively motivate your target audiences. But how do you put the right words in the most effective order to convince your potential target markets that the offering you are creating (or have produced) will benefit them?

Visual content, whether still pictures or video, draws our attention into a campaign, but usually the headline *sells* us to read further or click on the CTA. Words [generally] lead us into the marketing effort, *if* the messaging has value to us. Remember, **we are motivated to act by self-interest**. Give someone something they want, or think they need, and you'll likely have a sale (or, at least, get conversion on your CTAs)!

Copywriting is selling with words. So, ultimately, Copywriting IS marketing. They are one and the same. Perhaps the most difficult bit in creating marketing campaigns is writing *effective* copy—copy that converts, and/or sells the viewer. Most startups (and sadly, established corporations) don't productize their offerings up-front. They never Get Ready. Even their marketing staff are not intimate enough with what they are selling, or *who* will likely find value in the offering, and why, to get their target audience to act: try; subscribe; buy.

The first module of LSL Workbook 3—Copywriting, takes you step-by-step through the copywriting process. First, we review how to direct and manage each marketing effort with a **Creative Brief**. We'll explore how to generating ideas for campaigns, and then choose the right words, in the right order, to clearly, and concisely communicate your campaign messaging.

We'll examine how to write attention-grabbing headlines, that tout the USP (unique selling position) of each campaign. We'll explore copywriting grammar, to learn how to keep our words focused on writing copy content that sells <u>features and benefits</u> of your offering and company, that <u>fulfills a desire</u> of a <u>specific group of people</u>.

Make Your Idea the Next Big Thing

You are now empowered with knowledge, techniques, and process, to create your own product and company identities, and visual marketing campaigns, or direct those you hire to produce advertising and marketing with visual impact, that gets the greatest response.

LSL Workbook 3: LAUNCH, you'll learn how to apply the branded marketing material you created in this workbook to launch your new company and begin the sales process (think: conversion funnel).

All the branded identities and campaigns you created in Take <u>A</u>im, you now <u>FIRE</u> —Launch those campaigns at your target markets. Learn step-by-step how to launch your marketing campaigns, with consistent branding across all media, indirectly and directly at your potential audiences.

You'll begin by publishing your website, which is your virtual storefront, and should include all your company offers.

Next, you'll learn to launch your initial Social Media Marketing (SMM) campaigns, with management tools and proven strategies to increase brand awareness.

We'll drill down on where to find your potential target markets and users, both live, in-person, and online. We'll examine how to build social networks of 'friends' and followers of target audiences on your company's social media profile pages that are likely interested in your offerings.

LSL Workbook 3, you'll learn how to find and collect email addresses of potential customers, and create eblasts and email marketing campaigns that avoid SPAM filters, and motivates the targeted recipients to *act* on your CTAs.

You'll explore how to utilize website links, as well as special offers and incentives in your email campaigns to entice first adopters to try, subscribe, even buy, with your startup's launch campaigns.

Next, we'll review physical print media, and explore direct mail (snail mail) marketing, as well as creating brochures that your targets will *keep*, and utilize for reference. You'll learn to solicit PR, get press, ratings, do interviews, write articles for industry rags, do guest blogs and/or vlogs, to get other people to chat you up.

We'll examine the emerging world of big data analytics—*the* big thing in targeted marketing today. A/B [Spit testing] will be reviewed, to show you how to increase your response rates on any given digital marketing efforts. We'll even crack open the Recommendation phenomenon, that is now reflecting back at us our preferences and viewpoints with every web page we visit.

LSL Workbook 3: Launch, is the final phase of actualizing an idea into offerings of value, on which to build a sustainable company, for profit. It is also where you'll learn how to create and produce ongoing marketing and advertising that gets the greatest response throughout the life-cycle of your business. You'll use the marketing and advertising campaigns you created in this workbook, and create additional marketing efforts as well, to launch your new venture, and market your startup into a thriving company.

◆◆◆

LSB Workbook 2: PROJECT #X
Continual Marketing Efforts

To launch your own sustainable startup by the end of the **LSL Workbook 3**, you'll need marketing tools and campaigns to launch your new company. Be sure to complete all the projects in both LSM Workbook 1 and LSB Workbook 2 before moving on to **LSL Workbook 3—Launch**, even if you have to hire someone to create the campaigns for you. You need marketing material to launch with, both offline—print, networking and viral messaging—as well as PPC/SMM digital campaigns.

Make sure you are publishing professional-quality campaigns by utilizing the slides, and bullet point text in each module of this book (and throughout the LSE series) as **checklists** *before* launching any campaigns to motivate the greatest possible conversion with each marketing effort.

◆◆◆
◆◆◆◆◆

<u>F</u>IRE! And LAUNCH Your Startup

Once you've become *intimate* with your idea through the Productization process, then created branded marketing tools and campaigns to get the message of your great new offering to the people most likely to use it, you are ready to launch your initial marketing efforts.

LSL Workbook 3: <u>F</u>ire—LAUNCH, takes you through the process of publishing your pre-launch, launch, and beyond campaigns, but also gives you techniques, tips and best practice to create and produce digital and print marketing, as well as PR campaigns that get attention *and* motivates conversion (click; buy; try; engage (UX); sign-up; subscribe), throughout the life-cycle of your business.

Proceed to LSL Workbook 3—LAUNCH:

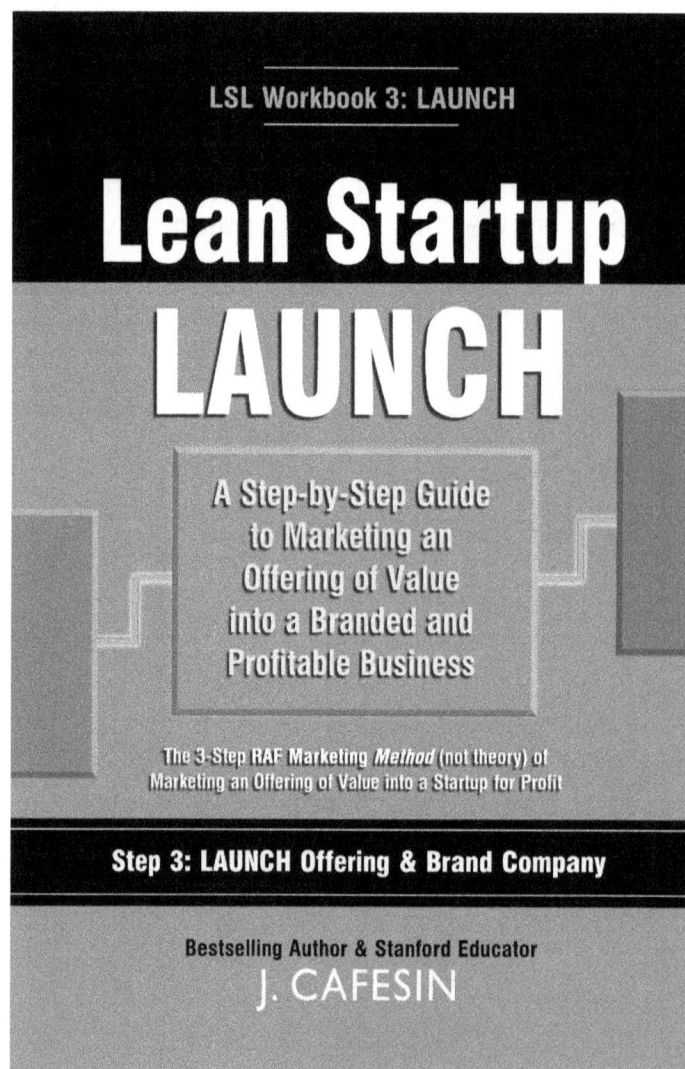

LSL Workbook 3: LAUNCH

Lean Startup
LAUNCH

A Step-by-Step Guide
to Marketing an
Offering of Value
into a Branded and
Profitable Business

The 3-Step RAF Marketing *Method* (not theory) of
Marketing an Offering of Value into a Startup for Profit

Step 3: LAUNCH Offering & Brand Company

Bestselling Author & Stanford Educator
J. CAFESIN

◆◆◆◆◆

-About the Author-

J. Cafesin is the founder of the **Lean Startup Entrepreneurial Series**, helping entrepreneurs and innovators actualize their ideas into startups, and market their offerings into sustainable companies.

A Stanford marketing educator, and MarCom specialist for over 20 years, she has helped facilitate the launch of many Silicon Valley startups, including Stac Electronics (sold to Altiris); Bay Networks (sold to Northern Telecom); MD2 (sold to Sybase); Tea Leaf (sold to IBM); The Learning Company (sold to Mattel); Southland Associates, and others. Her corporate clients have included Six-Flags; Bay Alarm Systems; Intuit; Change.org; Location Labs; CA Technologies; Genetech; CBS; NBC; Xerox FCU; 1st Nationwide Bank; and Hewlett Packard, among many others.

For updates on new blog posts, videos, upcoming live and online workshops in entrepreneurship, marketing startups, education, plus stories and insights into Silicon Valley life, find J. Cafesin on *Twitter, LinkedIn, Instagram*, and *Amazon.*

Have questions or comments about LSB Workbook 2, or the Lean Startup Series? Please email: connect@jcafesin.com.

www.ingramcontent.com/pod-product-compliance
Lightning Source LLC
Chambersburg PA
CBHW050452110426

42744CB00013B/1965